An Introduction to Systems Analysis Techniques

An Introduction to Systems Analysis Techniques

Second edition

Mark Lejk and David Deeks

PEARSON

Addison
Wesley

Harlow, England • London • New York • Boston • San Francisco • Toronto • Sydney • Singapore • Hong Kong
Tokyo • Seoul • Taipei • New Delhi • Cape Town • Madrid • Mexico City • Amsterdam • Munich • Paris • Milan

Pearson Education Limited
Edinburgh Gate
Harlow
Essex CM20 2JE
England

and Associated Companies throughout the world

Visit us on the World Wide Web at:
www.pearsoned.co.uk

First published under the Prentice Hall imprint 1998
Second edition 2002

ISBN-13: 978-0-201-79713-8

British Library Cataloguing-in-Publication Data
A catalogue record for this book can be obtained from the British Library

Library of Congress Cataloging-in-Publication Data
Lejk, Mark.
    An introduction to systems analysis techniques / Mark Lejk, David Deeks.--2nd ed.
      p. cm.
    Includes bibliographical references and index.
    ISBN 0-201-79713-5 (pbk.)
    1. System analysis. I. Deeks, David, M.Sc. II. Title.

    T57.6 .L45 2002
    003--dc21
                                           2002018945

10 9 8 7
09

Typeset by 3
Printed in Great Britain by Henry Ling Limited, at the Dorset Press, Dorchester, DT1 1HD

Contents

Foreword

A second edition of this popular text has been created because of the steady progress achieved in the field of information systems development. This progress has been given impetus by technology advances (particularly network technology) and by method adaptation arising from improved understanding of how to create successful information systems. We are still only 40 or 50 years into the business of creating computer-based information systems – a tiny period compared with the history of other established brands of human activity such as engineering, economic systems and political structures. However, users of the world do not have infinite patience and information systems project leaders are now expected to get things right – including the price and the date. Achieving this is no easy task. Quite simply there are no infallible approaches. An engineer can calculate the point at which a circuit or mechanical component will fail. Provided that the materials used are within specification and operational parameters are not exceeded then failure will be avoided. The information system designer is not so fortunate. The components for this system include people and groups of people. Unfortunately there are no reliable material specifications for these components and operational parameters are likely to evolve, perhaps unpredictably, throughout the life of the system.

Experience and technique are crucial in assessing requirements for a system for it is as easy to overindulge a user's whim as it is to pay insufficient regard to their needs.

The early phases of a project, when processes are being critically reviewed and solutions are being evaluated, must be handled with skill and objectivity. Later, during detailed design work, attention to detail must be complemented with constant reference to the fundamental goals of the project so that technicalities do not deflect its course.

Overall the task of the information systems analyst and designer remains one of the most challenging in the world of technology. The educational development of these professionals is important but difficult and this book will continue to make an impressive contribution to the task.

There is much wisdom in this book as well as a firm foundation of technique. The wisdom derives from the authors' in-depth experience refreshed by their continued involvement in series of real-life projects. Mastering the messages and the methods contained here will set the reader well down the road to professional competence.

R.T. Bell BSc PGCE
Pro Vice Chancellor
University of Sunderland
October 2001

Acknowledgements

We would like to acknowledge the help of the following in this project:

- All whose help we acknowledged in the first edition – without whom this second edition would not exist.
- Students and staff of the School of Computing, Engineering and Technology and the Business School who have provided ongoing feedback from the first edition. We have endeavoured to note and respond to every comment within this update.
- Those whose organisations' systems we have been allowed to use as examples, but who wish for commercial reasons to remain anonymous.
- Simon Stobart, who checked the accuracy of the chapters on object-oriented analysis, and made several useful suggestions.
- Angela Dixon, whose postgraduate assignment became the 'Pontefract General Infirmary' case study and who continues to collaborate closely with us.
- Helen Edwards, who played a key part in the original development of the 'Process Improvement for Strategic Objectives' (PISO) method and continues to provide valuable research advice.
- Clare Harvey, who gave enthusiastic assistance with PISO before leaving us for 'pastures new'.
- Last but by no means least our families, whose forbearance has allowed us to spend time on this project that could so easily have been spent with them.

Mark D Lejk PhD BA BSc MBCS CEng
David A Deeks MSc CertEd FIAP
School of Computing, Engineering and Technology
University of Sunderland
October 2001

Publisher's acknowledgements

We are grateful to the following for permission to reproduce copyright material:

Figure 4.19 from G. Taylor, *Computer Studies GCSE*, 3rd edn (1991) Macmillan, reproduced with permission of Palgrave.

Introduction

If you have picked up this book you must have at least a passing interest in systems analysis. Perhaps you are completely new to the subject, or perhaps you know a little already but need to learn more. Perhaps you are a seasoned systems professional who needs to brush up on techniques. Whatever your reason, we hope that you will read on and discover that, as with the first edition, our aim has been to make it as accessible as possible.

This second edition reflects the steady progress made in systems analysis in the few years since the title was first published. As ever more powerful systems and systems development languages are available, users have an increasing right to expect a system to do what they need it to do – rather than what the systems developer manages to get it to do. This puts an increasing burden on the systems analyst, who cannot shelter behind the excuse that 'the computer has to do it like that'.

We have again concentrated upon only a selection of techniques – most being those which are in widest use within business application development environments and commonly found in HND and degree (including the new foundation degree) computing courses as well as the ever-popular postgraduate 'conversion' ones. This new edition includes a look at the object-oriented approach – the increasing use of such techniques meaning that they play a correspondingly increasing role within taught programmes.

We cover all aspects in ways that have been found to work best with the students that we teach. This is not to suggest that there are no difficult bits – but simply that we would be hard pressed to think of ways to make them easier.

- For continuity purposes a student assessment system is revisited several times as different techniques are explored, but we have included other scenarios when we feel they do a better job.

- Whenever possible we describe the application of each technique in a series of clearly defined steps.

- We do not include large numbers of self-study exercises – but at the end of each appropriate chapter we *do* include at least one that links what has gone before to the reader's own experience. We have found this a particularly powerful way of ensuring that learning takes place. In our experience students never use conventional book-based exercises with 'model answers' as they are intended – being more likely to read the question and immediately look up the answer. We therefore concentrate on giving clearly worked 'case study' examples within the main text, describing problems and then showing step by step how to solve them.

- Each chapter ends with a short paragraph summarising what has been covered, and identifies recommended further reading or, as appropriate, useful web addresses. All such references have been chosen for their accessible style as well as for their academic correctness.

We spend quite a lot of time on data flow diagrams (DFDs). The reason is that this book is angled towards the 'business' end of systems analysis – the 'human' end – and DFDs are an extremely useful interface between user and computing practitioner. You will then find that while we cover some aspects of design, there is a lot more about analysis. This is because without a firm foundation in analysis techniques, even the most creative systems designer would find it difficult to communicate his/her grand schemes – a bit like expecting an artist to paint a picture, having been taught how to visualise a scene but with inadequate instruction in how to mix colours or create different brush strokes. In this second edition, we explore a new way of using DFDs in a particularly business-oriented way. This approach has become a popular choice for student projects at our university, and we have seen many students use it to bring about effective change within companies.

So, systems analysis is all about techniques, right? Techniques that allow the analyst to turn situations into diagrams, mess around with them a bit and turn them into systems? Well, partly right. But the fact is that you could become the best user of systems analysis techniques that the world has ever seen, and still not be a useful systems analyst – academically above criticism, but in practical terms of little use. The reason is simple. There are few opportunities these days for practitioners in any profession to work in isolation.

For the systems analyst there are two major areas of constraint. Firstly, there are decisions to be made as to which analysis approach best suits the circumstance in which the work is to be carried out. Secondly, it is usually necessary to work as a member of a team of people, bringing with it responsibilities of communication, co-operation, collaboration and negotiation not only with other team members but also with the world at large – the 'users'. Part 1 of this book is designed to help with such aspects. It begins with a brief background as to the alternatives available and then has something to say about the environment in which the analyst is expected to work, including practical help with regard to establishing objectives and managing a project.

Parts 2, 3 and 4 cover the techniques referred to earlier and in Part 5 we sum up everything – hopefully leaving the reader with a solid foundation in systems analysis, and practical abilities to offer the world at large: making choices, influencing decisions, communicating with people, applying techniques, working as an effective team member.

Welcome to the world of systems analysis.

Part 1

The systems development environment

Setting the scene 1

1.1 Introduction

The main objective of this book is to help you get to grips with systems analysis techniques. If this is literally *all* you want to do, then skip to Part 2. Part 1 is for those who are new to the concept of computer systems development, and/or would appreciate some explanation as to where systems analysis is found within the systems development process. Perhaps you are having initial thoughts of taking up a career as a systems analyst. The background that follows is by no means exhaustive, but is intended to give an initial feel for where systems analysis 'sits'.

To begin with, we need to get one fundamental point clear. Simply by using the term 'systems analysis', or referring to the role of 'systems analyst', to the computer systems development world at large we authors have already laid some implied cards on the table. We have effectively announced that we are talking about an overall approach to computer systems development that is known as a 'structured analysis' one. We have spent most of our working lives using such an approach.

In recent years, however, we have become increasingly interested in another approach – i.e. object-oriented analysis. Some consider this a new, and some by implication also better, alternative to structured analysis – and its use is increasing. We consider that rather than being competitors, each approach has a different range of strengths. Part 4 covers our exploration of the object-oriented approach.

There are many ways of approaching the development of a computer system, and this chapter refers to a few of the more important ones. It is worth noting, however, that on those occasions where a formal method is utilised (and much development takes place without one), the majority of business application computer systems are still developed using a strategy that employs structured analysis techniques in some shape or form. They are therefore found within most business computing undergraduate and postgraduate programmes of study.

1.2 Techniques, tools, methods, strategies

1.2.1 A hierarchy

Students who are new to computer systems development often become confused by the difference between one or more of the above. Some clarification is in order – see Figure 1.1 and the explanations that follow.

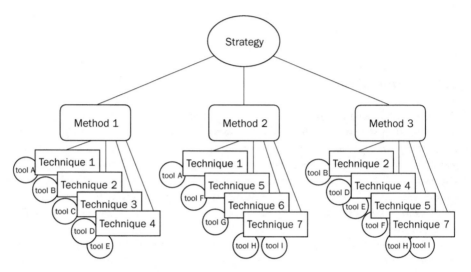

Figure 1.1 A systems development hierarchy

1.2.2 Techniques

Techniques are designed to do a particular job within the systems development process. As already explained, much of this book describes techniques for systems analysis – primarily structured analysis, but also object-oriented. Structured analysis techniques (covered in Part 2, further specific aspects in Part 3) include, for instance, data flow diagrams and entity models. Object-oriented ones (Part 4) include class diagrams and sequence diagrams. An appropriate technique is selected to achieve a required outcome.

1.2.3 Tools

Tools are often confused with techniques. It is helpful to think of a tool as being a device designed to assist in utilising a technique. One or more tools may be appropriate to one technique.

It is worthwhile to remember that tools of any kind require expertise in selecting the most appropriate ones, and skills in their effective use. Computer systems development tools are no exception. Consider a woodworker whose required outcome is to join one piece of wood with another. S/he needs to select a technique for joining the two pieces. Let us assume that the choice is to screw or nail them together. Having used his/her expertise to decide upon the technique most appropriate to the job being undertaken, further expertise is needed to select appropriate tools. If a nailed joint is chosen, the tool would be a hammer of an appropriate size/weight. If a screwed joint, appropriate drills and screwdrivers would be used. These days, of course, a combined power drill and driver could be utilised.

So tools – even power tools – do not replace the need for expertise, but simply assist in the practical execution of it. In the same way, systems development techniques can be undertaken using pencil and paper, a word processor, drawing software, or sophisticated computer-aided software engineering (CASE) tools. The systems developer must first be able to select the appropriate technique then understand how to apply it, before utilising the appropriate tool for the job.

The choice is sometimes a wide one. Select SSADM (by Select Systems), for instance, allows the rapid preparation of structured analysis diagrams with some abilities to directly generate program code (the 'SSADM' bit refers to the method supported by this software – see section 1.2.4 below). BAE Systems' Principia is another useful structured analysis diagramming tool. The Object Modelling Tool (OMT) is a CASE tool for object-oriented program development. Borland's Delphi is a Rapid Applications Development (RAD) programming tool based upon Object Pascal, allowing the quick and efficient creation of Windows-based applications. Blyth Software's Omnis is another – this being primarily directed towards the development of databases.

1.2.4   Methods

Methods (sometimes the term 'methodology' is used interchangeably, although this isn't strictly correct) embody a number of techniques, each chosen for its appropriateness to a particular task within the overall aim of the method. There are many published methods, as well as even more unpublished ones – the latter commonly derived through custom and practice within individual organisations and often consisting of extracts, perhaps just individual techniques, from a range of established methods. There is now a general decline in the rigid adherence to large-scale full-blown methods, and others are being developed that are more appropriate to the modern systems development environment.

We referred above to the Select SSADM CASE tool. SSADM stands for the 'Structured Systems Analysis and Design Method'. One of the well-known published structured analysis methods, it is the standard one approved for use within UK government IT departments. While this is by no means an SSADM textbook, as teachers at a UK university and because to avoid confusion we have to work to *some* standard, we have fairly closely adopted SSADM notation where appropriate to the described techniques.

For obvious reasons, methods evolve as new techniques keep pace with ever-advancing software and hardware developments; the methods most closely aligned with computer 'programming' are particularly sensitive to this. Jackson Structured Programming (JSP) for instance is a long-standing method for designing carefully structured computer programs, predominantly with the COBOL programming language. JSP's close relationship with COBOL has now seen its decline in the face of the rapid evolution of database development software such as Oracle and Microsoft Access.

Structured systems analysis methods map much more directly with software such as Oracle and Access than with the traditional 'batch processing' programming languages such as COBOL – particularly when using their techniques for the creation of normalised tables of data (see Chapter 8) and entity models (introduced in Chapter 7, seen again in Chapters 8, 9, 10 and 11).

The first published method for re-engineering business processes originated in the 1980s and was called, unsurprisingly, Business Process Re-engineering (BPR). Some organisations have reported that the use of BPR has had an amazingly positive effect – but many more have reported the opposite. A recent development that utilises structured analysis techniques for this purpose is Process Improvement for Strategic Objectives (PISO), developed here at the University of Sunderland. At the time of writing, PISO has met with success in the vast majority of well over 300 projects, with organisations large and small reporting significant improvements, apparently a considerably higher success rate than BPR. Research into the application and use of the method is continuing. In the meantime, in response to requests for PISO to be introduced to a wider public, in Part 3 we include an exploration of a couple of PISO case studies.

The Object Modelling Technique (OMT, confusingly sharing its initials with Object Modelling Tool) is, paradoxically, a method. It was pretty well the first published method to use the class and sequence diagrams referred to in section 1.2.2. We see these in detail when we explore object-oriented techniques in Part 4.

PRojects IN Controlled Environments (PRINCE) is the standard project management method for UK government IT departments and integrates directly with SSADM. We refer to PRINCE again in Chapter 2, when we look at project management more closely – although the principles within that chapter are general to all project management approaches.

1.2.5 Strategies

Strategies are at the highest level. A computer systems development strategy will be agreed within a particular organisation and may involve the use of certain methods for certain parts of the development process or for certain types of system, but other methods for other situations. One company's strategy for the development of small systems may be, for instance, to use an RAD approach using Borland Delphi. For large projects the same organisation could use a strategy that includes PISO to determine the overall systems requirements, followed by further selected structured analysis techniques, a 'buy v build' analysis, then procurement and/or programme development utilising appropriate software.

The above subsections give a very brief look at the choices available. If this is all completely new to you, don't panic. For the present, note simply that there are many techniques that use many appropriate tools, many methods that incorporate a variety of techniques, and that organisations can select from a wide range of everything when putting together a systems development strategy.

1.3   Approaches to systems development

1.3.1   Explaining the term 'approaches'

When faced with such a wide choice of systems development methods it is helpful to divide the alternatives into 'groupings', or 'approaches'. We have already 'divided up' the world of systems development in this way, when explaining that Parts 2 and 3 of this book cover techniques used by the 'structured analysis' approach and Part 4 techniques from the 'object-oriented' one. There are others. This section aims to give you a general awareness of this aspect.

1.3.2   Approaches covered by this book

The structured analysis approach
This overall approach was originally conceived in the early to mid 1970s. Structured analysis focuses upon what a system does rather than how it does it. This means that the emphasis is logical rather than physical, addressing what the system is meant to accomplish. Looking at it another way, it is based on the assumption that the procedures used within organisations are stable, whereas the data is stored and used in a way that simply supports them.

The main characteristics of structured analysis are the **top-down functional decomposition** of the system – and the fact that conversion from the physical to the logical view can be handled early in the development process. The traditional approach has always been that the physical view begins with document flow diagrams being prepared (we explore these early in Chapter 4), but this is based upon the assumption that the systems development involves manual systems being computerised. Increasingly, systems development these days involves early computer systems being replaced. The 'physical view' will frequently therefore include computer screen displays, or computer stores of data – so rigid adherence to the use of document flow diagrams would mean much being overlooked. Data flow diagrams (also introduced in chapter 4) are an advance over these, and allow the manual and computer aspects of a system to be shown side by side.

Using such diagrams, it does not really matter whether a structured analysis investigation begins with documents (thereby identifying **data flows**), or by talking to people (thereby identifying **processes** and **external entities**). One way or another, data flow diagrams are constructed that show the physical system (explained in Chapters 4 and 5) and allow progression to a view of what is logically *happening* (Chapter 9). Entity models (Chapters 7 and 8) are used to show entities and their relationships – that is, what is logically *there*.

It is usual for the structured analysis approach to provide three fundamental views of a system: process-centred, data-centred and event-centred. SSADM develops this approach to a level of considerable rigour, its intention being to produce documentation at every stage that will be understandable by a third party. Taken to the extreme this can even allow a variety of suppliers to combine in the development of a system, without necessarily even needing to know each other's identity. This feature makes it attractive where high security is an important factor – for instance in banking, or applications for the armed forces. Very few organisations these days use a full SSADM-style method, however – it is much more common to find selected techniques being applied as felt appropriate.

The object-oriented approach

This is one of the more important introductions of recent years. As explained earlier, techniques used by this approach are further explored in Part 4.

For someone new to the world of computer systems, the object-oriented view of computer systems development is perhaps one of the most difficult concepts to describe. In a sense it combines the structured analysis 'what a system does' view and the data-centred 'what information the system uses' view. It results in a number of standard **modules** within a system that have predetermined effects upon the data that is sent their way, being able to be called upon by any part of the system that requires that effect to take place.

'Modular' programming languages such as C++ and Visual Basic are most appropriate to the object-oriented approach – and another already mentioned is Borland Delphi. Borland claim that Delphi is unique in allowing structured, object-oriented and event-driven programming to be catered for within a single development environment. It can be argued that others such as (Java-based) JBuilder and C++Builder at least come close to achieving this, but such discussions fall outside of the remit of this book.

The object-oriented view creates systems that are easily catalogued and managed – but is most appropriate to situations of frequent 'repeat processing' (such as production line automation, car park access etc.) rather than the handling of large volumes of complex data typical within information systems and well catered for by structured analysis. When compared with the structured analysis approach, the object-oriented alternative arrives much more quickly at a system design, but one that is far less easy to share with users as it utilises notations that do not readily relate to the 'real world'.

It is unfortunate that a culture of 'structured versus object-oriented' seems to have developed in many quarters. Even books that purport to compare/contrast methodologies seem to tend to support one side or the other. Although this one is primarily a textbook on structured analysis, we see the two approaches as complementary, each with its own advantages and disadvantages, strengths and weaknesses. We hope you find our 'structured analysis view' of object-oriented analysis, as explored in Part 4, constructive and useful.

1.3.3 Approaches *not* covered by this book

The Systems Development Life Cycle (SDLC)

The SDLC is a logical approach to large-scale systems development. Some would describe it as a method, but as so many variations exist we are more comfortable calling it an approach. By mentioning it, there will be some readers who think that we have suddenly gone all 'old fashioned'! Don't worry, we haven't. We know that the SDLC originated in the 1960s, but it was really the first successful attempt at a fully documented approach to IT project development and has much to teach us. It is now viewed as traditional (or old-hat, depending upon your age) – but it is extremely comprehensive, ensuring that all stages of the development of a system are thought about, planned, monitored and completed. While it grew up in the era of large mainframe computer systems it can still provide a valuable checklist of things to consider, no matter what the environment.

With structured analysis, stage 1 of the SDLC will usually involve the decomposition of the higher levels of the system, further decomposition taking place in stages 2 and 3, and even as far as stage 4.

As you become familiar with the techniques described in Part 2 of this book, you will better appreciate how they fit in with the SDLC as shown in Figure 1.2.

(Typical systems analysis
techniques found in this book)

STAGE 1	**Preliminary investigation**	context diagram
	Gain clear understanding of current system,	data flow diagram
	summarise findings to management – including	entity modelling
	whether to proceed with next stage.	normalisation
STAGE 2	**Systems analysis**	context diagram
	Define business requirements (software) for new	data flow diagram
	system (hardware requirements finalised during	entity modelling
	and after design phase), prepare system	normalisation
	requirements report, evaluate alternatives,	
	prepare Request For Proposal (RFP).	
STAGE 3	**Systems design**	data flow diagram
	Define technical design, establish controls, prepare	entity modelling
	design documentation, use CASE tools/prototyping,	normalisation
	build project dictionary.	entity life history
		state transition diagram
STAGE 4	**Systems construction**	
	Create or select software required by new system,	
	design, choose supplier, train users and operators, test system.	
STAGE 5	**Systems implementation**	
	Get new system running, create final operating	
	documentation and procedures, begin to use system.	
STAGE 6	**Evaluation**	
	Check new system meets objectives, make adjustments.	

Figure 1.2   The traditional Systems Development Life Cycle

For the present, however, it is worth noting that for the analysis and design stages of large projects the structured analysis approach has often been mapped on to the SDLC – and this was probably an important factor in SSADM being so readily adopted in UK official circles.

While the SDLC can be separated into anything between five and nine stages, the most common are probably the six shown. The indication as to which techniques are appropriate to the stages is by no means exhaustive but is intended simply to give a feel for typical uses of some of the structured analysis techniques that you will find in this book.

The diagram should be read in context, for it has already been made clear that the systems analyst is much more than simply an expert in the use of techniques. He or she is involved at every stage of the development process, acting as user/programmer liaison, getting involved with training and user documentation, testing, evaluation, etc. Note also that the SDLC is a *cycle* – the review that takes place at the end can easily result in 'fine tuning' or the decision to add extra facilities, which can then begin the whole process again.

The full SDLC remains most appropriate to situations where there are predictable information systems requirements. This would include circumstances where users have a clear idea of their needs, or where there is an existing system with a clearly defined structure. Such a situation will be found in systems involving the entry of data from input documents, with high transaction and processing volumes, requiring validation of data input, encompassing several departments. The complexity will often necessitate a long development timetable, and development by project teams.

The SDLC approach is highly project manageable as the stages can be clearly identified, scheduled, monitored and controlled. Sometimes the creation of the project plan is seen as a separate step following stage 1, but this implies that stage 1 itself is not planned – and in any instance project planning and control is really an ongoing task implicit within the whole systems development process. We cover such aspects in Chapter 2.

The data-centred approach

This approach was another that originated in the 1970s. It is based on the premise that the basic *data* that an organisation uses is stable, whereas the *procedures* are not. It often comes under the umbrella term 'information engineering'. While SSADM for instance includes a data-centred view within an overall structured analysis context, the data-centred approach pretty well bases the whole development upon it.

In this approach, data becomes a separate resource within an organisation and processes become merely a means of transforming it. The design of the database becomes the most important aspect, with the development of the 'data dictionary' (with every data item clearly identified and defined) forming the initial major part of the development.

In an information engineering project, the views of a wide range of users are taken on board in order to gain consensus as to the precise definition and use of each item of data. This usually precedes any attempt to design the system processes. The data-centred approach therefore usually incurs a heavy 'front-end' loading in terms of cost and time, before results are produced. Once the initial investment has been made, however, it is said that systems can be developed more rapidly than with the structured approach.

The data-centred approach has tended to have a centralist, 'big computer' orientation – and usually with one systems consultancy/development team seeing the whole process through to the end. Many developments have floundered before the data dictionary was even completed. While completed systems still exist, the use of this approach probably 'peaked' before the mid 1980s – and patchy maintenance of the data dictionary in many of the remaining ones has in many cases left companies without the firm foundation for further development that the approach offers in theory. In our experience, very few new projects these days utilise the data-centred approach.

The soft systems approach

The approaches considered so far are amongst those often considered 'hard' – not in the sense of difficult but more in the sense of concrete, or precise. It is assumed that the system has a goal, that the problems are easily identifiable and that the requirements are largely known. All that is needed is some tried and tested techniques to set the ball rolling. But what if the problems are not clear? What if everyone recognises there is a problem but there is a lack of consensus as to what it is – i.e. there are several different points of view? What if there is a general sense that things need improving but no one knows what or how? This is where the **soft systems** approach comes in. It was developed by Peter Checkland from Lancaster University and provides a very sophisticated participative analysis of the problem situation.

Using cartoon-like diagrams called **rich pictures**, the participants build up a picture of the organisation under study and represent communication flows, processes, areas of conflict, external observers and interactions. The aim of this is to help in the construction of a 'root definition' that expresses very concisely what the system is. The method goes on to build conceptual models that support the requirements outlined in the root definition. By comparing these models with the original expression of the problem, it is possible to formulate some desirable changes and actions to improve the problem situation.

While a detailed introduction to the soft systems approach is beyond the remit of this book, we consider it worthwhile for any prospective systems analyst to be aware of the concept and have an idea as to what it can achieve. It can sometimes provide an extremely useful means of gaining initial understanding and consensus as to what is involved within an organisational area – before moving on to the more 'hard-edged' analysis approaches found within structured systems analysis, for instance. It is becoming popular (including in the most recent versions of SSADM) to recommend the use of soft systems as a possible 'front-end' to structured analysis approaches – as it helps very much in formulating the components of a difficult-to-identify problem and thus bringing clarity to the initial information requirements stage of such a development. It can also be used in the initial stages of PISO projects for helping to identify what the strategic objective is.

The rich pictures in Figures 1.3 and 1.4 were prepared by two groups of undergraduate Systems Analysis students in the School of Computing, Engineering and Technology at the University of Sunderland. They show their views of the student assessment system operating within their school.

A good rich picture should be easy for others to read, clearly showing the key aspects that the 'soft systems analyst' wishes to portray – that is, the communication flows, processes, areas of conflict, external observers and interactions mentioned above. Beyond this there are really no rules. Judge for yourself how successful the two examples are in achieving this objective.

1.4 More fundamentals

1.4.1 Prototyping

What it is

Prototypes are well known in engineering. Perhaps best known to the public at large are those that motor manufacturers produce. A prototype can be developed for a number of reasons, but the main ones really boil down to two:

1 To give a good idea of what an end-product will be like, without having to go to the trouble of making a completely finished working article.
2 To gain feedback, to enhance the finished product.

A prototype vehicle may be developed purely for the purpose of eliciting public reaction to the way it looks – in which case, it may have no engine, for example. On other occasions, a manufacturer may wish to test the reaction to a novel or newly developed feature – a new type of semi-automatic gearbox perhaps – and this will therefore be included. New design and manufacturing techniques are enabling ever more sophisticated prototypes to be developed, often with slight variations being made available simultaneously in order to judge the preferred one.

The same overall principles to the use of prototypes apply within computer systems development – with RAD techniques playing an increasingly large role.

Appropriate use

Traditionally, those who have supported prototyping have often been considered (sometimes justifiably) 'hackers' who have little understanding of 'proper' methods and who may produce a result quickly, but with little chance of its being any good in the long run. This has led to prototyping gaining something of a bad reputation. The rapid development possible with the latest application software can, however, allow legitimate and cost-effective use of the approach – as long as it remains within a structured development framework.

A large proportion of computer-based information systems is currently developed using a strategy that embodies structured analysis supported by prototyping. It is therefore gaining recognition as an approach that has its place within

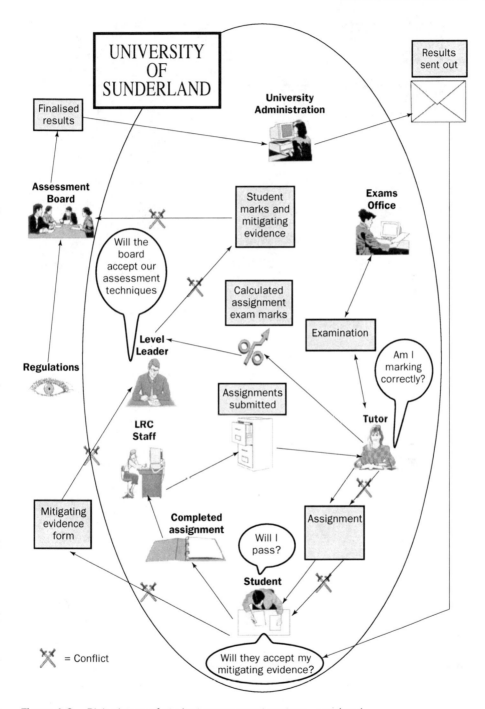

Figure 1.3   Rich picture of student assessment system – version 1

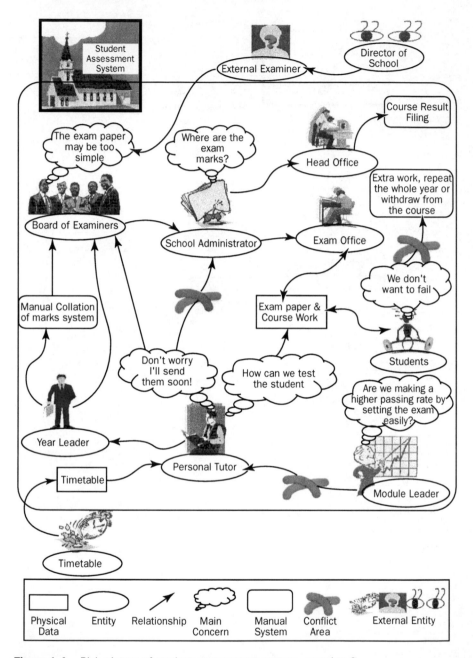

Figure 1.4   Rich picture of student assessment system – version 2

an overall strategy – for it can provide an important complement to the documentation provided by a structured analysis approach (more recent versions of SSADM formally acknowledge the role that prototyping can play, seeing it as an important part of the requirements specification stage).

User involvement

Prototyping has clear strengths. Fundamentally, it allows the demonstration of the system at various stages of the development process – involving users to ensure that the development is satisfactory before progressing to the next stage, and providing a useful platform to establish their requirements before having them check the next update. It is therefore part of an iterative, or evolutionary, approach and can be of considerable assistance in establishing user 'ownership' for a system, with important subsequent benefits regarding ease of implementation.

The traditional SDLC approach and the increasing use of prototyping may initially seem to be mutually exclusive. Look back at the SDLC stage 3 (Figure 1.2), however. Even within the SDLC as it was developed in the 1960s, prototyping was seen to have its place – albeit often a minor one. It is now so much easier to create a prototype than it was then, particularly with increasingly sophisticated computer-aided software engineering (CASE) tools, that the benefits are increasingly appreciated and acted upon. As already explained, at the same time as the analyst utilises appropriate techniques to document the proposed system in order to gain user acceptance, she or he can reinforce and clarify the intended design by demonstrating a prototype – with user responses being used as feedback into the whole development process.

Prototyping's most obvious early strengths were found to be within areas of unique application settings, or where developers had little or no design experience (this use probably more than any other initially gave prototyping its bad name among system professionals), or where costs or risks of error may have been high. These advantages remain. In these circumstances in particular, it can be an extremely efficient means of establishing user requirements – by gaining their feedback stage by stage as the system evolves.

Prototyping has also been seen to have a particularly important role to play where future users have no computing experience, as it has been shown to have a strong demystifying effect. Users who are involved in the systems development process are invariably more accommodating when the time comes to go live – and quite apart from anything else this can be an important commercial consideration for the software company developing a system for an important client. Prototyping offers another important advantage even before the 'official' development process begins – it can be used as a powerful accompaniment to a written system specification and/or quotation, by being able to *demonstrate* what can be done.

A major player

Prototyping has quickly become commonplace in all sizes of organisation, within the development of major or minor systems, 'in-house' or external. With increasing expectations of quick results, it has become established with the availability of high level programming and database development languages. It has been one of the systems development 'rising stars' of the mid-to-late 1990s, and along with the continued rapid evolution of user-friendly development software it is now a major player. We would now go so far as to say that any organisation large or small that develops systems *without* the use of prototyping, does so at its peril.

When using the prototyping approach, however, it is important first to consider how it can best be applied, bearing in mind that the objective is to make your intentions understandable to the potential user of the system.

Using effectively

As explained earlier, prototypes can vary from the simple to the much more complicated. An initial prototype may simply consist of a single screen in order to gain early agreement regarding use of colours and so on, perhaps progressing to a complete menu structure that still does not actually do anything. These give the prospective user a good idea of the **look and feel** of the proposed system, as well as demonstrating that the developer has had a good initial stab at determining the likely **facilities** that will be needed. The prototype up to this early stage may not even need to be developed using the intended software. For instance, presentation software such as Microsoft PowerPoint may be used in order to offer alternatives of what the system could look like (or even in some cases what it could feel like) and the screens that it could contain.

Subsequent to this, one key facility can be selected and developed completely, using the chosen development software. This is good for demonstrating the developer's ability to actually replicate the look and feel within a fully *functional* part of the system.

The use of the prototyping approach can then continue in the same vein – for as already explained, the best use of prototyping employs an iterative approach with regular reference to the users. The prototype thus steadily develops into a completed system with which the users are familiar, and for which they feel ownership. Such users will be much more supportive of the system when the time comes for implementation – or for pre-implementation tasks such as keying in lots of foundational data. And because they have been so closely involved in deciding what the system should look like and how it should actually work, system training will be minimalised.

Dangers of over-dependence

From what has gone before it should be evident that we are strong supporters of the use of prototyping. It represents a very user-oriented approach to systems development – and systems are, after all, for users. They are the experts in what a system should do, they are the people who will use it and who should have a strong say in how the system feels when they do so. As with most things in life, however, over-dependence can bring its pitfalls.

Consider the motor manufacturer who elicits the views of car users as to what the latest model should look like, how the interior may be trimmed and what sort of performance they expect for a certain price – but is still expected to engineer a cost-effective, easy-to-produce, reliable vehicle that carries the occupants in safety. Similarly, computer users are *not* expert in how a system should be constructed, how the workings should be designed, how to build-in reliability, upgradeability, and all the other aspects that need to be considered by the professional systems developer. Attempting to develop a system *only* on the basis of whether users are happy with it is a recipe for disaster. It is sometimes all too easy to slide into the habit of delivering continually updated prototypes to users, forgetting that the system needs the firm foundation that only a structured and methodical approach can provide. Prototyping fulfils an important role – but only within the context of properly managed systems development.

1.4.2   CASE (computer-aided software engineering) tools

From simple to sophisticated

This book assumes that all of the analysis techniques introduced by us can be tackled with only a pencil and paper, or a word processor with a simple drawing facility. Any cross-checking between diagrams will thus be done by manual, visual comparison. This is the best way to learn about the techniques, and is also often the way in which these techniques are put into practice on a day-to-day basis. As already explained, however, automated tools have evolved to help the systems developer – these coming under the broad heading of **CASE tools.** They range from simple diagramming aids to extremely sophisticated computer products that document and automate the whole development, even generating the final computer code. CASE tools can include such components as diagramming tools, data dictionaries, report or screen generators, program code generators and project management tools.

Upper and lower CASE

Upper CASE tools support the analysis and design stages, providing graphics and text facilities to create and maintain data and structured analysis and design techniques. They help document system requirements, develop and maintain data and process models, or even create simulated interactive user dialogues – this last facility often proving particularly useful for those analysts who aim to produce a first-time user-acceptable system. Some have built-in rules that provide error-checking and cross-referencing – for example by editing a data model and highlighting any detected errors.

   Lower CASE tools support the design and construction stages of the systems development process. Automatic code generators convert the results of the physical design into code that is suitable for the target hardware and software environment. The code that is generated should be relatively free from syntax errors.

CASE and the systems analyst

The most obvious way in which CASE can help the systems analyst is by alleviating the need to draw by hand the graphic representations of an existing system's specification or the design of a new one. Such a view of the advantages of CASE is, however, a superficial one – for an analyst could use an ordinary graphics package to do this. The principal features that characterise a CASE tool include one or more of the following:

- the ability to integrate other productivity tools such as project managers, cost-benefit analysis tools and spreadsheets;
- a quality assurance capability that checks for consistency and completeness;
- the ability to share diagrams and data with other systems;
- rapid prototyping.

The data dictionary

The functional capabilities of CASE products are built around a **data dictionary** that acts as the central repository for all of the products produced. This repository is really simply a database about an information system project. Not only does it store these products, it also acts as a quality control by making sure that the products are consistent with each other. It performs the functions of storing, organising, updating, analysing and reporting all data items and objects needed to create, enhance or maintain the information system. So, for example, data flows will be stored in the data dictionary and these data flows will contain data items that are stored in entities within the system. The data dictionary would store a description of this data item once only and link it to the data flows and the entity in which it plays a part. As a system develops and gets more and more complex, it is quite possible for the same thing to appear in more than one guise and for the analyst to think of them as two different things and give them two different names. A properly controlled and managed data dictionary should help in trapping such inconsistencies and problems.

The data dictionary is the single, authoritative source of every detail about a project. As such, it is a key asset to the project team. It is also invaluable when considering system changes associated with system maintenance.

During the **analysis** stage, the analyst may use an **upper** CASE tool to create and enter many objects into the repository (such as user requirements, process models, data models, report layouts, screen formats, data definitions etc.).

During the **design** stage, the analyst may use a **lower** CASE tool to access the data in the repository and automatically generate a first-cut physical design of the system, which is then reviewed and updated as necessary.

Once everything is finalised, a **lower** CASE tool may be used to **generate program code** – typically, anything between 25 and 99 per cent of code can be generated in this way. The remainder still has to be modified or added to by hand. Provided that everything that preceded the code generation was done correctly, the system should now meet the needs of the users.

Lack of standards

The main obstacle to widespread use of CASE tools has been a lack of standards. CASE tools are often incompatible with each other and do not interface properly with other software products. Some products are now emerging, however, that make a serious attempt to integrate with widespread analysis techniques and software. Already mentioned is Select SSADM, one example that allows a design created using structured analysis techniques to be turned into a Microsoft Access/Visual Basic-based fully operational system.

No substitute for expertise

A systems developer using a CASE tool is similar to a student using a word processor. It is still possible for the student to produce a poor assignment, including one that doesn't properly answer the question that was set – although the spelling and grammar should at least be OK. It is even possible for authors to write a poor book – although hopefully, you won't consider this one of them! In the same way, however, it is perfectly possible to use sophisticated CASE tools to create a system that does not fulfil user requirements.

This book's title makes it clear that the aim is to teach you systems analysis techniques – for if your use of the techniques is flawed, it does not matter how sophisticated the CASE tool is, you will still end up with mistakes. However, we do not wish to undervalue the importance of such tools. They are extremely widespread and very successful – and we have used them ourselves. Our advice is simply not to let the tools take over the development process. It is extremely important that the analyst is in control of the tool and not the other way round. We have witnessed analysts getting so carried away with the sophistication offered by some CASE tools that they have forgotten that the system is being produced for someone other than themselves.

1.4.3   Data and information

Not the same

A particularly important aspect that we wish to address is the difference between data and information. Much confusion exists concerning this, and in computer systems development the distinction is an important one.

For an information system to communicate it must provide **information** – but to do so it will need to process **data**. Data and information are not the same. As you will discover from this book, the analysis and design of computer systems involves techniques such as data flow diagrams depicting datastores, normalisation creating organised tables of data, and data models. You will probably have heard of the 'data processing department' and almost everyone these days has heard of a computer database. So it is data that we are gathering, data that we are processing – but it is information that we need, information systems that we are building.

It is the job of the systems analyst to determine what data an information system needs in order to produce the required information, and how this data should be stored and processed so that the information is clear and timely.

Use of the word 'data'

It should first be noted that the way the word 'data' is used within business and computer systems development runs the risk of offending any purists who have studied English or Latin, or mathematical science. Such people will be aware that it originates as a plural of the word 'datum' – i.e. the phrase 'the data are' would be correct. Within information systems and other areas of modern life the word 'datum' has disappeared and 'data' has become a 'mass noun'. We therefore say 'the data is' in exactly the same way as 'the information is'.

Information is data in context

A number of definitions exist for information and data, but our favourite way of defining both happens to be by combining them in a definition that we came up with ourselves(!), that is:

Information is data that has been put into context.

To understand this fully, consider a piece of paper carrying a list of numbers. The data on the paper means little until explanatory column headings or descriptions are added (such as invoice number, name, address) – that is, it becomes a document. A document becomes a document when it not only carries data but indicates what the data is, what the numbers mean. Or, returning to our definition, it puts the data into context.

Similarly, a computer screen full of data in the form of numbers or letters will only begin to convey information when these numbers or letters, individually or in groups, are given descriptions. As we pointed out earlier, a computer system does not store or process information, it stores and processes data – data that is put into context as information when processes display it on a screen or print it out as a document.

Male	Yes
Male	Yes
Female	Yes
Male	No
Female	Yes
Male	No
Male	Yes
Male	Yes
Female	No
Female	No

Figure 1.5   A table of . . . what, exactly?

To establish that data is presented as information a good test is to ask the question 'What was the question?' In the first column of the table in Figure 1.5, we can assume that the question was one concerning gender but there really is not enough clarity to be sure that the column contains information. Are we seeing the gender of the person being asked, or the gender of their partner, or the gender of their dog, or . . . what? And to what does the second column refer?

If we are now told that the table shows the responses of a number of people who were asked 'do you smoke cigarettes?', the data contained within it begins to provide us with information. The table itself only begins to provide this information, however, if appropriate headings are added to it, as shown in Figure 1.6. If you were handed this table as a 'document' or shown it as a computer screen display, it would begin to convey something – it would give information because the data has been put into context.

People who were asked 'do you smoke cigarettes?'	
Gender	Response
Male	Yes
Male	Yes
Female	Yes
Male	No
Female	Yes
Male	No
Male	Yes
Male	Yes
Fomale	No
Female	No

Figure 1.6   A table showing male and female responses to the question 'do you smoke cigarettes?'

This is of course a simple example – and it still gives us only minimal information. What cross-section of people was questioned? From what country? Were they queueing to buy cigarettes, or leaving a cinema, or taking part in a church service? The more complete the data, the clearer the information. To put it another way, there is ultimately *never* a requirement for data, but for information. The data serves only to provide us with the information we require – and efficient computer systems hold *only* that data necessary to provide this information.

Let us now assume that we need to know what percentage of those questioned are smokers. To establish the answer to this, a quick calculation tells us that 60 per cent of those questioned were smokers, and 40 per cent of those questioned were not. To carry out this calculation we have ignored the data in the 'gender' column. If this is the *only* information we ever need to know from this 'system' we can assume that the gender data can be discarded – there is no need for our system to capture it, store it, display it. If we need to be able to establish the relative numbers of male and female smokers, however, the 'gender' data is required.

While simple, the above example serves to differentiate between information and data, and the way in which data simply exists to meet the requirement for information – and it is the job of the systems analyst to develop an information system that captures the appropriate data, processes it appropriately and displays it clearly as information.

When in Chapter 4 we introduce you to data flow diagrams you will discover that these can depict physical or logical stores of data. Essentially, a physical datastore is somewhere that information is stored – most commonly as documents. This could typically be a filing cabinet containing invoices. A logical datastore is one held electronically on the computer, and we have seen that computers hold data rather than information. So physical datastores hold information, logical ones hold data.

1.5   Making complex choices

1.5.1   Introducing the weighted matrix

Here we address an aspect of the life of a systems analyst that seems rarely to be mentioned, yet can be vitally important. It is the need to be able to make clear decisions given a range of alternatives containing an apparently bewildering number of factors. What if it is your responsibility, for instance, to design an overall approach for the development of a large project within your company? How do you compare the advantages and disadvantages of the standard approaches available – or even decide whether to develop your own 'hybrid'? Or if your company prepares a tender document for third parties to submit proposals for a large systems development, how do you assess and compare the responses?

A simple solution can be found in a technique that, again, seems rarely to be covered by student texts – the weighted matrix. The purpose of the weighted matrix is to provide a straightforward means of comparing a range of options and coming up with a clear choice as to the best one to suit a particular circumstance. It is a deceptively powerful technique that allows almost objective decisions to be reached, based largely upon subjective judgement. It is increasingly common for companies to use such a method to decide which prospective systems supplier has proposed a best overall solution. Weighted matrices can become extremely complex, but we are interested only in the simplest two-dimensional type. This is represented by a straightforward 'table' or 'spreadsheet' layout of lines and columns.

1.5.2   A simple weighted matrix example

In order to appreciate what weighted matrices are and how they are used, we will use a simple example that concerns a student selecting a university. Such a choice is made on the basis of a range of factors – probably including the following:

- Distance from home/easy to get to
- Based upon visit
    - facilities
    - impression of lecturers
- Relevance of course content
- Surroundings/environment
- New/established course
- Prospects after course (is it 'recognised'?)
- Accommodation
    - price
    - quality
    - distance from university
- Daily travel to lessons (walk/price of transport)

A completed weighted matrix for the above example is shown in Figure 1.7.

Factors	Significance weightings	Scores		
		University 1	University 2	University 3
Distance from home/easy to get to	10	8	7	5
Based upon visit – facilities	15	12	14	10
– lecturers	10	6	8	10
Relevance of course content	15	14	9	12
Surroundings/environment	5	4	5	5
New/established course	10	5	9	10
Prospects after course	10	8	7	7
Accommodation – price	10	9	10	5
– quality	10	8	7	10
– distance from university	5	2	3	9
Travel to lessons	5	1	3	5
TOTALS	**105**	**77**	**82**	**88**

Figure 1.7 A weighted matrix to establish which is the most appropriate university

The above list appears in the first column, entitled 'Factors'. The 'Significance weightings' column is the key to how the 'weighted' matrix gets its name. It is here that the person preparing the matrix enters against each factor a figure that represents their own judgement as to the relative significance of each. The scale used does not matter – it is the relativity of the weightings which is significant. Those factors with the same 'Significance' value (e.g. note those with a '10') are considered by the student to be equally significant. Those with higher or lower values are respectively more or less significant. This is the subjective part of the process – a different student may well allocate a different set of values. The final stage is to enter the alternatives, and 'score' them. Note that each factor is scored out of the maximum significance weighting that has been allocated to it. The highest *total* score indicates the best university.

An important point to remember is that the person who prepares and uses a weighted matrix can genuinely be said to 'own' it. The technique does not simply allow the recording of scores against a mathematically established set of standards. Instead it records scores against a subjectively judged set of factors – factors selected by, weighted by and then judged by the creator of the matrix.

Weighted matrices are an extremely useful tool – and one thing is certain. A completed weighted matrix represents a rigorously analysed personal view of what it sets out to evaluate. If you should use one and not like the conclusion it reaches, the fact that it is *your* conclusion will be inescapable!

1.5.3 Commercial use of weighted matrices

As explained earlier, it is common for companies to select suppliers using a weighted matrix – particularly when the suppliers are responding to a detailed Invitation To Tender. The weighted matrix comes into its own in helping the client decide who should be awarded the contract – as this involves a large number of aspects that the client needs to consider in arriving at a clear choice as to the best solution for the company's needs.

Most clients who are in the habit of issuing Invitations To Tender – including those for software development – use a pre-prepared general weighted matrix that includes overall aspects common to any such process. They then add details to this, appropriate to the specific system being offered for tender.

To give you an idea of how complex a typical weighted matrix may become when used for the above purpose, refer to Figure 1.8. This is a real example, although the company name has been changed. It shows a completed weighted matrix for only *one* supplier's proposed system. Because of the complexity of the comparisons being made, the client has decided that each factor will be measured in *three* ways: by asking each supplier to prepare a Written Proposal (Prop), deliver a Verbal Presentation (Pres), and demonstrate a Prototype system (Prot). The client would prepare one of these matrices for each competing prospective supplier, and then compare the totals in order to select the one that would be awarded the contract.

If you should work for a software development company in future, your company's proposals could well be compared with your competitor's in this way. At least you now know!

SUPPLIER: Super Systems Ltd   SYSTEM: Release Management   Date: 23/3/01

FACTORS	Significance weightings				Evaluations			
	Prop	Pres	Prot	Total	Prop	Pres	Prot	Total
Evidence that requirements understood								
Data capture	5	0	0	**5**	4	0	0	**4**
Release/change details	5	0	0	**5**	3	0	0	**3**
Impact details	3	0	0	**3**	2	0	0	**2**
Risk assessment/containment	1	0	0	**1**	1	0	0	**1**
Issues/implementation plan	3	0	0	**3**	1	0	0	**1**
Regression plans	1	25	20	**46**	1	18	12	**31**
Status reporting	1	0	0	**1**	1	0	0	**1**
Hardware configurations	1	0	0	**1**	1	0	0	**1**
Management information	3	0	0	**3**	2	0	0	**2**
Service level measurement	3	0	0	**3**	1	0	0	**1**
Future growth	3	0	0	**3**	1	0	0	**1**
Business & application	1	0	0	**1**	1	0	0	**1**
TOTALS	30	25	20	**75**	19	18	12	**49**
Evidence that requirements met								
Data capture	6	0	0	**6**	4	0	0	**4**
Release/change details	6	0	0	**6**	3	0	0	**3**
Impact details	4	0	0	**4**	2	0	0	**2**
Risk assessment/containment	1	0	0	**1**	1	0	0	**1**
Issues/implementation plan	3	0	0	**3**	2	0	0	**2**
Regression plans	1	20	30	**51**	1	15	15	**31**
Status reporting	1	0	0	**1**	1	0	0	**1**
Hardware configurations	1	0	0	**1**	1	0	0	**1**
Management information	4	0	0	**4**	2	0	0	**2**
Service level measurement	4	0	0	**4**	2	0	0	**2**
Future growth	3	0	0	**3**	1	0	0	**1**
Business application	1	0	0	**1**	1	0	0	**1**
TOTALS	35	20	30	**85**	21	15	15	**51**
Evidence of skills available								
Project management/planning	0	2	0	**2**	0	2	0	**2**
Design/build/technical	0	3	6	**9**	0	2	3	**5**
Interpersonal	0	2	2	**4**	0	1	1	**2**
Team spirit	0	3	2	**5**	0	1	1	**2**
TOTALS	0	10	10	**20**	0	6	5	**11**
Look and feel of system								
Help text	0	0	2	**2**	0	0	0	**0**
Ease of use	0	0	7	**7**	0	0	3	**3**
Appearance	0	0	3	**3**	0	0	1	**1**
Suitability	0	0	8	**8**	0	0	4	**4**
TOTALS	0	0	20	**20**	0	0	8	**8**

Figure 1.8   Weighted matrix for evaluation of client proposals (*continued over*)

Figure 1.8 *continued.*

FACTORS	Significance weightings				Evaluations			
	Prop	Pres	Prot	Total	Prop	Pres	Prot	Total
Question handling								
Speed/confidence	0	4	0	4	0	3	0	3
Quality	0	6	0	6	0	3	0	3
TOTALS	0	10	0	10	0	6	0	6
Professionalism								
Style/appearance	3	5	2	10	2	5	1	8
Content	10	10	4	24	7	7	2	16
Flow	4	5	2	11	2	4	1	7
Clarity	4	5	2	11	2	4	1	7
Appendices	4	0	0	4	2	0	0	2
TOTALS	25	25	10	60	15	20	5	40
Lasting impression	10	10	10	30	6	5	5	16
OVERALL TOTALS	100	100	100	300	61	70	50	181

1.6 Communication is the key

1.6.1 Why communication is so important

We are all familiar with press reports of major systems that have failed to achieve the desired outcome. For every major one that gets reported, there are dozens of smaller ones that never gain such public notoriety. But what is meant by 'failed to achieve the desired outcome'? Usually it means that the prospective user has judged the system to a greater or lesser extent unusable. There has clearly been a breakdown in communications that has brought about a difference between the user's expectations of the outcome, and the outcome itself. This is the rationale behind the assertion that when deciding upon a strategy for systems development, the systems analyst should first consider how best to involve the user at every stage.

The most common reason for new systems to fail is poor communication somewhere along the line. Use of well-proven analysis techniques is a major factor in improving communication and thus ensuring mutual understanding at each stage of a system's development.

1.6.2 Communication skills

To put into context the use of the systems analysis techniques that are the main basis of this book, this chapter has been giving a brief overview of the environment within which these techniques will be applied. As implied by the above, however, working within this environment requires more than a knowledge of such techniques. The analyst needs to master a whole range of skills that can be considered generic 'communication skills'. These include 'fact gathering' ones such as interviewing, using questionnaires or leading discussion groups, and other more general ones such as handling meetings, preparing and giving presentations or writing reports.

Some people are naturally good communicators – others less so. There are several good texts that tackle communication skills, and one of our favourites is noted at the end of this chapter. While we need you to be aware of such matters, at this stage we want to encourage you not to feel intimidated by everything the aspiring systems analyst needs to know. We need you in a good, positive frame of mind as you embark upon the rest of this book! As we near the end of this chapter, simply remember that the fundamental requirements for a systems analyst are to be able to *think analytically*, and *communicate effectively*. Properly applied, the techniques in this book will assist with both of these requirements.

1.6.3   Ongoing involvement with users

We have seen that there is an important distinction that concerns the very essence of what 'communication' is all about – the difference between data and information. Generating pages and pages of systems design that no one will have the time to read may fool the unwary systems analyst into imagining that 'everyone has been kept informed', only to discover too late that users refuse to use a system that they find difficult to master.

The user should be given the opportunity to engage in the systems development process, considering carefully at each stage what is being offered, highlighting any perceived shortcomings and providing alternative suggestions from a user viewpoint. The person undertaking the software development must ensure understanding of what is being specified/discussed, and communicate clearly any queries or alternative suggestions from a software development perspective. Sensible systems analysts will commonly 'share' their techniques with users – helping them understand any diagrams drawn, and encouraging them to suggest improvements. It is the responsibility of the analyst function to be the bridge between the user and the software developer – ensuring that all communication is clear and acted upon. Active inclusion in the systems analysis process can be an effective means of doing this – it will be seen in Part 3 that the PISO method is one that formally recognises this kind of interaction.

As we have seen, the use of well-proven analysis techniques is a major factor in improving communication and thus ensuring mutual understanding between developers and users at each stage of a system's development – but there is one final, important point to note here and the next chapter expands on this. Successful systems development depends upon a planned and controlled project environment. The structured analysis techniques that form the main part of this book, and/or the object-oriented ones that we also spend some time on, can of course be used in isolation – but any project that attempts to do so without a degree of control is on course for failure.

1.7   Systems analysis principles

As we close this chapter, we want to leave you with a number of statements that encapsulate our view of what systems analysis is. At present, some may intrigue you. As you read on, our hope is that you will begin to appreciate what they mean. We will return to them and expand on them, in the closing chapter.

1   Systems analysis is problem solving.

2   Systems analysis involves research.

3   Systems analysis is about communication.

4   Systems analysis is different to systems design.

5   Systems analysis is about using techniques appropriate to the problem.

6   Systems analysis is about attention to detail.

7   Systems analysis is broader than computer systems analysis.

As we said in the 'Introduction' . . . welcome to the world of systems analysis.

This chapter . . .

. . . began by introducing the concepts of techniques, tools, methods and strategies within computer systems development. It introduced you to a number of approaches to systems development – structured analysis, object-oriented, the Systems Development Life Cycle, data-centred analysis, soft systems. It explained the use of prototyping and CASE tools, and made a distinction between data and information. It addressed the need for the analyst to be able to make complex choices and stressed the importance of clear communication within all of this, and the involvement of users. It ended by listing seven key aspects of systems analysis.

We have covered a lot of ground in this first chapter – but there is much more to come. It is our hope that you now at least have a much clearer idea of the systems development environment and the role played by the techniques that form the main part of this book, and that this introduction will assist you as you read on.

Whatever the approach, however, whatever techniques and tools, a systems development project will only succeed if it is planned and controlled carefully and professionally. This aspect merits further attention before we begin to cover systems analysis techniques in detail. The next chapter gives advice for the management of such a project.

Further reading

P. Checkland and P. Scholes, *Soft Systems Methodology In Action*, Wiley, Chichester, 1999.

J. Parkinson, *Making CASE Work*, NCC Blackwell, Oxford, 1991.
T. Warner, *Communication Skills for Information Systems*, Pitman, London, 1996.

Excellent general systems analysis books appropriate as a supplement to almost any chapter in this book:
J. Tudor and I.J. Tudor, *Systems Analysis and Design*, Palgrave, 1997.
P. Checkland and P. Scholes, *Systems Thinking, Systems Practice*, Wiley, Chichester, 1999.
D. Avison and G. Fitzgerald, *Information Systems Development (2nd edition)*, McGraw-Hill, Maidenhead, 1995.
S. Skidmore, *Introducing Systems Analysis*, Palgrave, 1997.
A. Dennis and B. Haley, *Systems Analysis and Design in Action*, Wiley, Chichester, 2000.

Web addresses worth a visit

www.rheingold.com/texts/tft
www.digitalcentury.com/encyclo/update/comp_hd.html
www.cet.sunderland.ac.uk/webedit/CET/reachout/piso.htm
www.smartdraw.com/resources/centers/software/ssadm.htm
www.borland.com/education/papers/eddelphi/eddelphi.html
www.principia.co.uk

Managing a systems development project

2

2.1 The role of the systems analyst

2.1.1 Background

Historically, many people have become systems analysts after working in the 'harder' end of the computing profession – programming, testing, debugging. Business areas that were 'computerised' were largely the simpler ones and involved relatively unsophisticated users often with little conceptual understanding of why things happened a certain way – they were simply paid to fill in this form, pass it to that person, and so on. It was therefore more realistic to train computer people to understand the business system rather than train users to understand the computer technology.

The dual role of 'analyst programmer' commonly evolved within such environments and is still found. Sometimes this is for reasons of expediency – a small company may have too few computer systems staff to enjoy the 'luxury' of separate roles. With the automation of ever more complex areas, however, and the general increase in computer literacy, the trend has now largely reversed with an increasing number of analysts never having been employed as programmers. Some have previously been so-called 'intelligent users' (a term with dubious implications, but often used!) while an increasing number have gained a computing qualification at university and have found systems analysis to be their chosen area of the profession. You may someday find your ambitions lead you to become a member of this latter group.

2.1.2 Personal qualities

It is a rare person who can claim equal success as both analyst and programmer, as each requires very different personal qualities.

For the programmer, interpersonal relationships are often not a primary requirement – the job can sometimes tend to be a fairly lonely one. Its frustrations are primarily found in the area of getting a computer system to work. The bright side is that the programmer who has just found and sorted out a 'bug' is usually allowed to look upon it as a moment of individual success.

As emphasised at the end of the last chapter, the systems analyst often has to be able to work in very different circumstances, calling upon the use of effective communication skills. Analysis can typically involve much discussion and nego-tiation and can thus depend heavily upon interpersonal relationships – with other analysts and also users who can sometimes be hostile. Unlike the computer program that finally 'works', there is nothing definite about analysis. The moment the design is said to be 'complete' will often be dictated by deadline rather than the satisfaction of *knowing* that it is. Also, in the most complicated systems so many compromises may be necessary that no one is completely happy with the result – and individual users may be so rankled by their own concessions that they fail to recognise what the analyst has achieved in gaining any agreement at all. In circumstances such as this, it is often the analyst's responsibility to negotiate for consensus.

It can be seen therefore that the systems analyst has a vital role to play at all times within a system's development, starting right at the beginning and staying with it through to the end. One of the first key requirements for the systems ana-lyst is the ability to decide which development strategy to utilise (that is, which systems development methods provide which appropriate techniques for the development to be undertaken) – and then which is the most appropriate means of controlling its use, managing the project.

2.2 Planning, control, progress

2.2.1 Working to a deadline

You still want to be a systems analyst? Good for you! – for it can be an extremely satisfying profession. One particularly satisfying aspect can be the opportunity to manage a project – pull it together, drive it along. The ability to do this begins with an ability to establish objectives.

The techniques in this book will equip you for analysing and solving a wide range of business and information system problems – but it will often be necess-ary to apply them to a tight deadline. This means that the analyst must be able to define and work to clearly stated objectives with a minimum of wasted time and effort, and commonly in co-operation with others as members of a team.

2.2.2 Balancing thoroughness and time

Key decisions that need to be made at the commencement of a project concern the balance that is necessary between the degree of thoroughness and the time available. As we have seen, many systems development and project control approaches have been devised, and the analyst will commonly play a key role in the decision as to which to use – the need being to decide upon a strategy that incorporates the most appropriate methods and techniques and tools to meet a particular requirement. We saw in the previous chapter how useful the weighted matrix could be for helping make such decisions. Any such decision should be based upon an assessment as to how best to gain the *fastest progress* through the *necessary* level of *planning and control*.

The important thing to remember is that the system requires **development**. There must at all times be monitoring and forward movement. Any development should take place as quickly and efficiently as the situation allows. Inappropriate adherence to long-winded approaches using large project teams is just as likely to lead to failure as the 'hacker' out for a quick and easy solution to a complex requirement. With the first, costs can escalate while an actual working solution remains out of reach. The second often leads to dissatisfied users who are left to find the design and programming faults in a system that has been passed off as complete and that turns out at best to have been a partially working 'prototype'. Is the project one in which extremely high quality and thoroughness are the prime considerations? Many set out to be, only to be hurriedly finished off as time and/or cost considerations begin to apply increasing pressure to have the system installed as quickly as possible.

2.2.3 Methods for project control

A number of formal methods for project control have been developed. We already referred briefly to one of the most famous in Chapter 1 – PRINCE (PRojects IN Controlled Environments). This is a structured project management method owned by the UK government's Central Communications and Telecommunications Agency (CCTA). It is directed and controlled by a Design Authority Board and supported by an active PRINCE user group. The methods are widely used in both the government and private sectors and in IT and non-IT applications. As with SSADM, with which it is associated, many organisations plan their projects on a basis that follows the overall PRINCE approach while not necessarily adhering to all of the details.

2.2.4 The need for clear objectives

Whether or not a formal project management method is utilised, the systems analyst who is leading a project needs a basic understanding of the need for clear objectives, and how to plan and control them. The remainder of this chapter seeks to provide such a foundation.

Clarification at the outset as to the real objectives results in a project where everyone is clear as to what is expected and one that has far more chance of remaining under control until the end. It is important to be able to think in a way that is 'objectives driven', and to use this approach to work as an effective team member and contribute to the overall management of a project. To give you the idea, we will introduce you to an approach called 'Management By Objectives' (MBO) – not because we are suggesting that you should adhere closely to it, but because it provides a useful way of beginning to appreciate just how important objectives are to the success of a project. Without clearly defined objectives, how do you know what is being asked of you?

2.3   Establishing what you are being asked to achieve

2.3.1   The theory of 'Management By Objectives' (MBO)

MBO is one of those techniques that grew up in the 1970s, surrounded by lots of hype. Management consultancies jumped on its bandwagon, and ran expensive courses to expound its virtues. While it is right to be wary of the objectives(!) of some of these consultancies, there is no doubt that the period did much to bring to the attention of British industry the need for a structured, focused approach. Many company executives reassessed just what their objectives were, and realigned company strategies to suit. It is the ability to clearly focus on objectives in this way that continues to keep many consultants in business – and they continue to be hired by those who have failed to develop such an ability.

In recent years a number of TV programmes have become popular that consist of an extremely tough objective being set, and then everyone becoming intent on seeing the job done – sometimes to the extent of working shifts of 20 hours or more, with little sleep in between. The participants share a common objective – and by each member dependably fulfilling their designated tasks and managing resources in such an organised and committed fashion, an amazing amount can be achieved.

2.3.2   The role of objectives

To appreciate how to manage objectives, it is first necessary to be clear as to what they are exactly. Have you ever realised that objectives rule your life? This morning you got out of bed. You did it because it was your objective to do so. In order to achieve your objective, you carried out a number of tasks – you turned back the covers, swung your legs out, put your feet on the floor, and stood up. But what was your objective *exactly*? It was probably that you should get out of bed by a certain *time*. If you continued to stay in bed past the time that you knew you should be up (in other words, you lost sight of your objective) you would inadvertently be achieving a different, shorter-term, objective – to remain cosy instead of face the day!

But what made you decide that you needed to get up by a particular time? It was perhaps because your objective was to get to the bus stop in time, to get to the university, to attend the day's lectures, to gain your degree, to get a good job . . . . You will note that these objectives are increasingly 'long-term'. The technique of moving from a shorter-term to a longer-term view of objectives and back again is known as 'adjusting the objectives horizon'.

As we 'raise the horizon' (that is, take a longer-term view), a fascinating thing happens in that shorter-term objectives become tasks of the longer-term objective. As we 'lower the horizon' the last task on that horizon resumes its status as an objective. Careful selection of the last task, that is, the objective, is vital – as all preceding tasks should be designed to focus upon it.

In the above example, the objective of getting out of bed became a task in achieving the objective of getting to the bus stop, which in turn became just one task necessary for achieving the objective of attending the day's lectures, ... and so on.

Some people always seem so organised. You can depend on them to do as they say, be where they need to be. Others struggle to find their way through each day, and soon seem to become overloaded with work. You can probably think of examples of both types – perhaps within your own peer group at university, or among your circle of friends – with similar abilities and even similar family commitments, and certainly with the same number of hours in each day! Broadly, they may have the same objectives – but the difference is that the organised ones have intuitively learned to *manage* them. Perhaps you can already identify which type you tend to be – most people are a bit of a mixture. Whatever your natural outlook, however, it is important to appreciate that by managing objectives, more can be achieved with the same effort. Or to put it another way, the same can be achieved with *less* effort. Because it is *personal* management, how you apply it is up to you.

2.3.3 The management of objectives

The career of 'systems analyst' is one where sooner or later it is necessary to be a member of a team, involved in the completion of, possibly, a sizeable project. Without a clear idea as to what the objectives of the project are, and then a means of managing the project to meet these objectives, the team will flounder and the project will not get completed satisfactorily.

You don't need to wait until you become a systems analyst or other type of team member before discovering the benefits of applying MBO, however. For the whole of your life you are going to be ruled by objectives. As we have seen, you cannot help it. You will gain tremendously by being able to identify what these objectives are, and then managing them. How should you go about it?

We shall first introduce you to the usefulness of MBO by imagining just one typical scenario that you could encounter as a student. Having done this, we will demonstrate the parallels between your own situation and that of a practising systems analyst.

Let us then suppose that you are a student undertaking an essentially practical module in which you have been made a member of a team. The following example is based upon the 'Information Systems Group Project' (ISGP), an undergraduate module developed by ourselves here at the University of Sunderland. The overall objective is to complete a fairly substantial project – lasting a whole semester, but broken down into two assignments. The teams of students are in competition, and there is a special team award for the best result for each assignment (you will soon see that this has a significant effect upon the objective). Each student must also take a time-constrained test.

There are therefore three major events to be considered:

- Time-constrained test (TCT)
- Assignment 1
- Assignment 2

The successful completion of each event represents the fulfilment of an objective. Each of these will require the completion of a whole series of tasks. But which will be the last one in each case? That is, which task represents the fulfilment of the objective? And what is the timing for each objective?

You establish that:

- the TCT takes place in semester week 6 – and your last task is to attend it;
- assignment 1 hand-in has a deadline of semester week 7 – and your last task is to submit the last part of it;
- assignment 2 hand-in has a deadline of semester week 14 – and again, your last task is to submit the last part.

In pure MBO terms there are now potentially three 'objectives horizons', based upon the timing of these events. If two of the events are targeted to happen at the same time there will be two 'objectives horizons', and if all events were planned to occur at once there would be only one.

Objectives Horizon 1 – take the time-constrained test

What is your objective for the test? How seriously do you take it? Do you simply want to scrape a Pass, or would you like to aim for something better?

Objectives Horizon 2 – hand in assignment 1

Should it be the team's objective to submit a 'good' one? With a bit of thought, and bearing in mind the competitive nature of the module, you may decide that your objective is to prepare the 'best' one. Surprisingly, neither of these objectives is really what the module is about – even the second is not specific enough because it does not consider who it is that makes the judgement. Your team's objective should be to produce the *winning* assignment – that is, the one the *assessor* thinks is the best. You will find that focusing upon an exact objective in this way is a vital part of the process and can have a profound effect upon all sorts of decisions as the project progresses. In this instance it should help you realise the importance of doing exactly what the assignment stipulates, and not wasting time unnecessarily refining areas not mentioned as being important.

If it is assumed that you will need to prepare for the test in some way, the fulfilment of the test and first assignment objectives will require work that is largely to be achieved in parallel. It will be necessary to regularly monitor progress and adjust the attention that each gets at any stage. Various techniques exist to help with this 'scheduling' of a project, with one of the most useful being covered in section 2.5.

Objectives Horizon 3 – hand in assignment 2

As for assignment 1, it is evident that the objective here must be to create the *winning* system.

Simply by carefully analysing what it is you are trying to achieve, you and your team have become 'objectives led' – and have identified the ingredient missing from many struggling companies. It is the ability to clearly focus on objectives in this way that keeps many consultancies in business – and fascination at what can be achieved by an objectives-driven team makes for compulsive TV viewing!

2.3.4　Tasks and roles

We have already realised that the fulfilment of each objective ends with the successful completion of the last task associated with it. Having identified objectives therefore, it is necessary to establish tasks – that is, the work required to achieve each objective, broken down into 'deliverable' stages.

Let us return to the above example. In preparation for the time-constrained test, it will undoubtedly be a good idea to attend lectures and tutorials, to ensure you have copies of all handouts, to check that you know the likely content of the paper, and to revise the required subject matter until you are happy that your understanding meets the standard that you have set.

Each lecture, each self-study period etc. can be considered to be a task. In MBO such a task is called 'time dependent': once the time has been spent, the task is complete. If revision of a particular subject area is chosen as being a task – perhaps checking understanding against last year's test – in MBO terms this would be said to be 'target dependent', because completion of the task is dependent upon achieving a certain level of understanding, no matter how long it takes.

To create tasks for the assignments you would follow the same process – the extra complication here being that the whole team is involved. If you read further you will soon appreciate how the team members would be allocated overall functional roles. Tasks would now be matched to members accordingly, possibly with some refinement of roles to compensate for any imbalance of workload. It would be important to keep on referring carefully to the assignment instructions. It may be that each assignment is to be broken down into separate components. Proper use of such information is the key to the allocation of members to roles and tasks – and this is fundamental to the process of changing a group of people into a team.

You didn't realise there was a difference? You will soon, but first let us apply the above scenario to a work-based one – for while the above may be very interesting, and may be useful to you while you are a student, what is it doing in a book that purports to turn you into a useful systems analyst?

Well, as explained in the introduction to this chapter, there are many parallels between the module-based scenario described above and the one in which you will be expected to work as a fully-fledged practitioner. While we can assume that you will then have attained a point in your career when the delights of time-constrained tests are best forgotten(!), you could be a member of a software development company given the opportunity to respond to an invitation to tender, in competition with other companies. The client expects a written proposal to be submitted, a demonstration of a prototype, and a short presentation. The written proposal is to be submitted two weeks in advance of the presentation and demo, both of which are to take place on the same day.

As with the student assignments, the overall objective must be clearly established – which is again the need to produce the winning solution, the one the
client likes best. It is then necessary to establish the objectives horizons. In this
instance the most obvious approach is to select two: the day on which the written proposal is to be submitted, and the day of the presentation and prototype
demo.

Once the MBO approach has been used to identify the tasks needed to complete an objective it is necessary to plan the completion of these tasks, firstly by
allocating them to appropriate members of the team. Often, sub-teams are
formed, each with the responsibility for establishing and working towards their
own objectives within the broader context.

MBO is a key to successful personal and team management. Once you get the
hang of it, be sure to mention this on your CV. Many companies appreciate its
worth and will be impressed that you know how to apply it. Before you can,
there are two more concepts that you need to be clear about – how to create a
team, and how to manage a project that uses one.

2.4 Getting organised

2.4.1 The difference between a group and a team

First we have to get definitions clear – so let's turn to the dictionary:

- Group – 'a number of persons or things placed or classified together'
- Team – 'a group of people working together for a common purpose'

(*Collins English Dictionary*)

The difference is that the members of a team **work together** to achieve a
common objective.

2.4.2 How to turn a group into a team

The first stage in creating a team is always to select the group members.
Sometimes when groups are formed within courses students are asked to choose
who they wish to work with. On other occasions students need do nothing in
this first stage because group members are chosen by staff – perhaps by allocating names alphabetically, or selection being engineered on some other basis.
This is certainly what happens in 'real life' – business-based project teams
inevitably being created on the basis of providing a wide mix of the necessary
skills. The ISGP module follows this model.

There are essentially three more stages that lead to the successful creation of
a team:

- Establish ground rules.
- Identify tasks.

- Based upon identified tasks, allocate roles. These may be largely organisational (primarily involved with the team itself – e.g. project leader, minute taker) or functional (primarily involved with the completion of the project – e.g. software developer, designer, hardware expert).

If you do all of the above you will be in a good position to **maintain** the team. This involves two essential ingredients – **communication** and **commitment**. Regular meetings and other contact, honest reports about progress, resolving conflicts, doing what you say when you say you will – these are the components that allow a group to work as a team.

Depending upon the size of the project, it is often recommended that the whole team meet together at least once per week – with meetings for sub-teams (e.g. the software developers, system designers etc.) in between as necessary. Full minutes of meetings are not usually necessary but a record of actions and comments on progress should be maintained for each. This should always record the date/time/venue of the meeting together with an attendance list and may typically contain details of techniques that have been used, which tasks have been progressed or completed, and which new ones are now to be commenced – with members clearly identified against actions.

Techniques may equip you to carry out fairly sophisticated systems analysis, to identify and plan objectives, but it is **communication, co-operation and collaboration** that will enable you to actually do the job.

2.5 Controlling it all

2.5.1 Introducing project scheduling

The planning of time is always an important activity when objectives have to be achieved by a given date – perhaps an anniversary present to buy, or an assignment to be done. It is particularly important when an objective demands that a *group* of people work in a co-ordinated manner. Proper organisation makes a tremendous difference to the effort required in meeting such objectives, allowing more time for family and social commitments.

The following instructions describe a simple set of procedures that provide an initial plan, and then a means of continuously monitoring progress – allowing timely adjustments to be made, and therefore preventing last-minute panics. While project management software packages such as Microsoft Project and CA Superproject are now commonly used to control projects, it is important that you understand the concepts that follow. You will not only gain an appreciation of how such packages work, but also have the advantage that should you ever consider them a bit 'heavy' for a small project you will have the 'paper-based' method to fall back on.

The first key point that should be noted is the difference between

- **elapsed** time (the time that passes during progress of the project), and
- **activity** time (the time actually spent carrying out the work involved).

2.5.2   How to go about it

Establish objectives

Begin by establishing 'terms of reference' – in other words, what is *expected* of you. These can be viewed as **external** objectives, or are sometimes called **imposed** objectives. There are three fundamental aspects to be found within such objectives: size, time to be spent and content.

A student should take care to note instructions such as

- 'in no less than 2000 words, investigate the benefits of . . .' (**size**)
- 'estimated time for assignment is 40 hours' (**time to be spent**)
- 'ensure that due regard is given to questions of reliability and security' (**content**)

Once these external objectives are established, identify any **internal** ones. These are objectives that you perceive as being necessary or desirable within the project, while not having been stipulated as a project requirement. It may be for instance that certain members of a project team would like to use the experience to gain further practice in programming skills, interview the client, or prepare and/or give a presentation. While there will always be jobs that no one wants and therefore need to be allocated by negotiation, where possible it is often a good idea to give people tasks that they have chosen, because they are then more likely to be committed to them.

Create a task list

All objectives, however determined, are achieved by carrying out certain **tasks**. Sometimes simply the terms of reference will indicate the tasks involved, whereas on other occasions – typically longer and/or group projects – the transition from objectives to tasks will need to be worked out carefully.

However the tasks are derived, the absolute rule is that every task should produce a **deliverable** – that is, something that can be 'ticked off' as having been achieved. A task called 'Continue reading Microsoft Access Manual' is not good enough – but 'Read Microsoft Access Manual chapter 2 and complete associated exercises', is.

The simplest task list will have the following headings:

- Task Reference (e.g. A, B etc.)
- Task
- Estimated Activity Hours/Elapsed Days (e.g. 16/2 for an 8-hour day)
- Actual Activity Hours/Elapsed Days (again, e.g. 16/2)

An example is shown in Figure 2.1. When completing the list note that it is recommended that

- every objective should involve a minimum of five tasks;
- no task should exceed around 10 hours of work (that is, activity time).

Task ref.	Task description	Estimated		Actual	
		Activity hours	Elapsed days	Activity hours	Elapsed days
A	Hold strategy meeting	4	1		
B	Prepare meeting minutes	2	0.5		
C	Distribute minutes				
D					

Figure 2.1   A simple task list

Keeping to these rules, you should be able to complete tasks often enough to maintain your interest, or (at least as important) to allow timely corrective action to be taken if necessary.

As each task is entered, firstly show the *activity* time only, as estimated *hours*. Then decide how many hours per day on average are going to be allocated to achieving the objective, and enter the *elapsed* time accordingly, as a number of *days*.

Create a schedule chart

The schedule chart is the means by which progress is monitored. Several types have been developed. While it is not felt necessary to actually illustrate more than one type here, it is worth giving a brief statement as to the strengths and weaknesses of a few.

- **Gantt charts** (so-called after their inventor) are perfectly adequate at showing straightforward *sequencing* of tasks. They are easy to prepare and read.
- **Network charts** were designed to address a weakness of Gantt charts, and clearly show *dependencies* of tasks upon one another. They are somewhat complicated to work out, however, and difficult to amend.
- **GASP charts** fairly successfully overcome the weaknesses of both of the above. They retain the clear graphical presentation of the Gantt chart, while allowing sequenced, parallel and dependent tasks to be easily portrayed. GASP stands for Graphical procedure for Analytical and Synthetical evaluation and review of construction Programs – or perhaps is what you do (i.e. gasp) when you are told the full title! Most project management software uses GASP chart principles, although often (wrongly) crediting them as being Gantt-based.

Creating a GASP chart is, fortunately, easier than remembering the words behind the acronym. The one in Figure 2.2 shows a chart as at day 5 of a project. The creation of such a chart usually proves to be illuminating in establishing the

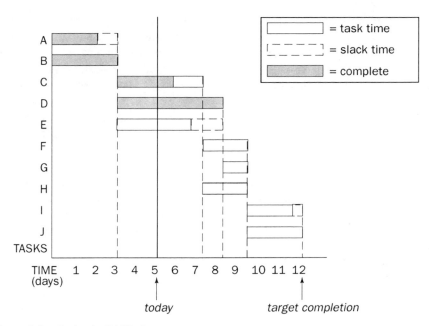

Figure 2.2   A simple GASP chart

content of a project – and once complete it provides a vitally effective means of monitoring and control.

According to the chart in Figure 2.2,

- tasks A and B are *complete*;
- task C is *ahead of schedule*;
- task D is *complete, ahead of schedule*;
- task E is *not started, and behind schedule*;
- tasks F–J are *not yet started*.

The stages in drawing the chart are as follows. First, draw an 'X' (horizontal) axis and 'Y' (vertical) axis, in the same way as for drawing a graph. List the references of all the identified tasks on the 'Y' axis, and mark days (1, 2, 3 etc.) on the 'X' axis. Then enter a 'bar' line for each task with its length appropriate to the elapsed days established at the task list stage – and do not overlook special days (such as family occasions) when no activity will be able to take place, adjusting to suit.

An important aspect when considering the starting point for any bar line is the need to decide whether the task is dependent upon any others. Using the GASP convention, dotted lines can be used to extend shorter bar lines up to what is called a 'milestone' or 'key point', denoted by a dotted vertical line. This is a stage at which all preceding tasks have to be complete before a subsequent (i.e. dependent) one can commence, and its position is fixed by the longest preceding bar line. Bar lines that have dotted sections thereby denote the 'slack' time in the project. The path through the tasks that incorporates all bar lines *without* dotted sections is the 'critical path' for the project. The reason for such a path through the project being identified as critical, is that because there is no slack time any delays in the actual execution of the tasks on this path are likely to delay the whole project. In the example above, the critical path would be described as B,D,G,J. If any of these tasks takes longer than planned, the only way that the project can be saved from running late is by one or more subsequent ones on the critical path being completed more quickly than expected.

When all task bar lines have been drawn, the total estimated days of the project will be indicated. By applying the expected start date, the projected completion date will be calculated. The terms of reference may, however, include a specified completion date. If so some adjustment of task activity times, or allocated hours per day, may be necessary. Always assume that the first version of the chart will not be the final one!

Note that the process described above uses primarily what is termed **forward scheduling** – that is, the tasks were entered on to the chart starting with the first one, and after all tasks were entered the likely completion date was determined. If this exceeded a known requirement for completion time, the chart was then adjusted. This procedure is most appropriate, however, to those occasions when you have been asked to *estimate* a completion time. On other occasions, the completion time is *stipulated* – and you are using the chart to determine how to meet the stipulation. For this it is most appropriate to use **backward scheduling**. This involves listing all of the tasks down the 'Y' axis in the same order as before, but then adding the bar lines beginning with the *last* task, and ensuring that it ends at the stipulated completion date (or a sensible time beforehand, to allow for problems). If it is discovered that one or more tasks should have begun before today, more time per day will need to be allocated – beginning with those tasks on the 'critical path'.

Whichever approach is used, when all adjustments are complete draw a neat version of the chart. This will now be used to monitor progress.

During the project

As soon as the project commences, mark the start date and therefore also the expected end date on the 'X' axis of the GASP chart. Then begin recording progress by shading in the bar lines – indicating the rough proportion of each task that has been completed. In this way, comparison of the shaded portions against the days on the 'X' axis will easily show whether the project is ahead of or behind time. As tasks are completed, enter the *actual* hours and days on the task list (see section 'Create a task list' above). As well as indicating how the current project is going, these actual times will prove useful when planning a similar future project (see Figure 2.3).

There is an approximately 90 per cent chance that the project will begin to run behind schedule, a 5 per cent chance that it will run on time, and a 5 per cent chance that it will run early. In 95 per cent of cases therefore, it will be

Task ref.	Task description	Estimated		Actual	
		Activity hours	Elapsed days	Activity hours	Elapsed days
A	Hold strategy meeting	4	1	5	1
B	Prepare meeting minutes	2	0.5		
C	Distribute minutes				
D					

Figure 2.3   Task list with actual times beginning to be added

necessary to adjust the schedule during progress of the project. The important thing is to *always work to the latest schedule* – that is, never be afraid to re-plan, and in particular never simply assume that it will be possible to catch up on a schedule that is running late.

2.5.3 Scheduling project teams

When controlling a whole team, a schedule chart should be created for each individual member – or if sub-groups are formed within the team, at least for each sub-group. An overall chart should also be created for the whole team, with each task identified with the team member or sub-group name. The team project manager should maintain regular contact with all team members, and keep the charts up to date. This is really where project management software comes into its own.

This chapter ...

... began by clarifying the role of the systems analyst. It went on to describe the concept of 'Management By Objectives', how to turn a group of people into a co-ordinated project team, and how to control it all. The purpose has been to give you an idea as to where systems analysis fits in the overall scheme of things. It can provide you with an absorbing and fulfilling career. Firstly, however, you need to learn the tools of the trade – the techniques that allow the analyst to analyse, communicate, influence and gain consensus. Parts 2, 3 and 4 cover such aspects.

A useful exercise

Imagine that you have to decorate a room.

1   List the tasks involved, creating a task list in the format shown.

Task ref.	Task description	Estimated		Actual	
		Activity hours	Elapsed days	Activity hours	Elapsed days
A	Decide overall colour scheme	4	1		
B	Work out amount of paint required	1	0.25		
C	Work out amount of wallpaper required				
D	↓	↓	↓	↓	

2   Prepare a GASP chart for these tasks, which should include an indication of at least two dependencies (note for instance that wallpapering cannot commence until the wallpaper has been obtained, and probably only after the painting has been done?).

Further reading

H. Plotkin, *Building a Winning Team*, Plotkin, Griffin Publishing, 1997.

K. Posner and M. Applegarth, *The Project Management Pocketbook*, Management Pocketbooks, 1998.

C. Bentley, *Practical PRINCE2*, Stationery Office Books, 1998.

D. Deeks, *The Information Systems Group Project* (Teaching Pack), Business Education Publishers, Sunderland, 1999.

Part 2

Structured systems analysis techniques

Spray and tree diagrams   **3**

3.1   Why spray and tree diagrams?

This chapter is a short but important one. We have written this book to introduce you to systems analysis techniques that will equip you to work as a computing professional. While most of the described techniques in this section
perform a major role within recognised structured analysis approaches, here we
describe two complementary techniques that play only a small part. When we
reach Chapter 6 you will find that the use of 'decision trees' is simply one of several techniques recommended when preparing elementary process descriptions
at the most detailed level of data flow diagrams. If none of this means anything
to you yet, don't worry – it will. In this chapter, however, we give tree diagrams
more prominence than they would seem to merit. So why are we doing this? The
reason is that the use of tree diagrams in a wider context can assist greatly in the
organisation and structure of information. Their use is often preceded by spray
diagrams, as these assist in the relevant information being captured in the first
place.

Spray and tree diagrams are therefore two different techniques, but complement each other and are frequently used together. They work in the same way
that our own thought processes do – firstly capturing information, then organising it. We do this all the time. A simple example would be the planning of a
shopping trip. We could first make a list of what was needed – we would be capturing the relevant information. We could then decide the most efficient way of
visiting the appropriate shops – we would now be analysing and organising the
captured information. Whether we plan shopping trips by writing lists or simply
by remembering what we need to buy will depend upon how many items we
need to purchase, and how good our memories are. The principle, however,
remains the same. We capture the information, then organise it.

The 1970s saw the introduction of Tony Buzan's 'Mind Mapping' technique,
based upon the spray/tree diagram approach. He has developed it to quite a
sophisticated level including the use of colour, images and symbols.

Spray and tree diagrams can act as a useful 'personal tool' between, for
instance, analysts in a team. An individual analyst can use the technique to sort
out ideas, and then communicate them in a clear and structured way to colleagues. Or a spray diagram can be created from a group 'brainstorming' session,

and then various tree diagrams created to show alternative structured views of the captured facts.

Spray and tree diagrams are also a useful study skill, as they can assist greatly in the learning of new concepts and techniques. They have many other uses. Time spent on this chapter will undoubtedly pay dividends later. We begin with spray diagrams.

3.2 Spray diagrams (the 'controlled brainstorm')

These are sometimes called 'scatter' diagrams – or even 'egg' diagrams. As explained above, they allow for the initial recording of the relevant information – that is, data **capture**. They also assist in the transition from disorganised facts into structured analysis.

To try one out, in the middle of a piece of paper write the title of a main subject to be analysed – try 'transport' to begin with – and draw a circle around it (or an ellipse – from which the egg diagram gets its name). Now think of anything you can that is even remotely associated with the subject (e.g. 'cars', 'buses', 'fares', 'airports'). As you think of each item, write it on the paper around the centre subject title, connecting each to the subject with a line. The example in Figure 3.1 is deliberately incomplete – use it as a basis and try to come up with as many entries as you can within five minutes or so. By formalising data capture in this way, it is often surprising how much information can be gathered in a short time.

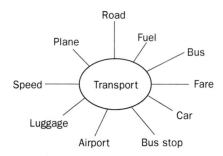

Figure 3.1 A basic spray diagram

When everything to do with the subject has been entered on the sheet, the entries should be examined for 'relationships', and roughly grouped together. As our example evolves in Figure 3.2, 'fare' is placed beside 'bus' and 'plane', but not beside 'car'. The diagram is now forcing you to **analyse** and helping you begin to **organise** the captured information (Figure 3.2).

You will find that this process often leads you to think of other entries and relationships overlooked during the first phase. In the example in Figure 3.2, 'diesel' and 'petrol' have been introduced as sub-groups of 'fuel', and 'route' has been introduced and related to 'bus'. 'Bus stop' and 'fuel' have been crossed out, because they have become sub-groups of other items.

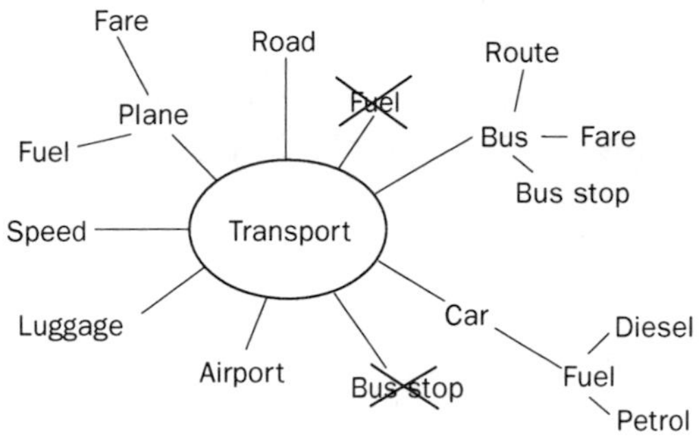

Figure 3.2   Spray diagram being developed

Introducing another item can radically change the diagram. If 'road transport' was an item, 'cars' and 'buses' could be linked with it and perhaps 'bicycles' then introduced and related. If 'motorised transport' was specified, however, only 'cars' and 'buses' would be part of this. You may like to reproduce the basic diagram above, adding other items and changing the structure as described.

Spray diagrams always end up a bit of a mess, with lots of crossings out as relationships are refined – but they carry out data capture, analysis and to an extent organisation, effectively. The relationships now have to be further refined and presented neatly, in order to complete the organisation and then **communicate** it.

3.3   Tree diagrams

3.3.1   Drawing one

As mentioned earlier, tree diagrams are often used within systems analysis for illustrating decision making, and as such are referred to as 'decision trees'. The earliest examples of tree diagrams date back hundreds of years and would, literally, be drawn pictorially like a real tree – with the main subject at the bottom and the groups and sub-groups branching upwards and outwards. This approach is still used sometimes, but within systems analysis their form has become more abstract, including usually turning the 'tree' horizontal as in the examples shown in Figures 3.3 and 3.4.

Continuing with the example shown in Figures 3.1 and 3.2 therefore, the main subject – in this case 'transport' – is now written at the *left* of the sheet, halfway down. By now copying and/or refining the items and relationships from the spray diagram, a simple graphic representation emerges of whatever was being analysed in the first place (Figure 3.3). As relationships are noted, it will be seen that groups and sub-groups are established – or even sub-sub-groups – and these can be shown using 'branching' lines. The important thing is that anyone should be able to understand it.

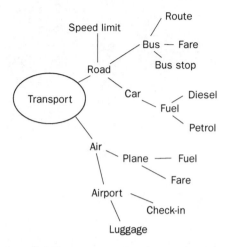

Figure 3.3   Resulting tree diagram

Sometimes it is tempting to create a tree diagram directly, without the spray diagram first – but this usually demands a re-draw anyway, to neaten things up. There are no hard and fast rules, however; as long as you end up with a tree diagram that includes all of the relevant items and relationships, you have *captured* the relevant facts, *analysed* them, *organised* them, and *communicated* your findings. It may even be that you are simply communicating your findings to yourself. If, for instance, the above exercise had been carried out because you needed to write a report about transport, the structure of the main body of the report would now be based upon the derived tree diagram. In the part-complete example shown in Figure 3.4, the numbers are beginning to indicate section and subsection numbers.

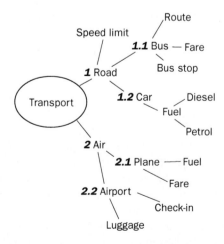

Figure 3.4   Tree diagram being developed as a basis for a report

3.3.2 More tree diagram applications

As a systems analyst you will often need to interview users, or attend conferences, presentations and meetings. From now on, instead of taking 'normal' notes, make a spray diagram of all the main points and associations – with the key subject in the middle. Afterwards, draw the tree diagram. If you become particularly adept at these, or the talk is a nicely constructed one, you can create the tree diagram directly. In either case, you will now have a structured summary.

If you are a student and have used lectures as your basis you will have a great 'revision aid' for the topic, to be used alongside handouts and textbooks. Even such as these can, however, benefit from the tree diagram treatment. If you have a handout or textbook chapter that you are finding difficult, make a tree diagram of it. You can also make a 'high level' tree diagram of a whole book or subject area. Or if you are trying to find out as much as possible about a particular subject, using a number of books all at once, capture what you read onto a spray diagram – you will then have a 'distilled' version of everything *all* of the books have told you, on one diagram. Turn it into a tree diagram and the facts will gain structure and be much easier to understand. Drawing it will in itself help you understand, and using it will help you revise.

Figure 3.5 shows the beginnings of a tree diagram illustrating the structure of three SSADM techniques. Even if you know nothing about the subject yet, the diagram communicates the structure and terminology in a clear and unambiguous way. As you continue through this book it may be an idea to return to the illustration now and again, and hopefully see it making increasing sense.

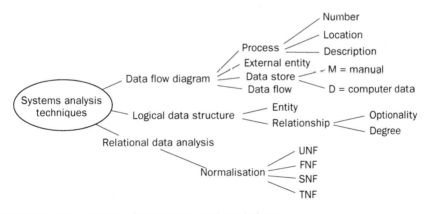

Figure 3.5 Tree diagram of systems analysis techniques

Spray and tree diagrams can help you plan a talk, design a system menu structure, draw up a questionnaire, prepare an interview, plan a project. You may well begin to wonder how you previously managed without them!

Look at the simple examples in Figures 3.6 to 3.8. They have deliberately been left a little short on detail so that you can see if you can add more to them. They are based upon the idea that you work for a software house and are involved in organising a small project team in responding to an invitation to tender. Firstly,

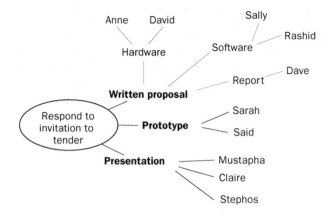

Figure 3.6 Tree diagram showing organisation of project

the whole project would need to be organised (Figure 3.6), then the database software to be used in the development of a system would need to be chosen (Figure 3.7) and a presentation planned (Figure 3.8). We hope that this has given you the idea.

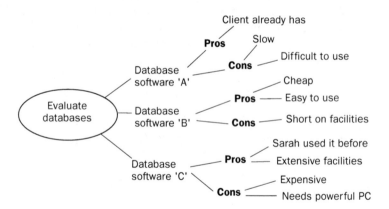

Figure 3.7 Tree diagram showing selection of development software

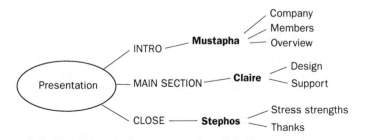

Figure 3.8 Tree diagram showing organisation of presentation session

This chapter ...

... began with a rationale for the spray and tree diagram approach. It then used a simple example to demonstrate the technique, and showed a number of further instances appropriate to the world of information systems. We hope that you have found the chapter useful. With spray and tree diagrams behind you, it should be possible to approach the rest of this book in a structured, efficient way as you discover more powerful structured analysis techniques. The less time you need to spend learning about these techniques, and therefore the sooner you can begin to put them into practice, the better. A tree diagram 'summary' of each chapter could be a useful way to reduce learning time.

Useful exercises

1   Prepare a spray diagram identifying items that you need to purchase over the next week, and then a tree diagram that illustrates an efficient way of making these purchases in one trip.

2   Prepare a 'personal revision' tree diagram of what has been covered so far in this book, creating groups and sub-groups that present the details in a logically organised manner. Your own structure may or may not represent the structure as presented by the written chapters – it all depends upon how you wish to organise the content.

Further reading

K. Williams, *Study Skills*, Palgrave, 1989.
A. Buzan, *The Mind Map Book*, Plume Books, 1996.

Web address worth a visit

www.buzancentre.com

Introducing data flow diagrams (DFDs)

4

4.1 Physical and logical views

4.1.1 An innate ability

It is always possible to view a circumstance in two basic ways – physically, and logically. We actually do it often, but probably never think about it. As we continue in our discovery of systems analysis it is a great help to recognise this innate ability that we all have, to operate in these two 'domains'.

The people in a room may for instance easily be identified by a physical characteristic such as hair colour, or those who are wearing jumpers or not. It would then be simple to create a tree diagram combining these groupings (Figure 4.1), thus representing one **logical view** of the **physical fact** that there was a variety of people in the room.

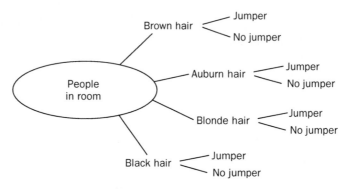

Figure 4.1 Tree diagram showing groupings of people in a room

It would be just as simple, however, to create a tree diagram showing marital status, qualifications, likes and dislikes, whether the person was a parent or not – or, if a classroom, whether a lecturer or student. This would again represent a logical view but this time based upon characteristics that could be said to be either not really physical at all, or at least less physically obvious. The successful 'unravelling' of facts by logical interpretation is a basic requirement of systems analysis. One of the advantages of tree diagramming is that it allows both views to be taken. These can be either separated as described, or combined. It would be possible to divide all people wearing jumpers into those who are married or not.

4.1.2   Applying relevant information

Physical buses – a logical need to travel home

This concept of physical and logical views may be tricky to grasp to begin with – but it is an important one. Logical views of a circumstance can vary tremendously, depending upon the information considered relevant. Imagine you aim to travel home by bus, and arrive at the bus terminus to find three buses there. They have different route numbers and you are fortunate – one is going your way. A simple physical view identifies them as all being red, all at the same bus terminus, whereas your logical view highlights the important piece of information that makes the difference – that is, the route number.

Now imagine the same sort of occasion but with slightly altered circumstances. At the bus stop is a minibus, a single decker and a double decker – but all have the *same* route number and it happens to be the right one (we did say 'imagine'!). In this fortunate situation you will probably simply choose the bus nearest the front of the queue that has seats available – ignoring the physical view that each is a different shape, and taking the logical view that the one at the front of the queue may get you home before the others.

Physical buses – a logical need to service them

Consider now that it is time for all three buses to have their service, and they are parked in the maintenance shed. The mechanic cares little which route number is displayed on the front of each – what he finds important is that one is a Volvo, one a Mercedes and one a DAF. He is therefore taking a *different* logical view. He is applying the information that is relevant to him, to a physical situation, and arriving at a logical conclusion – in this case identifying the differing service requirements. He has ignored all sorts of details irrelevant to the process that he is about to undertake – the route number is only one example. He cares little who was the last driver, how many miles the bus did this week, or how many passengers it carried.

You may recall the 'rich pictures' that we saw in Chapter 1 – these too were able to combine physical aspects such as processes and communication flows, with logical aspects such as conflict. It may be an interesting exercise to try creating a rich picture of the above scenario! Whilst such techniques can prove extremely useful in clarifying the overall components and interactions that make up a 'system', however, they do not provide the kind of analysis that the computer systems designer needs. As we will see, this is where data flow diagrams (DFDs) come in.

Three physical circumstances – one logical happening

Here is a final simple example of the concept of the 'two domains' that illustrates further how logic can often distil, or simplify, a view of something – and it is this feature in particular that can be useful to the systems analyst whose objective it is to create an efficient computer system. Consider a situation in which you wish to communicate with a friend. If the friend is sitting next to you, you simply speak. If you and your friend are at your respective homes you can telephone, or write. These are different physical situations, but from your logical viewpoint could be said to result in the same logical happening – that is, you communicate with your friend. You will see data flow diagrams being used to illustrate this example, later. The postman's logical view of the situation will not include the conversation and the telephone call. The telephone company will, however, consider only the telephone call to be relevant.

The key point to be gained from all of the above is that a logical view depends upon applying what is considered to be the *relevant information*.

Physical and logical views of business systems

Successful business information systems are those that provide the information relevant to that business. A major part of any systems analysis project is unravelling what information is relevant to the required outcomes, and what data needs to be held in order to provide this information.

Analysis of a business situation usually begins typically with people, documents, computer screens – a physical view – and is then followed by a focus upon the information required to meet the required business situation outcome – a logical view.

If you are finding the whole 'physical and logical domains' concept difficult, don't worry. For the moment, simply accept that these exist and that in common with tree diagrams and rich pictures, data flow diagrams allow us to graphically represent both.

4.2 Document flow diagrams

4.2.1 A predecessor of DFDs

Before we move on to DFDs, it is worth considering one of their predecessors. In the early years of computer systems analysis, when systems development inevitably involved the conversion of existing manual systems into new computer ones, an already existing technique called 'document flow diagramming' was adopted. It is fairly evident from the name that document flow diagrams only allow a physical view to be represented. As computer systems development increasingly involves replacing previous computer systems with enhanced versions, document flow diagramming is used less often. For those new to the whole concept of being able to diagram something that is happening, however, or with little experience of computer systems analysis, document flow diagrams can be a worthwhile introduction – particularly because they also provide a smooth conceptual transition to data flow diagrams.

4.2.2 Document flows and agencies

Document flow diagramming depicts where the document comes from, where it goes to, and what it is called. The **source** and **destination** of the document are commonly called **agencies**, and these are usually depicted using an 'elliptical' shape.

Returning to the example of communicating with your friend, a document flow diagram is limited to being able to illustrate the version of the communication that takes place via a written letter. This is the only one of the three alternatives (speak face-to-face, send letter, telephone) that involves transfer of information using a document. You and your friend are the 'agencies' and the letter is the document that 'flows' from one to the other, as shown in Figure 4.2.

Figure 4.2   A first document flow diagram

In business, the agencies would typically be departments within a company or outside contacts with the company. A simple example is shown in Figure 4.3. A purchase order is sent from the purchasing department to a supplier. The supplier delivers the goods to the stores complete with a delivery note, and sends an invoice to the purchasing department.

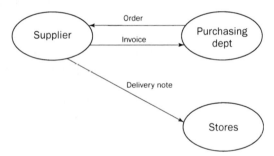

Figure 4.3   Document flow diagram of purchasing system

4.2.3   Using a document flow to improve a system

Document flow diagrams can often prove useful in identifying 'high level' inconsistencies/omissions. Examine the diagram in Figure 4.3, and read again the short system description that preceded it. Think about what is going on, and decide on the addition of one more document flow that would 'tighten up' the administration of the depicted system. Try to do so without looking at the solution in Figure 4.4 or reading on!

If you had a go, you may have realised that if the stores were to pass the delivery note back to the purchasing department, this department would have automatic confirmation of the validity or otherwise of the invoice received from the supplier. If you managed to work this out and found that the diagram helped more than the text, you have demonstrated to yourself that the diagram did its

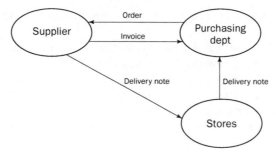

Figure 4.4   Document flow diagram of purchasing system – enhanced

job. It communicated the analysis that had originally taken place, made it easier to identify a shortcoming in the system, and finally allowed for the clear communication of a means of correcting it. This is the test of any worthwhile analysis technique, and something worth remembering.

4.3 Introducing data flow diagrams (DFDs)

4.3.1 A more powerful technique

So we have discovered a useful diagramming technique for depicting how a system works, in terms of the documents that it uses. But the limitations of this technique are surely evident. Documents are only one convenient way of carrying information in a form that is easily accessible to humans – advances in technology mean that electronic means are steadily supplementing paper-based ones, and people also converse with one another so the document flow diagram has always struggled to cope with such a thing as a 'verbal agreement'! These shortcomings were of course illustrated by the attempt to use the document flow diagram to illustrate your communication with your friend – it was able to illustrate only one of your three ways of passing on information. We are about to discover data flow diagramming – a technique that overcomes this difficulty. It largely manages this because, as implied by the name, it concentrates upon the data circulating around a system rather than on the information that a document carries (for a reminder about the difference between data and information, refer to Chapter 1, section 1.4.3).

Data flow diagrams concentrate upon the data needed to support the information requirements of a system – what data is needed, and the processes that convert it. DFDs are one of the most powerful and useful techniques available to the systems analyst. In the development of a new or enhanced computer-based system they are the interface between what is happening in the 'real world' of day-to-day business, and how these activities can be converted into suitable software.

4.3.2 DFDs and the two views

DFDs can be used not only to highlight procedural shortcomings, but also to recommend a system structure that will overcome them. The transformation from current inefficiency to future improvement is done in a series of steps that involve the 'unravelling' of what is logically happening within what is physically perceived to be happening. Using DFDs to create this transformation is not only extremely useful but also quite straightforward – yet there are many badly designed systems around simply because the analyst failed to appreciate this. A new system created without going through the logicalisation process will inevitably incorporate many of the shortcomings of the old one – and a brilliantly 'logicalised' DFD based upon a poor physical one will simply be built upon a weak foundation. Both 'views' are therefore equally important – and each is usually used twice within the development of a system, as explained below.

4.3.3   DFDs and the four stages

The physical view of the current system begins the whole analysis process, and the physical view of how it might be changed completes it. In the middle of this 'physical view sandwich', are two corresponding logical views. There are therefore usually four stages in the use of DFDs in the development of a system.

- Stage 1 – at the beginning of the analysis process a 'current physical' DFD is prepared that graphically represents the current system.
- Stage 2 – the 'current physical' DFD is logicalised to give a 'current logical' DFD, by removing all the physical constraints and thus giving an efficient view of what the system achieves, allowing the 'policy' behind the system to be clearly seen.
- Stage 3 – the design process begins, with new requirements introduced to the current logical DFD in order to create a 'new logical' DFD.
- Stage 4 – the design process ends with a 'new physical' DFD being prepared, to show how the new system will be implemented.

It is in the 'logical domain' therefore that the transition from old to new system takes place, and this indicates why the logical view is so important. Do not be too concerned if you are struggling with such concepts at present – all should become clear as we explore DFDs further.

4.4   Some first DFD examples

4.4.1   What you are doing at the moment

There is virtually no situation where a data flow diagram cannot be used to describe a circumstance. At present you are reading this book. You are indulging in an activity, carrying out a process that hopefully involves assimilating the data you are reading. We have tried hard to ensure that the book is designed and written in such a way as to present this data as information – but the book is merely a convenient way of holding, or storing, this data. In DFD terms it is a datastore. You could do various things with this assimilated data – perhaps tell a

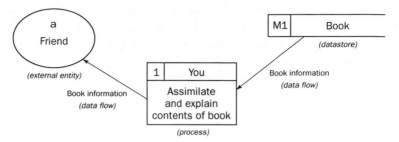

Figure 4.5 A first data flow diagram

friend 'face-to-face' what you have learned. You will again recall that the document flow diagram was unable to depict such a conversation – but the DFD can. Your friend would be seen as an 'external entity'. The data flow diagram would look something like the one in Figure 4.5, joining the process to the datastore and external entity using data flows that depict what data is flowing, and its direction. In order to describe this one activity, the four main elements of data flow diagrams have been introduced – that is, process, datastore, external entity, data flow. We will examine these in detail, shortly. For the present, let us return briefly to the example of the communication with your friend.

4.4.2   Three ways of communicating

As we keep being reminded, the document flow diagram was only capable of showing the instance where you send your friend a letter. We now see the big advantage of the DFD (*data* flow diagram): because all three versions of your communication involve the transfer of data, the DFD can show all of them.

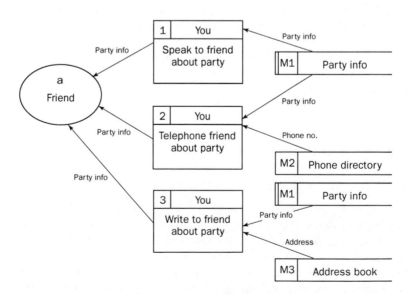

Figure 4.6 Communicating with your friend – physical DFD

The example in Figure 4.6 is therefore called a physical DFD, and it depicts three physical happenings – or, in DFD terms, 'processes'.

4.4.3 One logical happening

You will recall the importance of the logical view, however – and this is the next big advantage of DFDs. Figure 4.7 represents a first look at the way in which DFDs can be used to show the logical view of a situation, representing the same events but without any physical constraints.

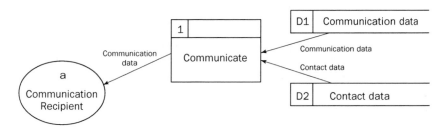

Figure 4.7   Communicating with your friend – logical DFD

The logical view that has been taken has assumed that the relevant aspect of the whole activity is to communicate information. It has therefore focused upon the need for someone (it now does not matter who) to communicate to someone (the communication recipient – that is, anyone who needs the information) by having available the data that is to be communicated (the communication data – whether it be about parties or anything else), and the data that indicates how to make contact (the contact data). To put it another way, because the logical view considered the passing of information to be the relevant fact, it now does not matter to the 'system' that it was you who was originally communicating, or that it was your friend who received the communication, or even that the communication was about a party. It would, however, still allow all the activities shown in the physical DFD to take place. That is the 'bottom line' test of a logical DFD – it strips away all physical constraints, but does not restrict the physical happening from taking place. The 'system' developed in the logical DFD is overall far less restricted in what it can do.

We hope that you are beginning to get the idea. Before you begin to create your own DFDs like those above, however, it is necessary to become properly familiar with their components.

4.5   DFD notation

4.5.1   Many conventions, four common elements

There are many conventions for the drawing of data flow diagrams, but all DFDs depict in one way or other the four elements in the diagrams we have seen already, that is:

1   The things that happen in a 'system' (**processes** – such as 'speak to friend about party', 'issue stock').

2   The data that moves when these things happen (**data flows** – such as 'party info', 'stock details', 'supplier details').

3   The stored data involved with the things that happen (**datastores** – such as address book, filing cabinet, card index, computer file).

4   The people or places outside the system, involved with the things that happen (**external entities** – such as friend, customer, supplier, invoice department).

The notation to use is down to personal preference, or may be imposed by the working environment. As explained in Chapter 1, for all of the 'official' structured analysis techniques in this book we use the conventions of the Structured Systems Analysis and Design Method (SSADM) as we find them to be rigorous and carefully designed.

4.5.2   Not to be confused with flowcharts

Before we continue, we need to make an important distinction between DFDs and some other diagramming techniques. In particular, many people who see DFDs for the first time already have experience of flowcharts, and imagine that DFDs are similar. Any similarity that exists is superficial, however; both use arrowed lines and boxes. Unlike flowcharts, **time** is not really an important consideration in data flow diagrams – for example, the first numbered process *need not* always occur before the second but it may. A DFD is *not* a flowchart – and structured systems analysis provides its own powerful techniques for showing time dependencies of processes, two of which you will meet in Chapter 11. Data flow diagrams simply show what the system *is* – the possibilities that exist within it, what happens to its data, where the data comes from and goes to and what datastores are referenced or updated as these happenings occur.

4.5.3   The four elements explained

To explore the four elements of DFD notation further, refer to Figure 4.8 and the explanations that follow. The figure shows a physical DFD of a sales system, deliberately very similar to the one that depicted the communications with your friend.

Processes (the rectangular boxes shown down the centre of Figure 4.8)

- These portray something actually happening, including any decisions that are made.

- Each is numbered, indicates the person or place carrying out the process, and describes in overall terms what happens there. Note that this decription must start with an imperative verb – e.g. *telephone* prospective client, *calculate* net pay.

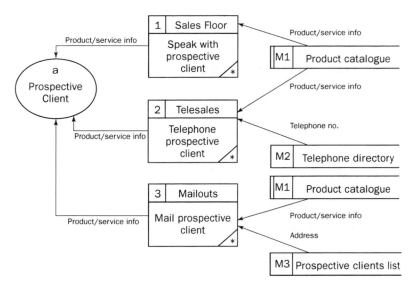

Figure 4.8   Physical DFD of a sales system

- Processes can be decomposed into sub-process, sub-sub-process etc. – allowing more and more detail to be exposed. An asterisk indicates that the 'bottom level' of expansion has been reached – we return to this aspect in section 4.6 of this chapter.

- The number of processes on a DFD should not usually exceed 7 or so – at least when you begin using them. If it does, the processes should be reviewed and certain ones combined.

- *When a DFD process is logicalised**, the person or place becomes blank – either 'disappearing' altogether, or becoming an external entity – see **External entities** below.

Data flows (the arrowed lines joining processes to other elements)

- These indicate the data flowing between the processes and the other elements – note that data flows must *always* go from or to a process.

- Each is named. Note that a data flow name must *not* include a verb. Data flows do not *do* anything – they simply exist.

- The arrows show the direction of flow.

- The data may be carried in the form of documents, or by any other means. No alteration of data can take place within a data flow – all changes are made by processes.

- *When a DFD is logicalised**, data flows that describe physical documents etc. are changed into pure data.

Datastores (the open-ended boxes at the right in Figure 4.8)

- These show data 'at rest' within the system.
- They carry a description and are numbered with an 'upper case' prefix – 'M' to indicate Manual files, or 'D' to indicate computer Data.
- *When a DFD is logicalised*, all of the datastores are given a 'D' prefix.*

External entities (the ellipse at the left in Figure 4.8)

- These indicate a person or place outside the system that is served by, or provides input to, the system.
- They are referenced alphabetically, usually in 'lower case'.
- *When a DFD is logicalised*, 'experts' who carry out processes are commonly 'transformed' into external entities.*

* See Chapter 9 for a full explanation of DFD logicalisation.

4.5.4 Some other points to note

- The relative positioning of the data flow elements is immaterial – that is, the diagram may be any convenient 'shape'. When beginning to draw DFDs, however, it is often advisable to follow the layout shown, with processes drawn first, in the middle, then datastores and external entities added as data flows are identified.
- Data flows must not cross one another; sometimes this creates the need to 'duplicate' datastores and/or external entities to make the drawing of the DFD feasible.
    - When datastores are duplicated, this is indicated as seen in M1 in Figures 4.6 and 4.8 – with an extra vertical line at the left end of the box.
    - When external entities are duplicated, this is indicated by a diagonal line in the top left corner of the ellipse as shown below. We will also see examples of this in subsequent DFDs. (If you're impatient, refer to Figure 4.20!)

    - Note: Processes are never duplicated.
- If any data *necessary to the functioning of the system* is transferred between external entities this may be shown using dotted line data flows. This is comparatively rare, but we include examples in Chapter 10, Figure 10.9.
- A broad arrow represents a **physical resource flow**, e.g. a movement of goods. This symbol is the least common one, and is in any instance only used in *physical* DFDs. The **resource name** is entered inside the arrow, as shown below.

Finished Goods

It is worth spending a moment clarifying the use of these, as students tend to either ignore them altogether or use them when they should not. There is actually a separate technique known as 'resource flow diagramming' where such flows are given great importance – typically for planning warehousing layouts etc. Within DFDs, however, their use is much more secondary, such flows only being shown if they trigger a movement of data while not themselves being accompanied by data. Perhaps the most common example is a successful delivery of goods to a customer that triggers the sending of an invoice. If the goods were accompanied by a delivery note the physical resource flow would not be shown – instead, a conventional data flow would be used to indicate the delivery note as the carrier of the data.

4.6 DFD levelling

One of the main requirements of preparing successful DFDs is to decide how much detail to show. The aim is simply to adequately describe what is going on. As explained earlier, DFDs can be expanded (or 'decomposed') into 'levels' – uncovering more and more detail by separating each process into sub-processes, then sub-sub-processes and so on. See Figure 4.9.

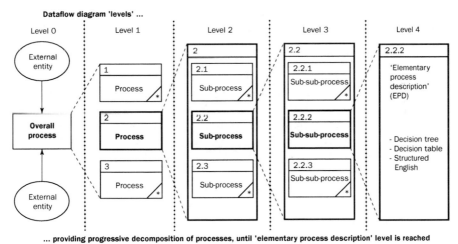

Figure 4.9   DFD levelling

- The highest 'real' DFD level is level 1.
- There is a level *above*, i.e. 'level 0', but this is often referred to as a context diagram. It contains only one process box with an overall description that covers the activities on the level 1 DFD, connected to external entities.
- The level *below* level 1, i.e. level 2, can include one DFD for each level 1 process, each showing that process further broken down.

- The level below that, level 3, allows the sub-processess to be broken down into sub-sub-processes, and so on.
- It is not always necessary or appropriate to decompose *all* processes at one level – as explained earlier, an asterisk in the bottom-right corner of a process box indicates that it is *not* being broken down further.
- The lowest level is reached when it is impossible to decompose processes any further, and consists of detailed descriptions called **elementary process descriptions** (EPDs). Such depth is only necessary when the analysis extends to defining the precise processing needs of a system. EPDs can be written in various ways – Structured English, decision trees, decision tables – or other methods, including narrative or flowcharts. They are explained fully in Chapter 5.
- Note the process numbering convention – each process within the boundary of the lower level DFD is identified by a decimal extension of the higher level identifier.
- A process box at a higher level becomes the DFD boundary for the lower level – and there must be consistency between DFD levels, with all the data going in or out of a DFD appearing on the higher level DFD.
- If a datastore is used only for that one process, it is placed within the boundary of that process, while a datastore used by other processes is placed outside the boundary.
- External entities are always shown as being outside the boundary of a lower level process, even if they communicate only with that process – because they are 'outside of the system'.

As we end this introduction to DFD levelling, there is one common question to get out of the way: how we define in practice what is our level 0, 1, 2, 3 etc. DFD. One simple answer is to draw a DFD that depicts your required set of circumstances, using a manageable number of process boxes, probably around seven maximum for those new to DFDs. If you feel you need more, combine some until you get down to seven (you will see more about this later). This is your 'level 1 DFD'. The process that covers all of the activity within your system is your level 0 process. The sub-processes of your level 1 DFD are of course your level 2 DFDs, sub-sub-processes level 3, and so on.

There is a considerable amount of detail in the above, and it is unlikely that you will have absorbed it all – but as you see the examples that follow it should begin to get clearer.

4.7 A worked example – the stock control system

4.7.1 Where to begin

The DFDs seen so far may have seemed straightforward enough to read but you may be somewhat overawed by the notation and levelling rules, and concerned that if you needed to draw a DFD of your own you 'wouldn't know where to start' – particularly if faced with the need to analyse the processes going on within a whole company.

Don't panic! As you progress through the next chapter we are confident that you will be ready to create real examples, developed by simply tackling the business problem in straightforward stages, thus creating data flow diagrams that are clear and useful. In this chapter, however, we are concentrating upon having you appreciate the *concepts* of DFDs rather than how to analyse a full-blown business situation. Let us return to the documents that a company uses. Because documents are physical they can be seen, handled, discussed – and analysed. Remember, they are a convenient way of carrying data – and it is data that we are interested in.

4.7.2   The document flow diagram

As explained earlier, document flow diagrams are becoming used less as technology advances. But documents are still of course in wide circulation as a means of carrying data, and document flows and data flows are therefore inextricably linked. We will therefore use a document flow diagram example to demonstrate that the processes that are going on inside it can be 'discovered' using a straightforward technique that also unearths the datastores and external entities involved, thus creating the data flow diagram.

Imagine that you are in a helicopter, hovering above an industrial estate. You have a pair of zoom binoculars with special lenses that when focused upon a particular company show you all of the departments – and even the customers and suppliers that the company deals with – laid out as a great big document flow

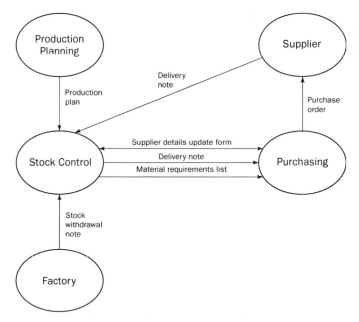

Figure 4.10   Document flow diagram of production area

diagram! You focus upon the production area and see the diagram shown in Figure 4.10. Do not worry if you cannot visualise what some of the documents are – all you need to appreciate is that **documents** (arrows) are moving between **agencies** (ellipses).

4.7.3   The context diagram

You now move the binoculars until the stock control department is in the centre of your view. Magically, the shape of this department changes into a rectangle – and at the same time you notice that the purchase order document flow has disappeared. The diagram you are now looking at is shown in Figure 4.11. It is called a **context diagram**. It is so called because it shows one department in context, ignoring any document flows that occur between other departments. In this case the purchase order has gone because it only flowed between purchasing and the supplier.

The stock control rectangle represents the 'boundary' of the system to be further analysed. The concept of the 'system boundary' is an important one. No matter what analysis approach is being used, it is important to be aware of the extent of the analysis being undertaken.

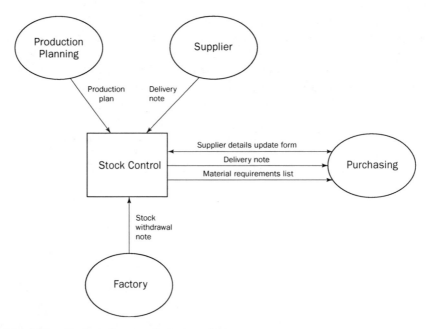

Figure 4.11   Context diagram of stock control

4.7.4   The DFDs

'Blank' documents, that is pre-printed headings without data, are as useless in business terms as the data without the headings. Together, as we saw in Chapter 1, section 1.4.3, we have information, but it is the data that flows – between departments, between people – and it is **processes**, that make it flow. Computers do not process documents, they process data. This is where data flow diagrams come in; with one small change, the context diagram in Figure 4.11 is transformed into a 'level 0 data flow diagram'. All it needs is for a process description to be added to the Stock Control box, as in Figure 4.12.

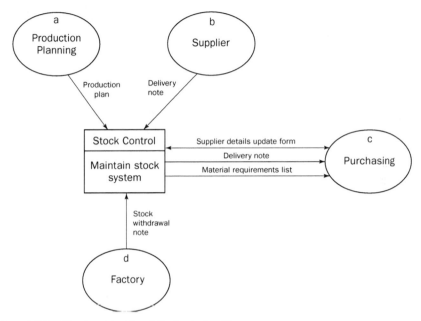

Figure 4.12   Stock control level 0 physical DFD

Note that

- because a level 0 DFD only ever contains one process, it is not usually numbered;
- a level 0 DFD does not incorporate any datastores, because any of these would be connected to the one and only process. They are therefore 'hidden' inside the only process box, waiting to be 'discovered' when the level 1 DFD is prepared;
- SSADM-style referencing has been added to the external entities.

To clarify the stage we have reached, and bearing in mind the advice given about recommended layout when beginning to draw DFDs, see the diagram in Figure 4.13 that has been 'laid out' to match the examples seen earlier – with external entities to the left of the process.

As explained above, datastores are not shown at level '0'. It is as we expand to more detailed levels that we begin to consider what data is needed to support the identified processes. Having established the boundary of the system to be analysed, we now 'zoom in' even further to discover what is within this boundary. We do so by creating a level 1 DFD equivalent to the book example. We need

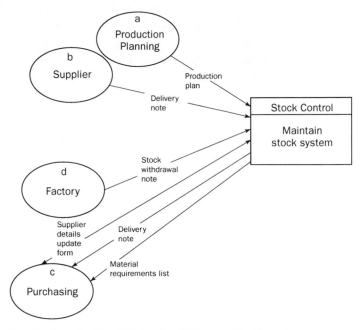

Figure 4.13   Stock control level 0 physical DFD – modified layout

to look at the different processes that together make up the overall stock control function, discover the data that flows to and from these processes, and establish where this data comes from and/or goes to – that is, the manual files, card indexes, computer systems, or other people etc. that support it. We will now complete a level 1 DFD of the above stock control system, just to give you the idea.

Imagine that, as an analyst, you have spoken with the people who together carry out the stock control function and have discovered more about what goes on within the department. You may well draw a DFD in the stages detailed below. As explained earlier, when creating data flow diagrams it is always best to first concentrate upon the processes, then identify the data flows and thus the related datastores and external entities. It is often useful when first starting to draw DFDs to get into a habit of entering the processes down the middle of the page, adding external entities to the left and datastores to the right as the data flows are identified. This encourages a step-by-step approach and tends to result in diagrams that are better laid out and easier to read, as illustrated below.

In Figure 4.14 we see the processes. In Figure 4.15 the data flows, external entities and datastores have been added. The diagram thus created – i.e. a level 1 DFD – gives a good overall idea of what happens within the stock control function and this may well be all that is required. In the same way as the overall process of the level 0 DFD led to the discovery of a number of level 1 processes within that, however, each of these level 1 processes can in turn be further expanded to reveal a greater degree of detail – that is, the sub-processes that take place at the more detailed level, as explained in section 4.6.

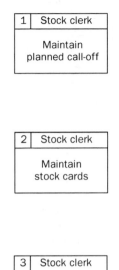

Figure 4.14   Stock control level 1 physical DFD – processes

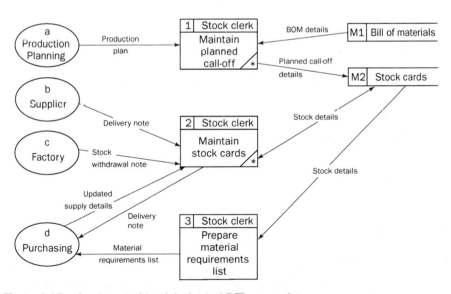

Figure 4.15   Stock control level 1 physical DFD – complete

Sharp-eyed readers will have noticed that processes 1 and 2 have an asterisk in the bottom right corner indicating that they are not going to be decomposed further. But what about process 3 'Prepare material requirements list'? What exactly is happening here? It could be as shown in Figure 4.16.

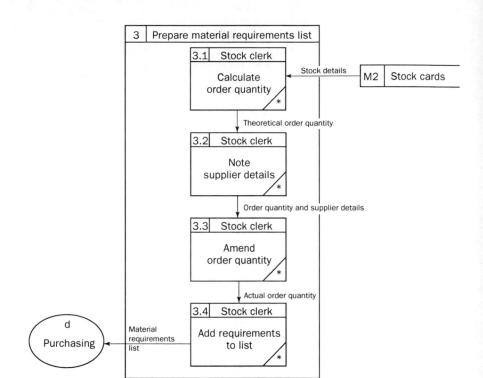

Figure 4.16   Stock control process 3 level 2 physical DFD

Do not be too concerned if you haven't got the hang of all the DFD notation yet. Neither are we expecting you to be a stock control expert(!) – but simply endeavouring to illustrate some DFD principles, in the hope that you are at least beginning to get the idea. DFDs are so important within systems analysis that we are trying to approach them in different ways to ensure that you understand them. The greater variety you see, the more you will get used to reading them. Because of this, the chapter ends with another couple of examples.

4.8   Two more examples of DFDs

4.8.1   The hairdressing salon

Take a look at the following level 1 DFD (Figure 4.17) and simply see whether you can understand what it is trying to tell you. If so, it should further convince you how useful DFDs can be as an analysis and communication tool – you have only just been introduced to them and already it should be pretty evident what is going on in this example. It is of course possible to draw DFDs that are confusing and difficult to read, but if you get used to reading examples that are clear, you are more likely to create clear ones of your own.

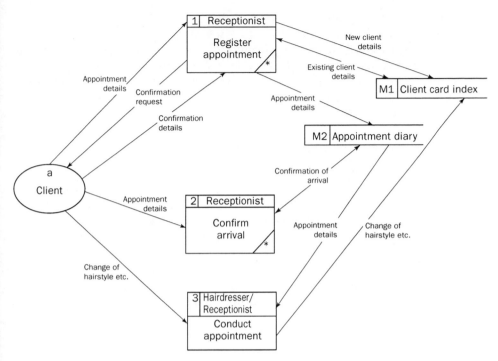

Figure 4.17   Hairdressing salon level 1 physical DFD

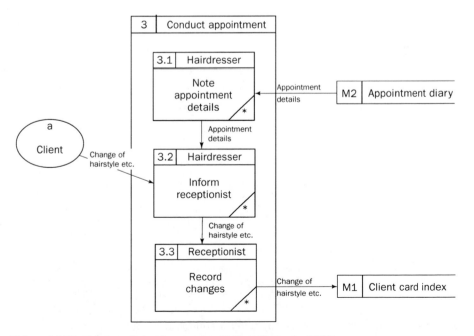

Figure 4.18   Hairdressing salon process 3 level 2 physical DFD

The level 1 DFD processes shown in Figure 4.17 could be further expanded into sub-processes in the same way as we saw happen with the stock control system. Again, asterisks on two of the processes indicate that they are not going to be expanded – but note 'Conduct appointment'. This is an interesting process because two people in the salon are involved in it – the hairdresser and the receptionist. By expanding it into sub-processes we discover who contributes what – see Figure 4.18.

4.8.2   The integrated accounting system

Finally, here is a comparison between a standard block diagram of an integrated accounting system – similar to the kind found in many textbooks used on accountancy courses – and a DFD of the same system. The block diagram is an excellent one of its type, and gives a good idea of the major components of the system. The systems analyst would need to know much more, however, and this is where the DFD comes into its own.

While you will find that the block diagram (Figure 4.19) is obviously simpler, the information that the DFD (Figure 4.20) contains is far more detailed and communicative. It tells you how the system *works*, rather than simply the elements it consists of.

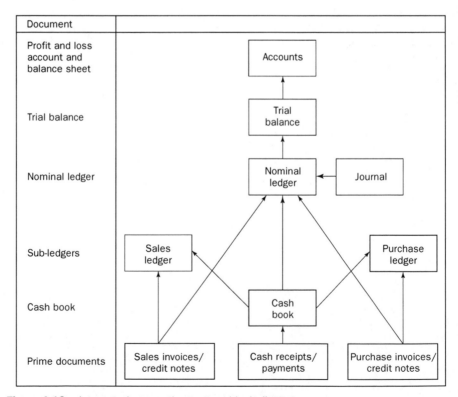

Figure 4.19   Integrated accounting system block diagram

Source: G. Taylor, *Computer Studies GCSE*, 3rd edn, (1991) Macmillan, New York, p. 164.

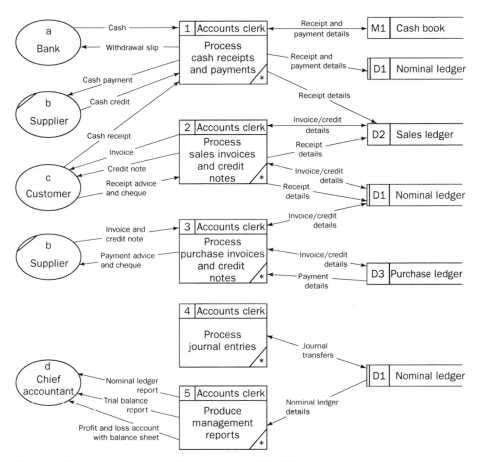

Figure 4.20 Integrated accounting system level 1 DFD

This chapter ...

... began by introducing the concept of taking either a purely physical view or a logical view of a circumstance. It then showed how the physical view as depicted by the movement of documents within a system can be communicated using the document flow diagramming technique. We then saw that documents exist only for the purpose of carrying data and introduced one of the most useful ways of diagramming what is going on – that is, data flow diagrams (DFDs). We hope you feel that you have gained a lot from this chapter. You may wish to go over it again and see how far you have come, either before or after tackling the exercises. Because of the importance of DFDs the next chapter continues with them, using detailed worked examples.

Useful exercises

1 Using Figures 4.15 and 4.17 as a guide, prepare a level 1 physical DFD based upon a 'system' that you yourself have taken part in – either as an employee or student.

2 Select one of the processes and using Figures 4.16 and 4.18 as a guide, prepare a level 2 DFD of that process.

Further reading

C. Britton and J. Doake, *Software Systems Development – a Gentle Introduction*, Alfred Waller, 1996.

Web addresses worth a visit

www.whatisreality.net
www.smartdraw.com/resources/centers/software/ssadm.htm
www.docm.mmu.ac.uk/online/SAD/

Creating DFDs

5

5.1 From theory to practice

5.1.1 Unreal and artificial

So far, we have seen why we need DFDs, the symbols used in their construction, the fundamental idea of different levels, and a number of examples. If you have completed the exercises from Chapter 4, you will also have had a go at creating your own. We are now going to lead you through two more worked examples. Before we start, however, we would just like to point out a serious problem we have when writing about DFDs for you as an aspiring systems analyst – the fact that it is all a bit unreal, or artificial.

There are two reasons for this. First, when we as authors are writing about a technique, we have to think of a scenario or example that we can use to illustrate the development of that technique. We therefore invent one or use one from our own experience and write it down on paper so that readers can use it to draw, say, a data flow diagram. The unfortunate thing with this is that, in producing the scenario, nearly all the work has already been done.

The really interesting part of systems analysis is in finding out what goes on in the existing system, and to do this you have to interview people, observe procedures, read documents, do some measurements and basically fact-find. To be successful at this, you need all sorts of characteristics other than the ability to draw a data flow diagram – skills like interviewing technique, diplomacy, attention to detail, patience etc. It is virtually impossible to learn these aspects of systems analysis from a book – you need to go on courses that involve role play and simulation, actively practise systems analysis and watch an experienced systems analyst in action. The drawing of the DFD is probably the *least* important part of the initial systems investigation; the really important part is getting the facts right and establishing a rapport with your users. The DFD is simply a technique that you use to describe what you have found, as well as being a good communication aid in its own right.

5.1.2 Context diagrams in context

The second reason is inextricably linked with the first. We introduced DFDs in the previous chapter by first showing the document flow diagram. We changed this into a context diagram and then expanded it into a level 1 DFD. We saw that we could expand DFDs to lower and lower levels until we were happy we had uncovered all of the necessary detail.

Although this is one of the best ways of introducing the concepts of DFDs, it may well not be as easy as that in practice. Imagine you have been brought into an organisation to do a systems analysis on the sales order processing system, which is largely manual. How, practically, can you start off the investigation by drawing a context diagram? You will need to know all the documents and other data flows that go in and out of the system, who sends them and who receives them – and you will need to know all of this from scratch. Impossible!! Basically, you can only interview one person at a time or observe one process at a time and so you will, of necessity, have to start at the detail end, talking to Fred or Nora about what exactly it is they do. Hence, while you will keep your eye on the higher level objective of producing an overall context diagram view of the system, you will be able to piece together snippets of the lower level DFDs as you go along, gradually building up the higher level DFDs, noticing inconsistencies and returning periodically to the lower levels. This 'bottom-up' approach to building DFDs is very common. It is rather like completing a jigsaw.

5.1.3   Functional areas and processes

One final word of advice before we start getting serious. You should always aim to come up with level 1 physical DFDs that contain one process box for each 'functional area'. For example, if you are investigating a large system made up of several departments, each department can be a level 1 process box. This makes sense as it is likely you are going to be investigating one department at a time. Then, when you start on level 2 DFDs, make the process boxes correspond to a person or a section in that department.

As you will see from the example that follows, this does not mean that the 'first version' of your physical DFD needs to follow this rule – but we strongly recommend that your final one does. You will discover in Chapter 9 that the whole thing becomes unravelled in any case when we logicalise the system. It is during the logicalisation process that you spot duplication and inefficiencies and sort them out. But to start with you need to document what actually happens, warts and all.

5.2   Example 1 – the boat building company

5.2.1   The scenario

This company is called Marine Construction – a firm that builds boats to a customer's specification. The description was obtained from interviews with the General Manager, who has a good overview of the whole process.

Customers send to Marine Construction a specification of the boat they want built. The Sales Office use this detail to make out a special form, BQ1, that includes the customer

EXAMPLE 1 – THE BOAT BUILDING COMPANY   **81**

specification as well as a deadline date for the quote to be ready. It is then sent to the Design Office who produce the drawing and material specifications and send this with a partially complete BQ1 to the Materials Office. They price up the material needed using their Material Catalogue and add this detail to the BQ1 before passing it to the Production Office. Here the required labour is estimated and, using the labour rates held in the Labour Rates File, the estimate is added to the BQ1. The BQ1 is now returned, with the drawings and specifications, to the Sales Office who complete it by adding on an appropriate mark-up by reference to the Sales Manager. Using the now complete BQ1 two copies of a formal quotation are prepared. One copy is sent to the customer and the other is filed with the BQ1, drawing and materials specification in the Quotes File. If and when the customer sends a letter of intent the relevant BQ1, copy of the quote, drawing and materials specification are retrieved from the Quotes File and sent to the Order Processing System.

5.2.2   Initial attempt at current level 1 physical DFD

An initial attempt at a data flow diagram is always influenced by the way the description is written. This one is written in a sequential manner, in that it basically follows a BQ1 around the system. Figure 5.1 shows a level 1 physical DFD based directly upon the description. As you study it, note the following:

- The BQ1 is having data added to it all the time so these updates have been called BQ1(1), BQ1(2) etc., through to BQ1(completed).
- Documents that are sent together are shown on the same data flows.
- The only external entities shown are the Customer (this is obvious) and the Order Processing System which is another system within the company but external to the Quotes System. If the whole Sales Order Processing System were being examined – including Quotations – then the Quotes System would itself be a level 1 process box in a much larger DFD.
- The Sales Manager is not an external entity as she or he is part of the Sales Office functionality in process box 5 and therefore 'part of the action', and could well become an external entity when the diagram is logicalised – but that is later.
- Only one datastore – i.e. the Quotes file – is shown on this level 1 DFD. There are other datastores in the description but this is the only one used by more than one process. The other datastores belong to one and only one process. At the moment we have not expanded these level 1 boxes into level 2. A datastore should only be shown on a DFD if it is used by more than one process at that DFD level. When the processes are expanded further at the next level, the datastores used by the sub-processes are thus exposed. When the level is reached where further expansion is not intended (indicated by the use of an asterisk in the bottom right corner of each process), all further datastores should be shown. This means that if only a level 1 DFD is to be drawn, *all* datastores should usually be shown. Exceptions to this include instances where a 'high level' DFD is being used simply to give an overview of a system's processes.

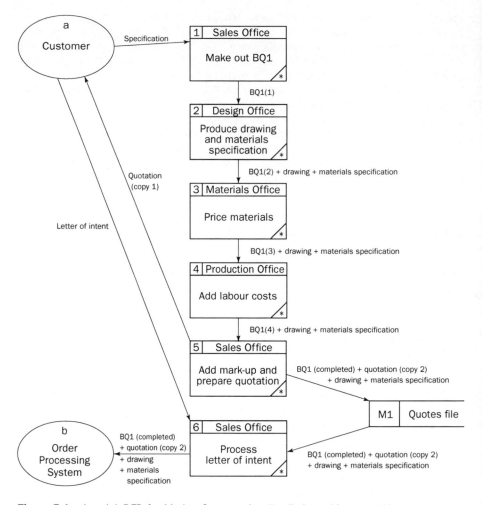

Figure 5.1   Level 1 DFD for Marine Construction ('walk-through' approach)

5.2.3   Second version of DFD – 'one process per functional area'

Figure 5.1 is an example of what is commonly referred to as the 'system walk-through' approach to drawing a DFD – in this case, it follows the BQ1 as it progresses around the system. It is pretty good at graphically representing the result of our initial investigation. We now return to the recommendation given earlier, however: to have each process box relate to one functional area.

Note that in Figure 5.1 the Design Office, Materials Office and Production Office all have their own process boxes but the Sales Office has three. The initial DFD is therefore redrawn to make the Sales Office like the others – so that each process represents only one 'functional area' – and the result is shown in Figure 5.2.

Sometimes it is difficult to decide on a 'functional area'. The following points should be noted.

EXAMPLE 1 – THE BOAT BUILDING COMPANY   **83**

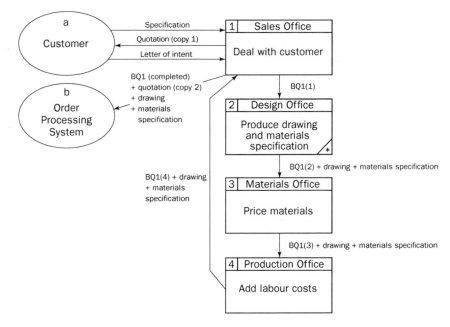

Figure 5.2   Level 1 DFD for Marine Construction (one process per functional area)

- *When the level 1 DFD covers several departments*, each department should be contained within one level 1 process box. The above is an example of this. This makes sense as it is easier to further analyse one department at a time – this being done when each process box in the level 2 DFD is made to correspond to a person or section within that department.

- *When the level 1 DFD represents one subsectioned department*, each subsection (which may be only one person) should, similarly, be represented by one process.

- *When the level 1 DFD represents one 'multi-skilled' department* (i.e. with all members covering all tasks), the tasks should be logically grouped into functions.

- *When the level 1 DFD represents only one person*, then similarly, their work should be logically grouped into functions.

Even if these guidelines are not closely followed, the whole 'system' later becomes unravelled, when it is logicalised (Chapter 9) – but the more refined the 'current physical DFD' is, the easier the subsequent logicalisation. It is during the logicalisation process that 'who does what' is questioned rather than assumed, and duplication and inefficiencies are highlighted and sorted out.

5.2.4   Level 2 DFDs

It is now necessary to consider whether to expand any of the level 1 processes to level 2. Obviously, the initial description of the Marine Construction quotations system was quite 'high level'. Is it worth expanding it further? The asterisk in the bottom right corner of process 2 indicates the decision that has been made – that processes 1, 3 and 4 are worthy of further investigation. To understand the decision to look at these further, we should be reminded that the purpose of such a DFD is to document what actually happens at present. The more detail it unearths, the less likelihood there is of unexpected 'discoveries' later in the project. As it happens, there is already enough information about the Sales Office found in the original level 1 DFD for us to have a good attempt at a level 2 DFD for this area. See Figure 5.3.

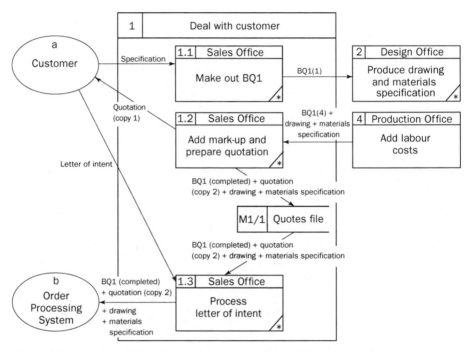

Figure 5.3   Level 2 DFD for Marine Construction Sales Office (derived from information already apparent in original level 1 DFD – see Figure 5.1)

As you study the DFD in Figure 5.3, note the following points regarding DFD 'levelling' (they may seem tricky to begin with, but will steadily make sense as familiarity with DFDs increases).

- A process box at a higher level becomes the DFD boundary for the lower level – and there must be consistency between DFD levels, with all data going in or out of a DFD appearing on the higher level DFD. Level 2 DFDs must be *consistent with* the level 1 DFD. In other words all the data going into and out of each level 1 process box must also go into and out of the level 2 expansion of that process. Data flows cannot suddenly be introduced or lost, as this would lead to uncertainty and inconsistency. Around the outside of the level 2 processes should be found all the external entities and

EXAMPLE 1 – THE BOAT BUILDING COMPANY   **85**

other processes and datastores that feed data into and receive data from the process.

- Each process within the boundary of the higher level process is numbered with a decimal extension of the higher level process number, e.g 1.1, 1.2 etc.
- If a datastore is used only for one process, it is placed within the boundary of that process, while a datastore used by other processes is placed outside the boundary (i.e. outside the process, but still inside the system). Note the reference number of the Quotes file M1/1. This refers to the first datastore in the expansion of process box 1 – further ones would be M1/2, M1/3 . . . etc. There is no rule regarding the order in which the datastores are numbered – it is common to simply begin with the one nearest the top of the page, or number them as they are 'discovered' during the analysis.
- External entities are always shown as being outside the boundary of a lower level process, even if they communicate only with that process.
- It will be remembered that the asterisk in the bottom right-hand corner of a process box indicates that this is a lowest level process and will not be expanded any further; in this case it will not be expanded to level 3.

In order to show processes 3 and 4 in more detail, more investigation is required. We will move on to the stage where this has happened. As noted earlier, no further expansion of process 2 is appropriate. It has been discovered that the Design Office relies heavily on the inspiration, expertise and experience of the designer and so cannot really be described except to say that the drawing and the materials specification are produced, and some details added to the BQ1. Further information for the Materials and Production Offices (i.e. processes 3 and 4) has, however, been considered appropriate, and is given below.

The Materials Office takes care to ensure that accurate costs are produced. Each material specified is checked against the Stock Card Index system. Where sufficient stock is available to fulfil this quotation then the most recent invoice is used for the quote. If there is insufficient stock then the Material Catalogue is used.

The Production Office people take similar care. The drawing and material specification are used to create a Work Schedule with each operation of the job identified in terms of equipment used, time taken and labour grade needed. The Work Schedule is prepared and clipped into a ring binder. Using this Work Schedule each operation is costed by reference to the Labour Rates file (a rate depends on the labour grade). In addition a cost is added depending on the equipment used (by reference to the Quarterly Cost Report) to give a total cost per operation.

Level 2 DFDs for the Materials Office (process 3) and Production Office (process 4) are shown in Figures 5.4 and 5.5. One final point to note is illustrated in particular in the Materials Office (i.e. in Figure 5.4): DFDs contain no decision symbol. As explained in Chapter 4, section 4.5.2, this is one clear way in which they are different to flowcharts, and is quite deliberate. Any decisions that are

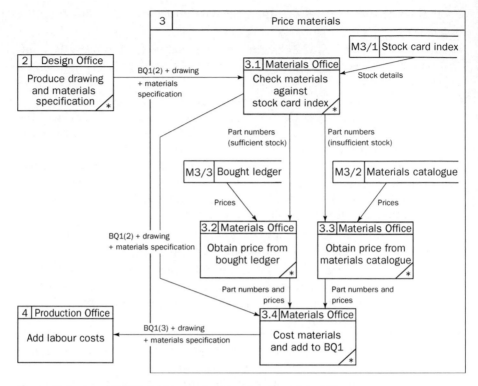

Figure 5.4 Level 2 DFD for Marine Construction Materials Office

made are described in the process description that accompanies each of the lowest level DFD processes. Process 3.1 in the Materials Office will, for instance, involve a decision as to whether there is sufficient stock of a material to meet the estimate. This is implied by the two data flows coming out of 3.1 called *Part numbers (sufficient stock)* and *Part numbers (insufficient stock)*. The data on both flows is exactly the same – it is a list of part numbers but the bracketed part is there to add meaning to the DFD. DFDs are, after all, intended to act as a communication tool.

5.3 Example 2 – the student assessment system

5.3.1 The scenario

The following example is about the system used to assess students on the second year of a degree course in business computing. The system was used in our university until recently and we have chosen it because it is fairly straightforward and yet has sufficient subtle little touches to make it interesting. We have simplified it slightly for the sake of clarity.

EXAMPLE 2 – THE STUDENT ASSESSMENT SYSTEM   **87**

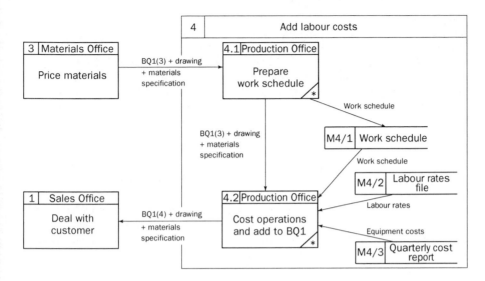

Figure 5.5 Level 2 DFD for Marine Construction Production Office

In the second year of the BA Business Computing course, students study six subjects:

Quantitative Methods
Systems Analysis & Design
Computer Systems
Software Engineering
Business Studies
Behavioural Studies

They are assessed in each subject by coursework and an end-of-year examination. The following description of the system is based around the roles of the various 'players'.

The subject tutor

Subject tutors first get involved when they are allocated to a subject by the timetabler. Subject tutors are responsible for setting courseworks (assignments) and giving them to students. The student completes the assignment and returns it to the subject tutor. They are then marked, the marks recorded and the assignments returned to the students with feedback. There may be a number of assignments per subject each with a different weighting (i.e. some assignments may be worth 50% of the coursework mark while others only 20%). Tutors record the marks in a variety of ways. Most use a spreadsheet while some still record them on paper. At the end of the year the subject tutor must calculate a final coursework mark for each student and pass a copy of these to the Year Leader.

Subject tutors are also responsible for setting an end-of-year examination. Once the paper is written and moderated (we shall ignore the moderation process for simplicity) the paper is sent to the Examinations Office who organise the time and place of the examination, arrange for the exam to be invigilated and then return the completed scripts to the subject tutor. The subject tutor then marks the scripts, records the mark and sends a copy to the Year Leader along with the coursework marks.

The Year Leader

The Year Leader is responsible for the final collation of marks for presentation to the Board of Examiners. The Year Leader produces a spreadsheet that shows, for each student, the coursework mark and the examination mark for each subject and the weighted average of these two marks (courseworks and examinations normally have a 20/80% weighting). Any fails are highlighted on the spreadsheet and the Year Leader brings copies of the spreadsheet to the Board of Examiners, together with any mitigating evidence received from the student.

The Board of Examiners

The Board is made up of all the subject tutors, the Year Leader (who is almost always a subject tutor as well), at least one external examiner and is chaired by the Director of School. The School Administrator is also in attendance to record decisions and take minutes. The Board looks at each student's marks carefully, takes into consideration any mitigating evidence and decides on the results for each student by applying a set of regulations. The regulations are complicated and will not be described here but basically students may be required to do extra work in some subjects or, in extreme cases, may have to repeat the whole year or even withdraw from the course.

The School Administrator

When the School Administrator receives the results from the Board of Examiners, he/she produces a Pass List which is passed to the Head of School. The results are then filed in a Course Results File. The Head of School signs the Pass List and returns it to the School Administrator who files it with the results. When all the results from all of the Boards of Examiners have been processed in this way, the School Administrator sends a copy of the results and Pass List to the Examinations Office.

Students who wish to have a copy of the results must submit a stamped addressed envelope to the School Administrator who sets up a file of such envelopes. A little while after the Board of Examiners, the School Administrator matches the results to the names on the envelopes and sends the results to the students.

5.3.2 Initial discussion

This description is very different to the one for Marine Construction. Have a close look at the two to see what the basic difference is.

Yes, this one is already broken down into functional areas. The Marine Construction description is very sequential – one thing happens after another. This one is different – it concentrates on the jobs performed by the various parties involved.

By preparing a description written in this way, we are making it easy to draw a data flow diagram according to our advice that a level 1 DFD should have each process box correspond to a functional area.

5.3.3 Initial attempt at current physical DFDs

In Figure 5.6 you will find a level 1 DFD. In Figures 5.7, 5.8 and 5.9 are shown the level 2 DFDs for processes 1, 2 and 4. It has been decided not to expand process 3 (Moderate and finalise results) at this stage, as the description of this

EXAMPLE 2 – THE STUDENT ASSESSMENT SYSTEM   **89**

process is best done in another way (as we will see in Chapter 6, 'Specifying processes').

Note in Figure 5.9 the dataflows 'Envelope' and 'Stamped addressed envelope'. It could be argued that these should be shown as *physical resource flows* as referred to in Chapter 4, section 4.5.4, but we have decided to leave them as standard dataflows.

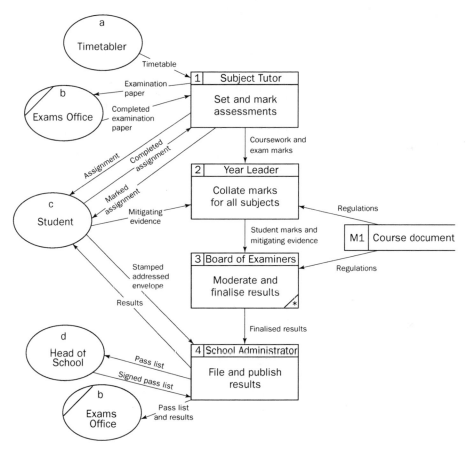

Figure 5.6   Level 1 DFD (current physical) for student assessment system

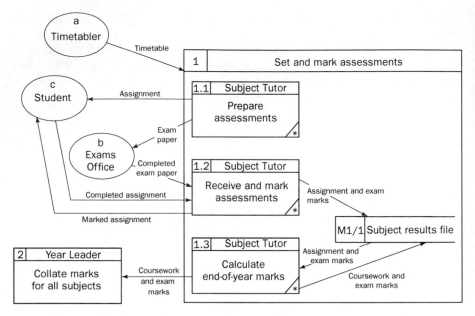

Figure 5.7 Level 2 DFD (current physical) for student assessment system process 1, 'Set and mark assessments'

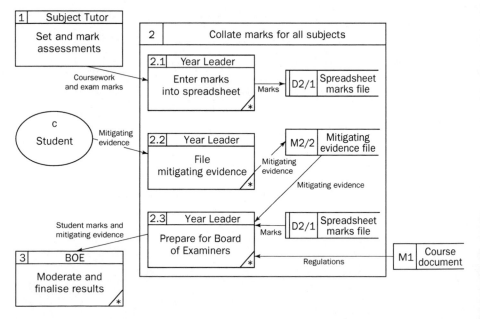

Figure 5.8 Level 2 DFD (current physical) for student assessment system process 2, 'Collate marks for all subjects'

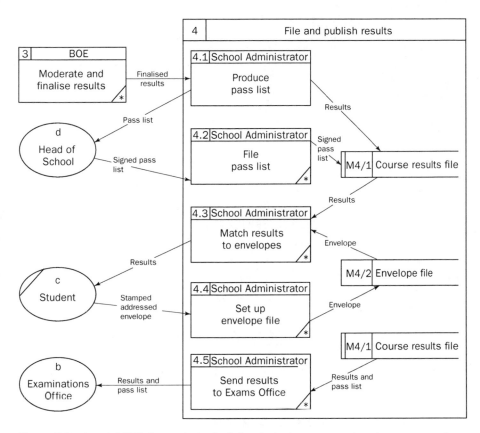

Figure 5.9 Level 2 DFD (current physical) for student assessment system process 4, 'File and publish results'

5.4 Further decomposition?

As was first explained in Chapter 4, section 4.6, DFDs allow progressive decomposition until a relevant level of detail has been exposed. Again, observant readers will have noticed that process 4.1 above has no asterisk, indicating that we are about to see just one example of this, given in order to illustrate a couple of related points already made but not so far seen in practice:

- sub-sub-processes within sub-process 4.1 should be numbered 4.1.1, 4.1.2 etc.;
- datastores within sub-process 4.1 should be numbered 4.1/1, 4.1/2 etc., with an M or D prefix as relevant. In this case there is only one, manual, datastore – thus designated M4/1.1 (see Figure 5.10).

We aren't going to decompose any of the other processes further, or go to any deeper levels, because the whole approach is simply a repetitive one and we are confident you should pretty well have the idea already.

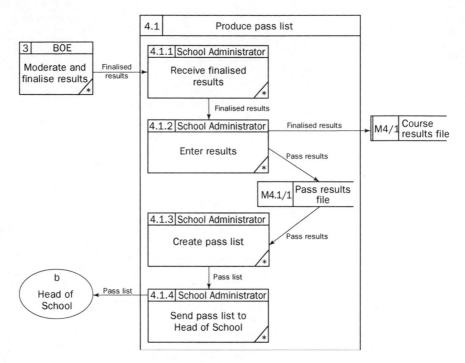

Figure 5.10   Level 3 DFD (current physical) for student assessment system process 4.1, 'Produce Pass List'

5.5   When is a level 2 a level 1, etc.?

In Chapter 4 when we first introduced the concept of DFD 'levelling', we referred to the question of how to define in practice what is a level 0, level 1, level 2 etc. for a given circumstance. With the examples that have followed, you should be starting to get the idea. It is an important aspect of data flow diagramming, however, and we need to make sure.

First let us return to the Marine Construction example for a moment. Refer to Figure 5.2 and imagine that we were only interested in the functions of the Production Office and not really bothered about the Sales, Design and Materials Offices. Our **system boundary** would now encompass only the Production Office. The level 2 DFD processes for the Production Office (as seen in Figure 5.5) would become level 1 DFD processes in our new scenario. In addition, the Materials Office and Sales Office which were **processes** in the original level 1 DFD would become **external entities** in the new way of looking at the system.

This idea of the system boundary is important. It depends exactly what it is you are interested in. In an earlier example (Chapter 4, section 4.7), we saw how the context diagram identified 'Stock Control' as being the part of a factory to be further analysed – that is, the stock control system defined the boundary of the further analysis. We also saw how the context diagram could be considered a level 0 DFD – and produced our level 1 DFD of that system by decomposing the Stock Control process box, then level 2 DFDs of the level 1 processes. For convenience, the level 0 DFD for the stock control system as first seen in Figure 4.12 is shown again in Figure 5.11.

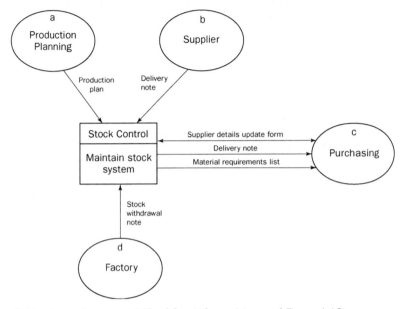

Figure 5.11 Level 0 physical DFD of Stock Control (copy of Figure 4.12)

If the system boundary was to be the whole production area, however, the other elements of the above diagram that are found within this area – i.e. Factory, Purchasing and Production Planning – would be shown as level 1 processes rather than level 0 external entities. Note that Supplier would remain

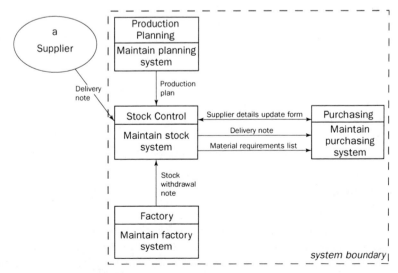

Figure 5.12 Level 1 DFD of production area

an external entity – being outside the production area system boundary (this is what defines an entity as being 'external'). See Figure 5.12. Similarly, the student assessment system seen earlier in this chapter could well be represented as only one process within a level 1 DFD that covered a whole university.

We trust that you are getting the idea!

5.6   A reminder about 'time'

We wish to re-emphasise another point originally made back in Chapter 4, and already touched on again earlier in this chapter. **Time** is not an important consideration in DFDs, and there is sometimes a danger of confusing DFDs with flowcharts. Remember that DFDs simply show what the system *is*, the possibilities that exist within it. Sometimes of course, *relative* time is an important part of a system and is successfully implied by a DFD's data flows. If there should be a data flow direct from one process to another, this will imply that the process at which the data 'arrives' is dependent upon the 'sending' process. The Marine Construction examples seen earlier in this chapter illustrate such a case – with the BQ1 form gradually having data added to it as it progresses from one process to the next. It is in systems like this that there is the greatest danger of slipping back into the habit of confusing the DFD with flowchart notation. Resist the temptation!

We hope that you are now gaining in confidence as far as DFDs are concerned, for we are about to discover what happens when the processes have been decomposed as far as possible – that is, when we reach the bottom level.

This chapter . . .

. . . began by explaining some problems with creating real DFDs for real systems and explained the idea of functional areas. It then went through two very different examples and guided you through the creation of a complete set of levelled DFDs for both scenarios. It gave further explanations regarding DFD levelling and ended by noting that DFDs are not intended to indicate time considerations. We want you to leave this chapter with a good understanding of creating a set of DFDs, including the appreciation that the different levels can be interchangeable if the boundary of the system expands or contracts.

A useful exercise

Return to the 'own experience' DFDs that you prepared at the end of Chapter 4. Refine and add to them based upon what you have learned in this chapter. Try to incorporate other processes and decompose at least three processes overall, with at least one to level 3. If necessary in order to establish the required detail, interview employees/fellow students.

Further reading

T. De Marco, *Structured Analysis and Systems Specification*, Prentice Hall International, Englewood Cliffs, NJ, 1980.
(This is one of the seminal works in structured analysis and, despite its age, still contains one of the best descriptions of the reasons behind data flow diagramming. The book is written in a very friendly style and we would recommend you having a browse as it is very inspiring.)

Web addresses worth a visit

www.smartdraw.com/resources/centers/software/ssadm.htm
www.docm.mmu.ac.uk/online/SAD/

Specifying processes

6

6.1 Introduction

6.1.1 Reaching the bottom level

DFDs are a very powerful way of describing processes. But they cannot completely describe the way things are done. When we reach the bottom level of a DFD we still need to write about what exactly it is that goes on in this bottom level. Often decisions are made or operations repeated and to describe this we need a way of writing accurately, unambiguously and completely. These process descriptions are contained in **elementary process descriptions** (EPDs), and this chapter will show you some ways of writing these.

6.1.2 Precise, accurate, unambiguous and complete

The sort of language required in systems analysis descriptions is very different to everyday English, in fact different to the style of language we are using in this book. You may have noticed that we repeat ourselves quite a lot – we have mentioned logicalisation several times for example and yet not explained what it involves. We have also warned more than once about the dangers of confusing data flow diagrams with flowcharts. We are doing this because repetition is an acknowledged educational tool – remember at school when you did several mathematics examples that were all basically the same? Repetition reinforces things. We are trying to get you to realise that logicalisation is really important by repeating it a lot. If you repeat yourself when you are describing a system, you are wasting time and effort and may well end up with inefficiencies. System descriptions should be **precise** and **accurate**.

Have you ever watched a skilled politician talking on the television? You may believe that they have been told never to answer a question directly. Often their answers can be interpreted in a number of ways: they are ambiguous. They do this deliberately so they can appeal to a range of voters and adapt their stance to events outside of their control. Also, it is often what they *do not* say that is more interesting than what they do say. They conveniently miss things out: their answers are incomplete. Ambiguity and incompleteness in system descriptions are potentially disastrous. You cannot have a computer system that does not know what to do or cannot make up its mind. System descriptions need to be not only precise and accurate, but also **unambiguous** and **complete**.

There are a number of techniques that are used in systems analysis to capture procedures precisely. Just remember that they are geared to precision and as a result would appear very turgid and unsophisticated to an everyday reader. They are not meant to be like conversational language.

6.2   The problem with ordinary English

Let us start with an example.

A product is passed as fit for sale if it passes a mechanical test and an electrical test and has the correct dimensions. If it fails the mechanical test or the electrical test (but not both), it is sent back to the workshop for repair. In all other cases, the product is rejected.

At first sight, this may seem a fair and realistic description of a quality control process. However, it is inaccurate, and if followed exactly could lead to products being passed as fit for sale when, in reality, they should not. According to a literal interpretation of the policy, a product that has incorrect dimensions and has failed the electrical test would be sent back to the workshop for repair simply because it passed the mechanical test.

The writer means to say that a product must have the correct dimensions even to be considered as being fit for sale. Because 'and has the correct dimensions' is the end of the first sentence, the writer has subconsciously assumed that this condition carries across to the start of the second sentence. The description can be written more accurately as follows.

A product is passed as fit for sale if it passes a mechanical test and an electrical test and has the correct dimensions. If it has the correct dimensions and fails the mechanical test or the electrical test (but not both), it is sent back to the workshop for repair. In all other cases, the product is rejected.

Although this description is more accurate, it suffers from being long-winded and cumbersome and considerable concentration is required on the part of the reader. The difficulty with ordinary English is that inconsistencies and inaccuracies are easily hidden in the words and creating an unambiguous and accurate description can lead to lengthy narrative.

6.3   Structured English

6.3.1   What it is

There is no hard and fast definition of structured English. It varies in style between its users and it varies in formality depending upon the target audience. It is basically an attempt to remove the 'background noise' words from narrative descriptions. It strips the description down to its bare essentials and removes ambiguity, redundancy and inconsistencies.

All forms of structured English are based on the logical constructs of

- sequence;
- selection;
- iteration.

6.3.2   Sequence

A sequence construct is simply a list of one or more actions or events, which are performed in order, and is represented by one or more imperative statements. For example:

Multiply Price by Quantity-Sold giving Net-Price
Multiply Net-Price by 0.175 giving VAT
Add VAT to Net-Price giving Gross-Price

All the actions are performed in the order given and they are all written in line. To illustrate the variations in style and syntax that abound, another way of writing the same sequence may well be:

Calculate Net-Price = Price * Quantity-Sold
Calculate VAT = Net-Price * 0.175
Calculate Gross-Price = Net-Price + VAT

6.3.3   Selection

A selection construct (sometimes called a decision construct) occurs when there are a number of alternative policies that can apply depending upon the result of some condition and only one policy is selected.

Again, different forms of structured English have different ways of implementing this but nearly all include the IF. . .ELSE statement. Some terminate this with an ENDIF, i.e. IF. . .ELSE. . .ENDIF. Examples are below:

IF dimensions not OK
    Reject product
ELSE (dimensions OK)
    IF mechanical test OK
        IF electrical test OK
            Pass product
        ELSE (electrical test not OK)
            Repair product
    ELSE (mechanical test not OK)
        IF electrical test OK
            Repair product
        ELSE (electrical test not OK)
            Reject product

Note the indentation and use of brackets which aid the reading and understanding of the description. An even more formal variation of writing this is below:

```
IF dimensions not OK
    Reject product
ELSE
    IF mechanical test OK
        IF electrical test OK
            Pass product
        ELSE
            Repair product
        ENDIF
    ELSE
        IF electrical test OK
            Repair product
        ELSE
            Reject product
        ENDIF
    ENDIF
ENDIF
```

The above is getting pretty close to the program code found in some programming languages. Multiple selections are sometimes implemented using the CASE construct. An example of this is as follows:

```
Select CASE
    CASE 1 (0 <= Net-Price < 100)
        Set Discount to 0
    CASE 2 (100 <= Net-Price < 200)
        Set Discount to 10%
    CASE 3 (200 <= Net-Price < 300)
        Set Discount to 15%
    CASE 4 (300 <= Net-Price < 500)
        Set Discount to 20%
    CASE 5 (Net-Price >= 500)
        Set Discount to 25%
```

6.3.4 Iteration

An iteration construct (sometimes called a repetition construct) occurs when an action or series of actions are repeated subject to a condition that governs the continued repetition.

It is implemented by such formats as REPEAT. . .UNTIL:

```
REPEAT
    Add Invoice-Total to Overall-Total
    Add 1 to Number-of-invoices
UNTIL no more invoices
Divide Overall-Total by Number-of-invoices giving Average-Value
```

or WHILE. . .ENDWHILE:

```
WHILE more invoices
    Add Invoice-Total to Overall-Total
    Add 1 to No-invoices
ENDWHILE
Divide Overall-Total by No-invoices giving Average-Value
```

or for less formal forms of structured English by FOR ALL or FOR EACH:

```
FOR each invoice
    Add Invoice-Total to Overall-Total
    Add 1 to No-invoices
Divide Overall-Total by No-invoices giving Average-Value
```

6.3.5 Variations on structured English

Code-like structured English as outlined in the previous sections may well be easy for an experienced analyst or programmer to understand as it is close to program code. There are even more formal variations such as pseudo-code that address such aspects as initialisation and termination, file handling, use of flags etc.

However, to a normal user, the structured English met so far may simply be 'too much'. One of the main aims of systems analysis is to involve users as much as possible; presenting them with rigid, formalised processing logic may very well put them off.

It is in this area that a return to a more narrative or report-like style may be appropriate but it should still be in a concise unambiguous form. In many cases, it may be necessary to convert the description into structured English first and use this as the basis for a more accessible form of presentation. It should be possible to express a structured process description in a narrative or report-like style without the loss of logical precision but it is not easy. As most users will be familiar with the more formal presentation found in reports, this approach is often successful.

The example of the quality control policy description could be written:

1   If a product does not have the correct dimensions, reject the product.

2   If a product does have the correct dimensions, consider the mechanical and electrical tests as follows:

2.1 both tests satisfactory – pass product;

2.2 both mechanical and electrical tests unsatisfactory – reject product;

2.3 either mechanical or electrical tests unsatisfactory (but not both) – repair product.

The above description, although perhaps a little verbose and long-winded, is accurate and in a form with which most ordinary users can identify. Note that the description is equivalent to structured English and uses some of its concepts (such as indentation).

6.4 Decision tables

6.4.1 What they are

Decision tables are useful when a combination of decisions has to be made in order to establish a result. They have been around for a long time and are still widely used. They are not peculiar to computer-related areas and variations upon them occur widely in the real world. Such tables are made up of four quadrants as illustrated in Figure 6.1.

Condition stub	Condition entry
Action stub	Action entry

Figure 6.1   Decision table quadrants

There are a number of types of decision table:

- limited entry;
- extended entry;
- mixed entry.

6.4.2 Limited entry decision tables

Conditions are entered into the table as direct questions to which the answer can only be Yes (Y) or No (N). All the possible combinations of Ys and Ns are placed in the condition entry quadrant of the table and each vertical set of Ys and Ns is called a rule. The possible results or actions are placed in the action stub and the relevant action(s) resulting from each rule are marked in the action entry quadrant with an 'X'.

Let us examine the product quality control problem. First identify the **conditions**. These are:

Correct dimensions?

Passed mechanical test?

Passed electrical test?

Note that it is important not to include mutually exclusive conditions such as 'Failed mechanical test?' as this is catered for by a 'N' answer to 'Passed mechanical test?'

Next identify the **actions**. These are:

Accept product

Repair product

Reject product

Finally determine the **number of rules** using the formula 2^N where N is the number of conditions. Hence, in this case, there are $2^3 = 8$ rules.

The decision table can now be constructed as in Figure 6.2. Note how the Ys and Ns are laid out in a set pattern to ensure that all combinations are catered for.

Correct dimensions?	Y	Y	Y	Y	N	N	N	N
Passed mechanical test?	Y	Y	N	N	Y	Y	N	N
Passed electrical test?	Y	N	Y	N	Y	N	Y	N
Accept product	X							
Repair product		X	X					
Reject product				X	X	X	X	X

Figure 6.2   Product quality control decision table – version 1

Examination of the table shows that redundancy exists. If the answer to the first question is N, the answers to the second and third questions are irrelevant. Redundancy occurs when two or more rules lead to the same action. It may be feasible to eliminate unnecessary conditions by inserting a '–' entry in appropriate places as in Figure 6.3.

Correct dimensions?	Y	Y	Y	Y	N
Passed mechanical test?	Y	Y	N	N	–
Passed electrical test?	Y	N	Y	N	–
Accept product	X				
Repair product		X	X		
Reject product				X	X

Figure 6.3   Product quality control decision table – version 2

The ELSE rule can be used to simplify a table even further. It is useful when the majority of sets of rules lead to the same action or set of actions. It is illustrated in Figure 6.4.

Correct dimensions?	Y	Y	Y	E
Passed mechanical test?	Y	Y	N	L
Passed electrical test?	Y	N	Y	S
				E
Accept product	X			
Repair product		X	X	
Reject product				X

Figure 6.4   Product quality control decision table – version 3

6.4.3   Extended entry decision tables

Where the conditions are all inter-related to each other, limited entry decision tables can be very unwieldy. For example the table in Figure 6.5 shows the alphabetical grades associated with percentage marks awarded in an assessment.

Mark 0–34?	Y	N	N	N	N	N
Mark 35–39?	–	Y	N	N	N	N
Mark 40–49?	–	–	Y	N	N	N
Mark 50–59?	–	–	–	Y	N	N
Mark 60–69?	–	–	–	–	Y	N
Mark > 69?	–	–	–	–	–	Y
Grade F	X					
Grade E		X				
Grade D			X			
Grade C				X		
Grade B					X	
Grade A						X

Figure 6.5   Assessment policy decision table – limited entry

By limiting the kinds of entry we have created an over-complicated view of the situation. An **extended entry** decision table replaces the condition entries of Y and N and the action entries of Xs with actual values as in Figure 6.6.

Mark	0–34	35–39	40–49	50–59	60–69	>69
Grade	F	E	D	C	B	A

Figure 6.6   Assessment policy decision table – extended entry

6.4.4   Mixed entry decision tables

Both limited and extended entry lines may be used in the same table but a mixture cannot occur within a single line, as shown in Figure 6.7.

Regular customer?	Y	Y	Y	N	N	N
Order value £	0–99	100–500	>500	0–99	100–500	>500
Discount given	0	15%	20%	0	10%	15%
Free gift			X			X

Figure 6.7   Sales policy decision table – mixed entry

6.5 Decision trees

We have already seen how useful tree diagrams can be, in Chapter 3. We now come to their most common use within the recognised systems analysis techniques, as an alternative to a decision table. They tend to be easier to understand because they are virtually self-explanatory. As with decision tables, they can be presented in a variety of ways. Returning to the product quality control example, slightly varying decision trees are shown in Figures 6.8 to 6.10.

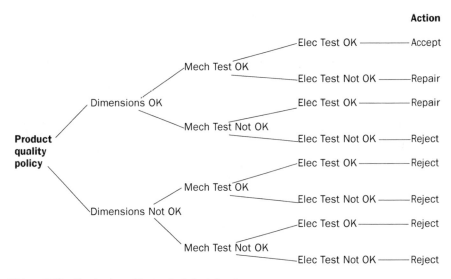

Figure 6.8   Product quality control decision tree

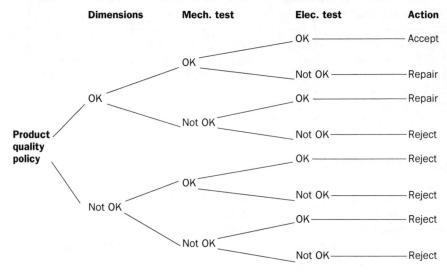

Figure 6.9   Product quality control decision tree (using 'column headings')

The examples in Figures 6.8 and 6.9 are very symmetrical structures but they can be reduced in a similar manner to decision tables as in Figure 6.10.

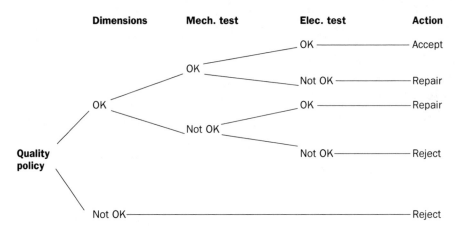

Figure 6.10   Product quality control decision tree (with reduction)

6.6   A worked example – the end-of-year assessment system

6.6.1   Background

We will now demonstrate the application of what has gone before, by considering an example that concerns the end-of-year assessment of students on the second year of a four-year degree course in business computing. The procedures describe the processing involved in processes 2.3 and 3 of the student assessment system introduced in Chapter 5, section 5.3.

Students study six subjects:

Quantitative methods

Systems analysis and design

Computer systems

Programming

Business studies

Behavioural studies

Students are assessed in each subject by coursework and an end-of-year examination. For all subjects except programming, the coursework counts for 20% and the examination 80% of the final subject mark. In programming, the coursework counts for 40% and the examination 60%.

After the examinations, the Year Leader receives from each subject tutor a list of all coursework and examination marks. A document must be prepared for the Board of Examiners showing for each student coursework marks, examination marks and overall subject marks for each subject. This document should also highlight any failed marks. The rules for determining failure are as follows.

A student has failed a subject if

• the coursework mark is below 40%, or

• the examination mark is below 35%, or

• the subject mark is below 40%.

Note that it is possible for a student to pass the coursework and the examination but to still fail the subject. The Board of Examiners has certain guidelines that are used to decide the fate of students. The Board does, however, have the power to condone marks if the student has justifiable reasons for not doing well (such as medical problems etc.). However, we shall concentrate on the formal rules that apply and ignore any exceptional circumstances.

If students fail three or more subjects they are allowed to repeat the year unless they already are repeat students in which case they are required to leave the course. A repeat is either internal or external. If any of the subjects failed include a failure in coursework or in the overall subject mark, the student can only repeat internally, i.e. they have to resit the year on a full-time basis. If the subjects failed are entirely due to poor performance in the examinations and all the coursework marks and overall subject marks are satisfactory, the student is given the choice of repeating internally or externally. External repeats are only required to resit the examinations in the following year.

If students fail 1 or 2 subjects, they are allowed to be reassessed in those subjects before the start of the next academic year. If students fail a coursework, they are given extra coursework. If they fail an examination they must resit it. If they fail the overall subject mark, they have to resit the exam and do extra coursework regardless of the marks obtained in each element. The subsequent results of these students are considered at a later Board of Examiners but the procedures involved will not be discussed.

6.6.2 Representing the narrative description

The above description is quite long-winded and probably contains some omissions, inconsistencies and ambiguities. However, it is meant to contain enough information to enable a reasonable understanding of the procedures employed. The procedures are represented as a fragment of the data flow diagram first seen in Chapter 5, Figure 5.8. See Figure 6.11.

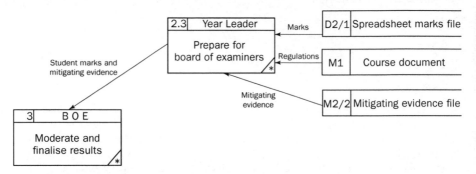

Figure 6.11   Fragment of level 1 DFD for student assessment system (from Figure 5.8)

We will now take each process in turn, and see how they may be described. To begin with, we describe process 2.3 in two ways – first in a fairly formal style of structured English (Figure 6.12), and then in a more 'user-friendly' manner (Figure 6.13).

```
REPEAT
  REPEAT
    Write Course-mark and Exam-mark on to result-sheet
    IF Subject = 'Programming'
      Calculate Subject-mark = 0.4* Course-mark + 0.6* Exam-mark
    ELSE (Subject not = 'Programming')
      Calculate Subject-mark = 0.2* Course-mark + 0.8* Exam-mark
    Write Subject-mark on to Result-sheet
    IF Course-mark <40
      Write '*' next to Course-mark on Result-sheet
    IF Exam-mark <35
      Write '*' next to Exam-mark on Result-sheet
    IF Subject-mark <40
      Write '*' next to Subject-mark on Result-sheet
  UNTIL no more subjects
UNTIL no more students
```

Figure 6.12   Process 2.3 'Prepare for board of examiners' (formal style)

Do the following for each student:
  For each subject:
    Step 1 Write the Course-mark and Exam-mark on to Result-sheet
    Step 2 Calculate Subject-mark as follows:
          2.1 Subject is Programming
              Subject-mark is 40% of Course-mark + 60% of Exam mark
          2.2 Subjects other than Programming
              Subject-mark is 20% of Course-mark + 80% of Exam mark
    Step 3 Write the Subject-mark on to Result-sheet
    Step 4 Highlight failures by placing an asterisk next to the failed mark on
          the Result-sheet. Failures determined as follows:
          4.1 Course-mark $<40\%$
          4.2 Exam-mark $<35\%$
          4.3 Subject-mark $<40\%$

Figure 6.13   Process 2.3 'Prepare for board of examiners' ('user-friendly' style)

Process 3 is more involved than Process 2.3. It is described in Figure 6.14 where it combines basic constructs of structured English with decision tables.

The example in Figure 6.14 illustrates the hybrid nature of some structured descriptions – using an appropriate mixture of ways to best describe what is going on. At all times, the target audience must be borne in mind. This is the single most important factor in determining the style used in specifying processes.

We trust that by this stage you really feel as though you are getting somewhere with DFDs and the processes that they contain. Our aim has been to give you a good fundamental understanding of their usefulness and how to create them. We are going to leave DFDs for the present but we return to them in Chapter 9 where we discover what they have to offer in terms of working out the logical happenings within a physical system, and how important this is to the systems design objective. We then explore them even further in Chapters 12 and 13 when we see them being put to uses beyond assumed computer systems development.

For the next two chapters we stop concentrating on what makes the data *flow* – that is, the activities that take place within a system and which drive the data around it. Instead we turn our attention to the data itself – its organisation, its structure. We show how the systems analyst answers questions such as what datastores (or files) a system needs, what data each should contain, and the relationships that need to exist within and between these datastores.

Do the following for each student:

Step 1   Determine the number of failed subjects:

         A subject is failed if any of the following are asterisked:
- Course-mark
- Exam-mark
- Subject-mark

Step 2   Determine student results:

         CASE 1   (Number of subjects failed = 0)
                 Student has passed the year

         CASE 2   (Number of subjects failed = 1 or 2)
                 For each subject determine the result according
                 to the following decision table:

Course-mark <40	Y	N	N	**E**
Exam-mark <35%	N	Y	N	**L**
Subject-mark <40%	N	N	N	**S**
				E
Redo coursework	X			X
Resit exam		X		X
Subject passed			X	

         CASE 3   (Number of subjects failed > 2)
                 Determine result according to the following
                 decision table:

Repeat student?	Y	N	N	N
Any Course-mark <40%	–	Y	N	N
Any Subject-mark < 40%	–	–	Y	N
Leave course	X			
Internal repeat		X	X	
Internal or external repeat				X

Figure 6.14   Process 3 'Moderate and finalise results'

This chapter ...

... began by explaining the problems with specifying processes and then introduced you to structured English. It went on to the various types of decision tables and decision trees. It ended with a couple of fairly complicated examples illustrating the hybrid nature of many structured process specifications.

A useful exercise

Return to the 'own experience' DFDs that you prepared at the end of Chapter 5. Select at least three appropriate lowest-level processes and prepare an elementary process description for each, utilising a different technique (decision tree, decision table, structured English) for each.

Further reading

S. Skidmore, *Introducing Systems Analysis*, Palgrave, 1997.

Web address worth a visit

www.docm.mmu.ac.uk/online/SAD

Entity modelling 7

7.1 Processes and data

In systems analysis it is necessary to view a system not only either physically or logically as explained in Chapter 4, but also in terms of either processing or data. Processes are the activities that are performed in the system and are described by DFDs, decision tables and structured English. By data, we mean data stored within the system that is needed by the system in order for it to function.

Data is often used by processes in a variety of ways. Processes can add to data, remove it, change or update it or simply refer to it. In efficient systems, data is always **organised**. So in a sales order processing system there are likely to be customer details stored together in a **Customer file** (or **Customer datastore**), product details in a **Product file** (or **Product datastore**) and so on.

These files/datastores will themselves be organised into some sort of **order**. Each customer may well be allocated a **Customer Number** and the file will probably be organised in Customer Number sequence to help in searching. With ever more powerful systems development software, such considerations are increasingly looked after automatically. However, this does not mean that these considerations can be ignored, for the speed and efficiency of a system will be helped greatly if a skilled analyst has organised the data structure in the most appropriate way for the required processing. It is a little bit like assuming that because a car has an automatic gearbox, the design engineer need exercise no care over the design of the gear ratios to match the engine characteristics.

The different files in a system are often linked or cross-referenced – and proper consideration of which should be linked to what plays a vital part in the design process. For example a customer may well order a particular product on a regular basis and if this fact can be stored somewhere in the system, the ordering process may be speeded up.

This chapter looks at ways of identifying things that need to be stored in a system and the relationships between these things. We will start with some basic concepts.

7.2 Entities and attributes

7.2.1 Entities

The most important concept in entity modelling is that of an **entity**.

An entity is a thing of interest to a system about which data is kept.

In computer systems, an entity is normally equivalent to a file. For example, in a hospital administration system, some likely entities are: Patient, Doctor, Operation, Ward. Each of these things are of interest to the system and will have data stored about them. Look at the following list and decide which you think are likely candidates for entities. Think about whether it is likely that data will be stored about each of them.

(a)   a member of staff in a personnel system

(b)   a book in a library system

(c)   a customer's address in a sales system

(d)   a customer in a sales system

(e)   a National Insurance number in a payroll system

(f)   a patient in a medical records system

(g)   the library in a library system

The only entities in the above list are (a), (b), (d) and (f). Each of these is likely to have data stored about them. Some likely data items for each of these are:

(a)   name, address, date of birth

(b)   book title, author, publisher

(d)   name, address, credit limit

(f)   National Insurance number, date of birth

Option (c) is not an entity. A customer's address is data *about a customer* and so is an **attribute** (see section 7.2.2 later), not an entity.

In the same way, option (e) is not an entity as National Insurance number is an attribute of an employee in a payroll system.

Option (g) is tricky. A thing is only an entity if it is possible for there to be more than one occurrence of it in the system. As there is only one library in, say, a school's library system, it is not an entity. However, if there were several libraries, such as in a local authority, or some universities, then the library would be an entity.

7.2.2 Attributes

Having introduced the term attribute, we need to define it.

An attribute is an item of data held about an entity. It is equivalent to a data item.

In computer systems, an attribute is equivalent to a **field** on a **record**. A record is equivalent to an **entity occurrence**.

A special and very important type of attribute is the **key attribute**.

A key attribute uniquely identifies a specific occurrence of an entity.

For example, in a sales system, customer name and address are attributes of the entity customer. The key attribute is likely to be a Customer Code or Customer Number which is unique to each customer. See if you can choose likely key and non-key attributes for the following entities:

(a)   a car in a vehicle registration system

(b)   an employee in a payroll system

(c)   an item of stock in a stock control system

For (a), the key is likely to be the car's registration number, with non-key attributes such as car make, car model, date of manufacture etc.

For (b), the key is likely to be employee number or payroll number with non-key attributes such as name, address, department, tax code etc.

For (c), the key is likely to be a stock number (or part number) with non-key attributes such as description, amount in stock, price etc.

7.2.3   Selecting entities

Deciding upon entities is not always as easy as you might think. Sometimes, suspected entities turn out to be really attributes and vice versa. A good place to start is to look at all the **nouns** in a description of a system and think deeply about whether data is likely to be stored about them or not. You may like to have a go at the following description. Start by selecting all the nouns and think about whether each noun is a likely entity or attribute or neither. The description is a very simplified account of a vehicle breakdown and rescue service that employs engineers to help its members when they have trouble with their vehicles.

Each engineer is allocated one van (which is driven up to a certain mileage and then replaced). Each member has only one address but perhaps many vehicles. Each visit is to deal with only one vehicle. A member can be visited more than once on any given date, and there may be many visits to a member on different dates. A member may only be covered for some of the vehicles they own and not for others.

The nouns in the description are: *engineer, van, mileage, member, address, vehicle, visit* and *date*. The likely entities are:

engineer – possible attributes include name, address and telephone number;

van – possible attributes include registration number and mileage;

member – possible attributes include membership number, name, address and telephone number;

vehicle – possible attributes include registration number, make and model;

visit – possible attributes include date of visit, purpose of visit and cost of visit.

For the other nouns in the description:

mileage is likely to be an attribute of the entity *van*;

address is likely to be an attribute of the entity *member*;

date is likely to be an attribute of the entity *visit*.

7.3 Entity relationships

7.3.1 Identifying relationships

What makes entity modelling such a powerful and interesting subject is the fact that entities are **related** to one another. Let us look at some of the entities in a particular sales order processing system that supplies and fits kitchens.

A sale always starts with a customer receiving an estimate. The estimate then becomes an order. An order can be for one or more stock items. Each stock item belongs to a certain stock category (e.g. taps, sinks, cupboards etc.).

We will leave it at that even though there is obviously a lot more to the system such as invoices, payments and so on. By looking at the nouns in the description and using some common-sense, we can arrive at a list of likely entities together with their key and some non-key attributes – see Figure 7.1.

In a personnel system, an *employee* is related to a *department* because an employee belongs to a department and a department contains a number of employees. You would expect this system to be able to tell you which department a particular employee works in and which employees are in a particular department. In our kitchen supply system, we would probably have several relationships between entities. In the table in Figure 7.2 an 'X' has been used to indicate a relationship between two entities. Because the relationships are shown in a grid, each one appears twice. So, an 'X' is placed in both places where Estimate and Order intersect. Why are these entities related?

The relationships are written out below:

An Estimate becomes an Order

An Estimate is issued to a particular Customer

Entity	Key attribute	Some non-key attributes
Estimate	Estimate Number or Order Number	Date Customer Code Stock Item Codes
Order	Order Number	Same as Estimate
Customer	Customer Code	Customer Name Customer Address Credit Limit
Stock Item	Stock Item Code	Description Number in Stock Supplier Code
Stock Category	Category Code	Category Description

Figure 7.1   Entities with their key and non-key attributes

	Estimate	Order	Customer	Stock Item	Stock Category
Estimate		X	X	X	
Order	X		X	X	
Customer	X	X			
Stock Item	X	X			X
Stock Category				X	

Figure 7.2   Relationships between entities

An Estimate refers to Stock Item(s)

An Order is placed by a Customer

An Order refers to Stock Item(s)

A Stock Item belongs to a particular Stock Category

Please bear in mind that this is all a little loose and is really intended to get you to understand the general idea. The above relationships are still 'one-way'. It is more complete to say that an Estimate becomes an Order *and* an Order is derived from an Estimate. This makes the relationship 'two-way'. Also, you may well think that a Customer is related to a Stock Item because a Customer orders Stock Items. However, they are linked via the entity Order. It should become clearer as we explore the topic further. The chapter on normalisation (Chapter 8) really sorts out any problems we may still have with which entities are linked.

7.3.2 Degrees of relationship

There is more to this than meets the eye. It is not enough to say that two entities are related. We need to say to what degree they are related. For example, can a Customer only place *one and only one* Order, and can an Order be placed by *one and only one* Customer? The answer to the first part is 'no' and the answer to the second part is 'yes'. A Customer can place several Orders if they so wish but one Order can only be placed by one Customer. Each of the relationships can be analysed in this way giving the following relationship statements.

1   A Customer can be issued with *one or more* Estimates and an Estimate is issued to *only one* Customer. This is known as a one-to-many relationship and is drawn as shown in Figure 7.3.

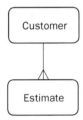

Figure 7.3   The one-to-many relationship between Customer and Estimate

The 'crow's foot' goes at the 'many' end of the relationship. It is usual to show the 'many' end beneath the 'one' end. This type of relationship is often called the master/detail relationship and the master should go on top. It is permissible to break this convention, however, if the overall shape of a final entity model requires it.

2   A Customer can place *one or more* Orders and an Order is placed by *only one* Customer. This is another one-to-many relationship, as shown in Figure 7.4.

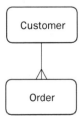

Figure 7.4   The one-to-many relationship between Customer and Order

3   An Estimate can become *only one* Order and an Order is derived from *only one* Estimate. This is known as a one-to-one relationship and is shown in Figure 7.5.

Figure 7.5   The one-to-one relationship between Estimate and Order

Because both sides of the relationship have the same degree, it is normal to draw it horizontally. Again, this convention can be broken if the final entity model demands it.

4   An Estimate refers to *one or more* Stock Items and a Stock Item may be present on *one or more* Estimates. This is known as a many-to-many relationship and is shown in Figure 7.6.

Figure 7.6   The many-to-many relationship between Estimate and Stock Item

Here there are two 'crow's feet' as the relationship is many-to-many. Again, this is usually drawn horizontally like the one-to-one relationship.

5   An Order refers to *one or more* Stock Items and a Stock Item may be present on *one or more* Orders. This is the same as the last one – a many-to-many relationship. See Figure 7.7.

Figure 7.7   The many-to-many relationship between Order and Stock Item

6   A Stock Item will belong to *only one* Stock Category and a Stock Category will contain *one or more* Stock Items. This is a one-to-many relationship again – see Figure 7.8.

7.3.3   Optionality

Some relationships are **mandatory** and some are **optional**. For example, in our sales system, some customers may be on file even if they do not have a current estimate or order (i.e. regular or account customers). However, an estimate

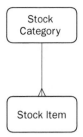

Figure 7.8 The one-to-many relationship between Stock Category and Stock Item

cannot exist without a customer. The complete relationship is shown in Figure 7.9 – and note also that it is good practice to include a description for each entity's relationship with the other, writing these against the line joining the two entities. The dotted line indicates that this part of the relationship is optional. The full line indicates that this part of the relationship is mandatory (or compulsory).

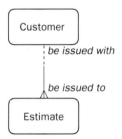

Figure 7.9 The one-to-many relationship between Customer and Estimate, showing optionality and including relationship descriptions

The relationship should be read as follows:

One Customer *may* be issued with *one or more* Estimates and one Estimate *must* be issued to *only one* Customer.

As explained above, it is normal to write the descriptions of the relationship against the line joining the two entities. Note that these descriptions *must not* include any words or phrases that are already indicated by the relationship line (e.g. 'may', or 'one or more') – but they must include all other words needed to complete the sentence (e.g. 'be' – see 'be placed by' in Figure 7.10).

The rest of the relationships for the sales system can now be represented as follows:

1   One Customer *may* place *one or more* Orders and one Order *must* be placed by *only one* Customer (Figure 7.10).

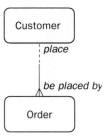

Figure 7.10   The one-to-many relationship between Customer and Order, showing optionality

2   One Estimate *may* become *only one* Order and one Order *must* be derived from *only one* Estimate (Figure 7.11).

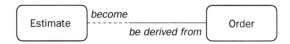

Figure 7.11   The one-to-one relationship between Estimate and Order, showing optionality

3   One Estimate *must* refer to *one or more* Stock Items and one Stock Item *may* be present on *one or more* Estimates (Figure 7.12).

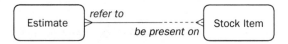

Figure 7.12   The many-to-many relationship between Estimate and Stock Item, showing optionality

4   One Order *must* refer to *one or more* Stock Items and one Stock Item *may* be present on *one or more* Orders (Figure 7.13).

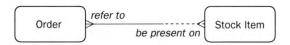

Figure 7.13   The many-to-many relationship between Order and Stock Item, showing optionality

5   One Stock Item *must* belong to *only one* Stock Category and one Stock Category *must* contain *one or more* Stock Items (Figure 7.14).

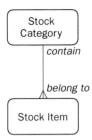

Figure 7.14   The one-to-many relationship between Stock Category and Stock Item, showing optionality

7.3.4   Entities and entity occurrences

We often find that some students get a little mixed up at this stage. Look back at Figure 7.10, the one-to-many relationship between Customer and Order. When told that one Order *must* be placed by *only one* Customer, we sometimes hear the comment 'Surely there is more than one customer'. Of course there are several customers in the system. Each particular customer is an **entity occurrence** of the entity Customer. The entity Customer is, if you like, the **idea** or **map** of a customer and describes the data items stored for the customer. The details of the actual occurrences of Customer then map onto these data items with real values. So, even though there are several customers in the system giving several occurrences of the entity Customer, it still remans true that one occurrence of an Order can only be placed by one occurrence of a Customer.

7.3.5   Further examples

Try the following four exercises. The entities are in capital letters. Connect the entities together with relationships. Show optionality and describe the relationship against the lines. Check your answers with the solutions given in Figure 7.15.

1   An EMPLOYEE may be a MEMBER of the company's sports club that is exclusive to the company's employees.

2   A ROOM may have a number of telephone EXTENSIONS but may not have any. A telephone EXTENSION must belong to a ROOM.

3   A COURSE must have a number of STUDENTS enrolled on it and a STUDENT must be enrolled on only one COURSE.

4   A STUDENT must be enrolled on only one COURSE and a COURSE must have STUDENTS enrolled on it. Each COURSE must have a number of MODULES and a MODULE can be part of more than one COURSE but must be part of at least one COURSE. Each MODULE must have a LECTURER as subject leader but a LECTURER may not necessarily be a subject leader or may lead more than one MODULE.

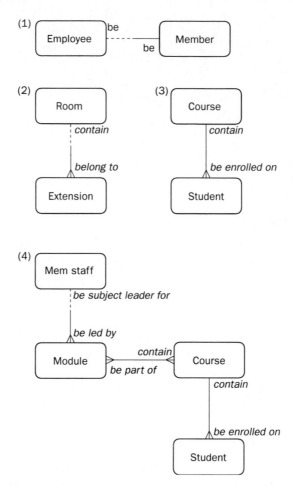

Figure 7.15 Solutions

The last example shows a model with four entities. When the entities in the system are connected together in this way, the diagram is called an **entity model**. It is worth noting that the terms **data model** and **logical data structure** are also sometimes used instead of the term **entity model**. They mean the same thing.

7.3.6 Many-to-many relationships

When a system is first investigated, it is often the case that many-to-many relationships appear to be present. We have already seen some in this chapter. However, these relationships *always* imply a missing or **link** entity. An example will illustrate this point.

In a doctors' practice where there are a number of doctors, a doctor can have appointments with a number of patients and a patient can have appointments with more than one doctor (even though they generally have one regular doctor). At first sight this seems a candidate for a many-to-many relationship.

One Doctor *may* have an appointment with *one or more* Patients and one Patient *may* have an appointment with *one or more* Doctors. See Figure 7.16.

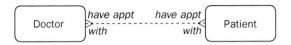

Figure 7.16   Many-to-many relationship between Doctor and Patient

Note that both sides of this relationship are **optional** – which may initially surprise you. It is possible, however, for a doctor's details to be stored in the system before they have had any appointments and similarly for a patient. It is simply a question of time, and this time factor often introduces optionality into a relationship that at first sight would appear to be mandatory. We look at the above example in more detail in Chapter 11, where we see that the time factor has implications for various aspects of systems development.

There is a 'missing' entity – hidden in the relationship description. You must ask the question 'Is there an entity in the system to cope with the situation where there is *only one* Doctor and *only one* Patient?' The answer is obviously Appointment and this is the missing link entity. The many-to-many relationship is then **resolved** as in Figure 7.17.

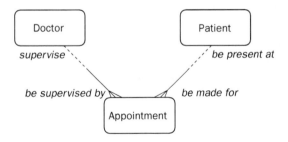

Figure 7.17   Resolution of many-to-many relationship between Doctor and Patient

A many-to-many relationship is always resolved in this way, with each of the original entities forming a one-to-many relationship with the link entity. Remember the many-to-many relationship between Order and Stock Item we met earlier in the chapter? (See Figure 7.18.)

To resolve this, we have to think about the 'thing' where one Order and one Stock Item meet. This is the individual lines of the order called Order Line. The resolved relationship is as shown in Figure 7.19.

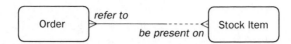

Figure 7.18 Many-to-many relationship between Order and Stock Item

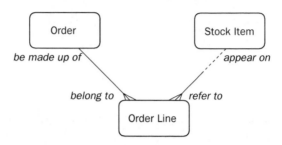

Figure 7.19 Resolution of many-to-many relationship between Order and Stock Item

If you look at the ways in which Figure 7.16 was transformed into Figure 7.17, and Figure 7.18 into Figure 7.19, it is not too difficult to see a set of rules emerging for the resolution of many-to-many links.

Rule 1: A many-to-many link *must always* be resolved by creating a new link entity.

Rule 2: The link entity is joined to each original entity by a one-to-many relationship with the 'many' end at the link entity.

Rule 3: The half of the relationship nearest the link entity is *always* mandatory (i.e. a solid line).

Rule 4: The other half of the relationship has the same optionality as in the original many-to-many relationship.

Rule 5: If it is difficult to name the link entity between entity A and entity B, simply call it A/B Link.

Rule 6: Finally, name the relationships.

7.3.7 Multiple relationships

In some situations, two or more different relationships can exist between a pair of entities. For example, a university lecturer may be the sponsor for one or more student projects (that is, he or she comes up with the idea for the project in the first place). However, the sponsor may not supervise the project and lecturers may well supervise projects that they have not sponsored. Hence there are two different relationships between Lecturer and Project – see Figure 7.20.

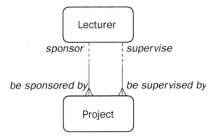

Figure 7.20   Multiple relationships between Lecturer and Project

7.3.8   Exclusive relationships

It is possible for a master entity to have detail entities that are mutually exclusive and vice versa. For example, a Customer is either issued with Invoices for each transaction or a Statement at the end of the month, never both. The relationships are exclusive – only one can exist for a particular customer. It is drawn as shown in Figure 7.21, with the exclusivity being shown by an **exclusive arc**.

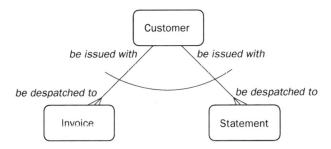

Figure 7.21   Exclusive relationships between Customer and Invoice, and Customer and Statement

7.3.9   Supertypes and subtypes

Certain groups of entity types can share common attributes with each having their own unique attributes. For example, Campus Student and Distance Student will all have an identifier code, name and address, course code etc. If these were to be included as entities within one university system, for much of that system's processing both could obviously be simply regarded as a Student, while in certain instances the differentiation would be necessary. Campus Student and Distance Student would be regarded as **subtypes** of the **supertype** Student. First note Figure 7.22, which shows how these would be drawn.

Subtypes inherit the attributes of their supertype as well as having attributes of their own. Because of this large commonality of attributes they can often share one file in a system (e.g 'Student file'), with another of the file attributes

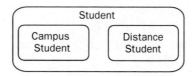

Figure 7.22 Student supertype containing Campus Student and Distance Student as subtypes

being an indicator to identify which type a particular record is ('Campus Student' or 'Distance Student'). Each subtype can have relationships with other entities in the system, including *different* relationships with the *same* entity as in the example shown – see Figure 7.23.

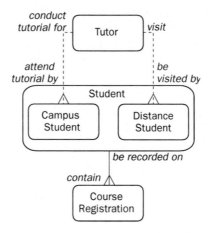

Figure 7.23 Student supertype and subtypes linked in different ways

The number of subtypes within a supertype may not be limited to two. For example, GP Practice, Clinic and Hospital share an obvious overlap of rationale. If these were all to be included as entities within one system, they might be considered to come under the overall category 'Health Care Provider'. See Figure 7.24.

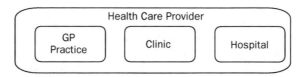

Figure 7.24 Health Care Provider supertype containing GP Practice, Clinic and Hospital as subtypes

We return to these concepts in Chapter 14, when we consider the 'object-oriented' view of systems.

7.4   Building an entity model

7.4.1   The example

We will approach this section by developing an entity model for an example system. The example system is described below.

A company that rents out country cottages for holidays uses a system to keep track of bookings made by customers in relation to particular cottages. Each cottage belongs to a specific owner and each owner is dealt with by a sales representative. However, not all sales representatives are allocated owners; a number of these representatives are responsible for a set of regions instead. A region is a geographic location that is made up of a number of areas in which the company has holiday cottages. Each cottage belongs to a particular class and each cottage will contain facilities (e.g. central heating, shower, games room etc.). The same facility may of course be available in a number of different cottages.

7.4.2   Selecting entities

Examination of the system description yields the following as likely entities:

Customer, Cottage, Booking, Owner, Sales Rep., Region, Area, Class, Facility.

7.4.3   Identifying relationships between entities

It is often useful to draw a grid with both rows and columns containing the entity names. At the intersections, we put the nature of any relationship. See Figure 7.25.

As you can see, each relationship is shown twice. The row entry is the 'first' entity in the relationship and the column entry the 'second'. So, for example, the relationship between Area and Cottage is 1:M (one-to-many), whereas Cottage to Area is M:1 (many-to-one). M:N stands for many-to-many. For those who are curious enough to wonder why, the fact is that M:N originally stood for many-to-numerous where the 'many' was the greater (e.g. an M:N of Patient to Doctor would indicate that there were more patient than doctor records to be held in a system) but this use has pretty well disappeared.

7.4.4   Drawing the relationships

Each relationship is now drawn as shown in Figure 7.26. The diagrams include optionality and relationship names. The optionality has been derived from a combination of common sense and careful inspection of the system description.

	Cus	Cot	Bkng	Ownr	S Rep	Regn	Area	Cls	Fcty
Customer			1:M						
Cottage			1:M	M:1			M:1	M:1	M:N
Booking	M:1	M:1							
Owner		1:M			M:1				
Sales Rep				1:M		1:M			
Region					M:1		1:M		
Area		1:M				M:1			
Class		1:M							
Facility		M:N							

Figure 7.25   Entity relationship grid

7.4.5   Completing the entity model

We are now in a position to join the whole thing together as shown in Figure 7.27. Note the introduction of the exclusive arc, and the resolution of the many-to-many relationship between Cottage and Facility.

7.5   Further examples

To conclude this chapter, try these two examples and compare your answers with the solutions that follow in Figures 7.28 and 7.29. The entities are in capital letters.

Library system

There must be at least one BOOK COPY of each BOOK TITLE in the system. Each BOOK TITLE must belong to one particular CATEGORY but a CATEGORY can exist in the system if there are no BOOK TITLES belonging to it. LOANS are stored in the system only if they are current (i.e. when a book is returned, the record of the loan is removed). A BORROWER can have several LOANS (or none at all) and each LOAN is for one BOOK COPY.

Project management system

A computer consultancy undertakes a number of PROJECTS. A PROJECT is for either an external CLIENT or an internal DEPARTMENT. A PROJECT must be for one or the other. A CLIENT or DEPARTMENT may have several PROJECTS on the go. Some DEPARTMENTS and CLIENTS are stored in the system even if there are no current PROJECTS for them. A PROJECT is split up into STAGES and there must be at least one STAGE stored in the system for each PROJECT. CONSULTANTS are allocated to each STAGE of a PROJECT. One CONSULTANT may be involved with several STAGES and each STAGE may have several CON-

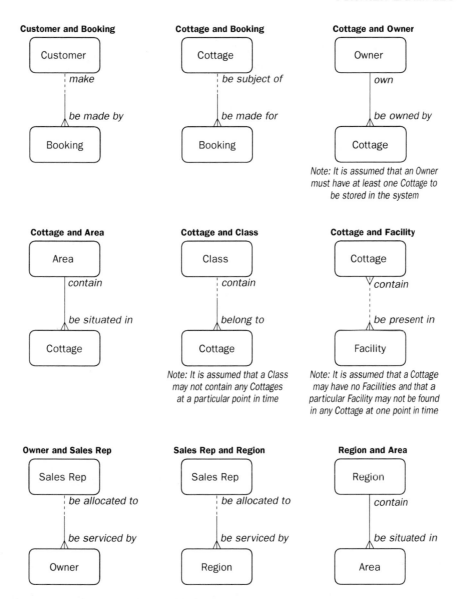

Figure 7.26   The entities and relationships

SULTANTS. CONSULTANT details are still stored in the system even if they are not allocated to STAGES. For each PROJECT, one of the CONSULTANTS must be the project leader. A CONSULTANT is not necessarily a project leader but they can only be project leader for one PROJECT.

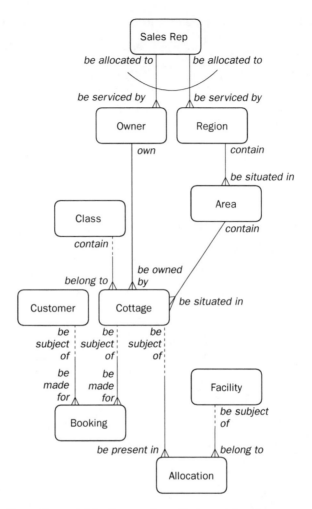

Figure 7.27   The entity model for the country cottage rental system

This chapter . . .

. . . began by introducing you to the concept of entities and attributes. It then looked at the different ways in which entities can be related to each other in terms of one-to-one, one-to-many and many-to-many links. The concept of optionality was introduced followed by a method of resolving a many-to-many relationship. Some special types of relationship were covered and we finished with an example of how an entity model is built. Entity modelling is a very important topic and the next chapter takes it even further, delving into the mathematically based concepts behind the topic known as 'normalisation'.

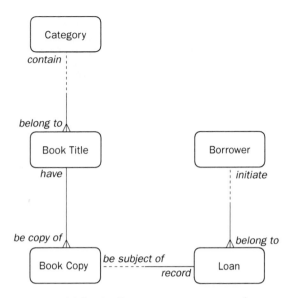

Figure 7.28 The entity model for the library system

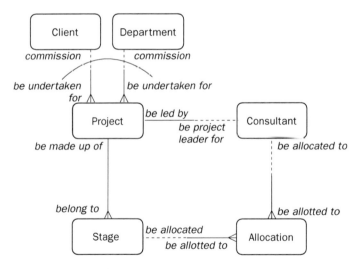

Figure 7.29 The entity model for the project management system

Useful exercises

1   Draw an entity model of the 'vehicle breakdown and rescue service' description found in section 7.2.3.

2   Bearing in mind the datastores in your 'own experience' DFDs from the exercises in Chapters 4 and 5, create an appropriate entity model of approximately 4–7 entities.

Further reading

D. Howe, *Data Analysis for Database Design*, 3rd edition, Butterworth-Heinemann, 2001.

Web addresses worth a visit

www.smartdraw.com/resources/centers/software/ssadm.htm
www.sum-it.nl/cursus/dbdesign/english
www.doc.mmu.ac.uk/online/SAD

Normalisation 8

This chapter follows on from the previous one on entity modelling and is very much linked to it. If you do not yet feel comfortable with the entity modelling concepts described, it may be worth reading the previous chapter again before continuing.

8.1 Introduction

Normalisation is the only part of the larger subject of **relational data analysis (RDA)** which we cover in this book. RDA has its origins in set theory and is based on the work of Codd in the early 1970s. It is not intended to go into the theory of RDA here but there are several good books that deal with the subject in some depth. One is recommended at the end of this chapter.

A relation is a term that describes a table of data items and, for our purposes, it is the same as an entity. You will hear the words relation, table and entity used interchangeably in systems analysis. You will also hear the term 'relationship', which refers to the relationship *between* these.

By applying normalisation, we end up with a set of relations (tables, entities) – and a means of establishing the relationships between them. The advantage of organising our data in this way is that we remove data duplication and ensure efficient data access. By storing a data item once only, we not only save disk storage space but also ensure data integrity.

8.2 What is a 'relationship'?

8.2.1 The entity model

In the entity modelling chapter, we finished with an entity model for a system that deals with the booking of country cottages. Part of that entity model is shown in Figure 8.1.

You will remember that the construction of this entity model was quite methodical but we did warn you that the whole thing was a little 'loose'. Let us explain what we mean by this.

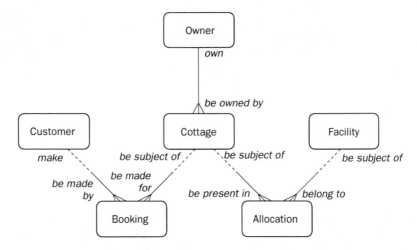

Figure 8.1 Part of the entity model for the country cottage rental system

There is obviously a relationship between Cottage and Owner because an Owner owns a Cottage. Also a Customer makes a Booking and so there is an obvious relationship here. In fact, one cannot really argue with any of the relationships in the entity model. However, what if someone suggested that there was a direct relationship between Customer and Owner because a Customer really makes a booking with an Owner? They would be correct that a relationship existed – but not a direct one. Customer and Owner *are* linked, but the link is *through* the two other entities Booking and Cottage.

When the entity model was developed in the last chapter, you were very much guided to the answer by the way the description was written, but what if it is not so obvious? The approach used in the last chapter was rather subjective. There is a more systematic, even mathematical, way of deriving a correct entity model.

8.2.2 Computer system relationships

In the cottage booking entity model, the relationships represent the ways in which the entities interact from a system point of view. So, a Customer makes a Booking and a Booking is made for a Cottage. When we initially investigate a system, it is this sort of 'business' relationship we are interested in. However, in a computer system the relationships mean something very much more precise than this. If the holiday cottage entity model were stored in a computer system, it would mean that the entities were linked within the computer system. So, if the Cottage details were to hand on a computer screen or in a computer program, the system would be able to get *directly* to the Owner details for that Cottage. Similarly, it would be possible for the system to get *directly* from an Allocation to the Facility or the Cottage.

The way this is done depends upon the type of database management system used. The most common and widely used type of database is called a **relational** database (for example, Oracle) and this is the type we will describe in this chapter. In a relational database, the Cottage and Owner would be linked by a **foreign key** as shown in Figure 8.2.

Figure 8.2   Cottage and Owner linked by foreign key

Within the Cottage entity would be stored the key of the Owner of that Cottage which is <u>Owner Code</u>. This provides the link to the Owner entity for that Cottage. <u>Owner Code</u> is a foreign key as it is not a key in the Cottage entity but is a key in the Owner entity. Note that the key fields are <u>underlined</u> and an asterisk * is placed to the left of a foreign key. In addition, the crow's foot is at the foreign key end of the relationship.

In a relational database, Allocation would be linked to Facility and Cottage by a **compound** key as shown in Figure 8.3. Note that the crow's foot is at the compound key end of the relationship. A compound key is made up of two or more **simple** keys – in this case <u>Facility Code</u> and <u>Cottage Code</u> to provide a unique identifier for an entity. If you think about it, both <u>Facility Code</u> and <u>Cottage Code</u> are needed to uniquely identify an Allocation. <u>Facility Code</u> on its own is not enough as a Facility can be present in several Cottages. It is very often the case that a compound key is the key for a **link** entity between two other entities that have a many-to-many relationship. This is the case with Allocation.

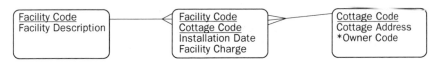

Figure 8.3   Cottage and Owner linked by foreign key

You can see the links are similar for a foreign key and a compound key. The thing that causes the link is a data item or data items. All of the links in a entity model are forged in this way in a relational database and for the fragment of the holiday cottage system, it is shown in Figure 8.4.

But how do we get to the situation where we know which entities have simple keys, which have compound keys and which contain foreign keys? The answer is by using the technique called **normalisation**.

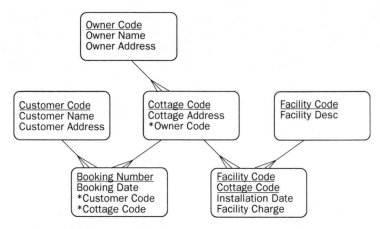

Figure 8.4   The country cottage rental system, showing use of key attributes

8.3   Normalisation of documents

8.3.1   Introduction

Before we launch into this topic, we want to admit that it can be a difficult one to master. Students often struggle with it. Our reason for its inclusion is a sound one, however – and we have done our best to make it as understandable as possible. Analysts who know how to apply normalisation are at a considerable advantage when it comes to drawing entity models that are reliable and complete.

We will use an approach of ours that you should be getting used to by now – that is, by going through a couple of examples and then analysing exactly what it is we have done. Both are taken from a student records system, present in some shape or form in most universities. The university in the examples operates a modular system where students study modules and gain credits for these modules until they have enough credits to qualify for a degree. The exact nature of these modules depends upon the course on which the student is enrolled, but generally speaking a particular module can be part of more than one course.

8.3.2   The student transcript

The document
Humans come into direct contact with data largely via input or output documents or computer screens. As we saw in Chapter 1, section 1.4.3, it is such 'human–computer interfaces' that translate the data into information. The system of which these form a part must store the data in some way, in order to provide these inputs/outputs. One of the outputs from the system we are considering is a 'student transcript' document that details the modules so far undertaken by each student and the results obtained, and this forms the basis for the example in Figure 8.5. Before we move on to the next subsection, see if you can

apply what you have learned in Chapter 7 in order to identify the entities contained within this document.

Student Number:	1078654X
Student Name:	David Green
Course Code:	G105
Course Title:	BA Business Computing

Module Code	Module Title	Number of credits	Grade Point	Result Code	Result
BUS119	Business Operations	20	10	P	Pass
COM110	Intro. to Computing	20	8	P	Pass
COM112	Application Building	20	3	RE	Refer exam
COM114	Software Engineering	20	2	DC	Defer coursework
COM118	Computer Law	10	9	P	Pass
COM120	Systems Analysis	20	3	RCE	Refer cwk and exam
COM122	HCI	10	7	P	Pass

Figure 8.5   The student transcript document

The entity model

We would consider Student, Course and Module to be definite candidates for entities. The rest of the data items seem to be attributes of Student or Module or both. If you thought differently, study Figure 8.5 again. If you still cannot see how we came to these conclusions, refer again to Chapter 7, section 7.2.

An initial attempt at the entity model might therefore be as shown in Figure 8.6. As we learned in the last chapter however, we have to resolve the many-to-many relationship. The model is therefore modified as in Figure 8.7.

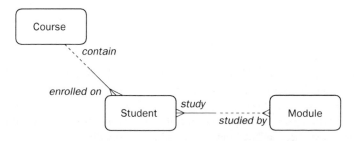

Figure 8.6   Initial attempt at entity model for student records system

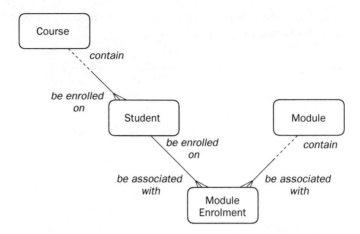

Figure 8.7 Entity model for student records system, with many-to-many resolved

But is this correct? We have used common sense and possibly intuition to arrive at this. Let us go about this more systematically and **normalise** the data. We will do so one step at a time.

Un-normalised form (UNF)
The first step in normalisation is to write the data in **un-normalised form** (UNF) as shown in Figure 8.8. For the moment, do not worry about the 1NF, 2NF and 3NF columns. The purpose of these will become clear as we go along.

UNF	UNF level	1NF	2NF	3NF
<u>Student Number</u>	1			
Student Name	1			
Course Code	1			
Course Title	1			
Module Code	2			
Module Title	2			
No. of Credits	2			
Grade Point	2			
Result Code	2			
Result	2			

Figure 8.8 Student transcript – un-normalised

You will notice that the UNF column contains the data item names for all the data items in the document. The first one, Student Number, is underlined because this has been chosen as the **key attribute** for this document. The key uniquely identifies the data and as each document is produced for *one and only one* student, the Student Number is a good choice of key.

The first four attributes in Figure 8.8 start in the same column position and are given a UNF Level number of 1. After the fourth attribute, the rest are indented slightly and given a UNF Level of 2. This is because the document contains a **repeating group** of data. For a given value of the Student Code, the module data repeats giving several lines, one for each module. Of course, the Student Name, Course Code and Course Title do not repeat for a given Student Number – they can only have one value for each student and so they have a UNF Level number of 1.

After writing out the data in un-normalised form in this way, the next stage is to **remove the repeating groups**.

First Normal Form (FNF or 1NF)

The repeating group of data is largely to do with modules. The first step is to pick a key for the repeating data (i.e. each line of the module data) which uniquely identifies each line *within* the document. The obvious choice is Module Code.

First Normal Form is then derived by separating out the repeating data as shown in Figure 8.9.

UNF	UNF level	1NF	2NF	3NF
Student Number	1	Student Number		
Student Name	1	Student Name		
Course Code	1	Course Code		
Course Title	1	Course Title		
Module Code	2			
Module Title	2	Student Number		
No. of Credits	2	Module Code		
Grade Point	2	Module Title		
Result Code	2	No. of Credits		
Result	2	Grade Point		
		Result Code		
		Result		

Figure 8.9   Student transcript – First Normal Form

What has happened here? We have ended up with two groups of data items, which you can see are the starting points for evolution into entities. All the UNF Level 1 items are taken across to 1NF together and here you can see the beginnings of a Student entity. The repeating data is taken out separately and given the key of Module Code, but the first key, Student Number, is taken down with it. This is a **compound key** and is made up of two or more **simple keys**. Basically, if the Student Number were not part of the key of the second group of data items, we would have student data and module data and no link between the two. The Student Number in the compound key provides the link between the two groups of data items.

In First Normal Form, repeating groups of data are separated.

Second Normal Form (SNF or 2NF)

In Second Normal Form, we look at groups of data items that have more than one element to the key. In other words, we look at compound keys (there is a similar type of key called a composite or hierarchic key and we deal with this in section 8.6).

Basically, we look at each of the non-key attributes and see if they really depend upon both of the elements of the compound key or just one of them. The group of data items we are to examine is shown below:

Student Number
Module Code
Module Title
No. of Credits
Grade Point
Result Code
Result

Let us look at each of the non-key attributes in turn.

- Module Title is obviously an attribute of a Module entity and has really got nothing to do with the Student Number. Hence we say that Module Title is *determined by* Module Code.
- No. of Credits refers to the size of the module and hence is also determined by Module Code.
- Grade Point is the grade a particular Student gets for a particular Module. Hence we need both keys to determine Grade Point.
- Result Code is the code for the result a particular Student gets for a particular Module and again needs both keys.
- Result is similar to Result Code at this stage of the normalisation process.

The normalisation table up to 2NF is now given in Figure 8.10. We now seem to have a Student entity, a Module entity and a link entity which is the one with the compound key. Another word for these groups of data items is a **relation** and we will define this term a little later.

In Second Normal Form, data items that depend on only part of a key are separated.

Third Normal Form (TNF or 3NF)

In Third Normal Form, we look at all the attributes and see if they are really dependent upon the key. If not, we decide upon a more suitable choice of key for these attributes.

In our example, there are two such questionable attributes. Course Title obviously really depends upon Course Code, and Result really depends upon Result Code. In other words a Course Code has only one Course Title and a Result Code

UNF	UNF level	1NF	2NF	3NF
Student Number	1	Student Number	Student Number	
Student Name	1	Student Name	Student Name	
Course Code	1	Course Code	Course Code	
Course Title	1	Course Title	Course Title	
Module Code	2			
Module Title	2	Student Number	Student Number	
No. of Credits	2	Module Code	Module Code	
Grade Point	2	Module Title	Grade Point	
Result Code	2	No. of Credits	Result Code	
Result	2	Grade Point	Result	
		Result Code		
		Result	Module Code	
			Module Title	
			No. of Credits	

Figure 8.10   Student transcript – Second Normal Form

has only one Result. We take these two groups of data items out in 3NF and end up with the table shown in Figure 8.11. A point to note is that the keys of the groups taken out are also left behind as foreign keys (marked with an asterisk) to maintain the link between the entities.

UNF	UNF level	1NF	2NF	3NF
Student Number	1	Student Number	Student Number	Student Number
Student Name	1	Student Name	Student Name	Student Name
Course Code	1	Course Code	Course Code	*Course Code
Course Title	1	Course Title	Course Title	
Module Code	2			Course Code
Module Title	2	Student Number	Student Number	Course Title
No. of Credits	2	Module Code	Module Code	
Grade Point	2	Module Title	Grade Point	Student Number
Result Code	2	No. of Credits	Result Code	Module Code
Result	2	Grade Point	Result	Grade Point
		Result Code		*Result Code
		Result	Module Code	
			Module Title	Result Code
			No. of Credits	Result
				Module Code
				Module Title
				No. of Credits

Figure 8.11   Student transcript – Third Normal Form

We will give the entities the following names: Student, Course, Module Enrolment, Result and Module. The name of the entity with the compound key, Module Enrolment, reflects the fact that both Student and Module are involved in this entity. You often find that compound key entities are difficult to name as they contain data relating to more than one entity.

In Third Normal Form, non-key attributes that are dependent upon other non-key attributes are separated.

So, we have ended up with five entities, one more than in our first stab at the problem as indicated by the entity model in Figure 8.7. The extra entity is the Result. This is really a simple 'look-up' or 'conversion' table.

By undertaking the analysis in this rigorous way, we have a set of entities, or **tables**, that are said to be well normalised. This is normally as far as we need to go. There is a Fourth Normal Form and a Fifth Normal Form but these are rarely found, especially if the first three stages have been done properly.

Third Normal Form tests

There are a couple of tests that we can apply to check whether the relations really are in Third Normal Form:

Test 1: For each of the non-key attributes, is there just one possible value for a given value of the key?

For the majority of the non-key attributes the answer is obviously 'yes'. For example, one Course Code can only have one Course Title and one Student Number and Module Code together can only have one Grade Point. However, the foreign key Course Code in the Student entity makes you stop and think. Is a student only allowed to be on one course? In this sort of situation, you have to go back to the system users and ask them. In this case, for simplicity's sake we have assumed the answer is 'yes' and so everything is all right. If the answer were 'no', the entity model would become a lot more complicated as Student to Course would be many-to-many and you would have to check that the Modules studied were for the correct Course and so on.

Test 2: Do all of the non-key attributes depend *directly* upon the key?

Again, in this case, the answer is 'yes' for all the non-key attributes. However, because we only normalise a sub-set of the complete system data when we analyse a document, it is often the case that a non-key field *really* depends upon another key. For example, if we wished to record a student's tutor for a particular module in the above normalisation, we may well have ended up including it in the compound key entity as follows:

<u>Student Number</u>
<u>Module Code</u>
Grade Point
*Result Code
Tutor Name

However, strictly speaking, the tutor is really determined by the Tutor Group of which the student is a part and so should be removed from this entity and placed in another one for Tutor Group. The Student will also be linked to this Tutor Group. This example will be developed fully in section 8.6 on composite keys later in the chapter. This is a case of **transitive dependence** where an attribute does have a unique value for a given key but is *really* dependent on another key that is itself dependent on the first key.

Construction of Third Normal Form (3NF) entity model

An entity model for these entities can now be constructed as in Figure 8.12. It is easy to see the pattern here. The individual elements of the compound key become the many end of a one-to-many relationship with the entities that have those elements as their simple keys. Entities with foreign keys become the many end of a one-to-many relationship with the entity that has this foreign key as its simple key.

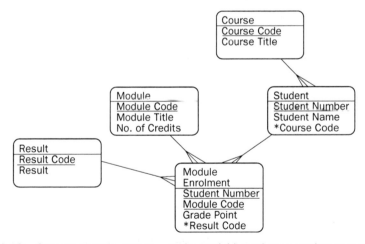

Figure 8.12   Student records system – entity model based upon student transcript Third Normal Form

This is somewhat complicated to put in writing and it is useful to think of it visually. The crow's foot can be thought of as a 'grab' and the simple keys 'grab' the asterisk of a foreign key and also 'grab' any compound keys of which they are a part. Notice that, unlike the entity models we built in the last chapter, we omit optionality and relationship names in the 3NF entity model, simply because we do not have sufficient information to derive them. These will be added at a later time (see section 8.7).

Summary of stages of normalisation

The following stages include some 'tips' which refer to the completed normalisation table in Figure 8.11.

- Write out data in un-normalised form (UNF). Always underline the key field (see <u>Student Code</u>). Always indent the repeating data and give it a level of 2.
- Convert to First Normal Form (1NF) by separating repeating groups. When going from UNF to 1NF, all the data items with a level of 1 are just copied across to the 1NF column. When going from UNF to 1NF, the repeating group is copied across to the 1NF column and a key for the **repeating group** is chosen (in this case <u>Module Code</u>), but the original key (<u>Student Number</u>) is brought down with it to make a **compound** key.
- Convert to Second Normal Form (2NF) by separating data items that depend on only part of a key. When going from 1NF to 2NF, any relation with a simple key (i.e. just one underlined data item) is copied straight across unchanged (in this case the <u>Student Number</u> relation).
- Convert to Third Normal Form (3NF) by separating any attributes not directly dependent upon the key – those which instead depend upon other non-key attributes. When going from 2NF to 3NF, make sure that, if you take a relation out (e.g. the <u>Course Code</u> and the <u>Result Code</u> relations), you leave a copy of the key behind as a foreign key.
- Apply the Third Normal Form tests.
- Construct the Third Normal Form entity model.

You may find it useful to remember the following memory jogger when creating First, Second and Third Normal Forms:

- repeating groups
- part-key dependencies
- non-key dependencies

The above tips are the simple ones. How you get from 1NF to 2NF for a compound key relation cannot be explained in one sentence, so you will need to really study the working; similarly for going from 2NF to 3NF.

8.3.3   The module class list

The document

It is possible, in fact very likely, that the same data used in the student transcript example would be used to produce other documents for other users of the system. The previous example contained data presented for the benefit of the student. The module leader might well want the same data but presented in a different way – for example a module class list as in Figure 8.13.

Module Code: COM120
Module Title: Systems Analysis
Number of Credits: 20
Lecturer Code of Module Leader: MLEJ
Lecturer Name of Module Leader: Mark Lejk

Student Number	Student Name	Course Code	Course Title	Grade Point	Result Code
0156786	Simon Adams	G105	BA Bus Comp	9	P
9876455	Jennifer Barker	G105	BA Bus Comp	3	RE
2341235	James Bull	G106	BSc Comp	2	RCE
3493426	Deborah Cameron	G105	BA Bus Comp	15	P
.	.	.	.	.	.
.	.	.	.	.	.
4561239	Susan Williams	G108	BSc Info Tech	3	DC

Total number of students: 76

Figure 8.13   The module class list

You can see that this document contains most of the data in the previous example, but some extra data has been added and a little has been missed out. For example, the code and name of the module leader are included. The module leader is a lecturer and a lecturer can take on several roles, such as module leader, personal tutor, course leader, or simply a tutor who supports the module leader. However, in the system, a lecturer is stored under Lecturer Code and the exact roles of the lecturer need to be shown. You will also notice that the document only contains the Result Code and not the Result description. This is because the module leaders deal with Result Codes frequently and know what each one means. Finally, this document includes a Total for the number of students on the module.

The normalised document

Normalisation of this document produces the result shown in Figure 8.14 (ML stands for Module Leader).

If you compare this normalisation to the previous one, you can see that the final 3NF entities are virtually the same and any differences are due to differences we have introduced to the data in the first place. So, the Course and Student entities are identical to the first normalisation. In the Module Enrolment entity, the compound keys have the elements Student Number and Module Code in a different sequence but they are still the same. Also, the Result Code is not marked as a foreign key in the second normalisation as the Result description is not present in the document. A new entity, Lecturer, has been introduced together with a foreign key in Module that links to it.

The other new thing to come out of this is that the No. of Students disappears in Third Normal Form. This is because the attribute can be **calculated** by adding up the number of students on a module and need not therefore be stored.

UNF	UNF level	1NF	2NF	3NF
Module Code	1	Module Code	Module Code	Module Code
Module Title	1	Module Title	Module Title	Module Title
No. of Credits	1	No. of Credits	No. of Credits	No. of Credits
Lec Code of ML	1	Lec Code of ML	Lec Code of ML	*Lec Code of ML
Name of ML	1	Name of ML	Name of ML	
No. of Students	1	No. of Students	No. of Students	Lecturer Code
Student Number	2			Lecturer Name
Student Name	2	Module Code	Module Code	
Course Code	2	Student Number	Student Number	Module Code
Course Title	2	Student Name	Grade Point	Student Number
Grade Point	2	Course Code	Result Code	Grade Point
Result Code	2	Course Title		Result Code
		Grade Point	Student Number	
		Result Code	Student Name	Student Number
			Course Code	Student Name
			Course Title	*Course Code
				Course Code
				Course Title

Figure 8.14 The normalised module class list

As we go through a system, normalising inputs and outputs, it is always the case that not all the data items for each entity will appear on each input or output. We have to rationalise the entities as new data items determined by the same key crop up and we gradually collect together the complete set of data items for each key.

However, the main point to come out of this is that, from whichever point we start the normalisation, the final Third Normal Form entities should be consistent. This is why the technique is so powerful and so frequently used.

8.3.4   Combining the student transcript and class list

If we combine the results of the two normalisations we have done so far, we end up with the 3NF entity model in Figure 8.15.

You can see that this structure will get more and more detailed with new entities appearing and new data attributes added as further inputs and outputs are normalised. Hence, normalisation is known as a 'bottom-up' and rigorous technique compared to the 'intuitive' entity modelling seen in Chapter 7 which is very much a 'top-down' and subjective technique.

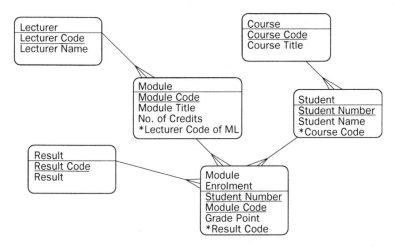

Figure 8.15 Student records system – 3NF entity model based upon student transcript and module class list

8.4 Normalisation and relational data analysis

You may remember that we explained at the beginning of this chapter that normalisation is only one part of the larger subject of relational data analysis (RDA). We do not intend going into RDA in any depth in this book, but it is useful to touch on it briefly here as it provides useful 'cross-check' rules for confirming the validity of normalised data.

You will also be aware by now that a relation is a term that describes a table of data items and, for our purposes, is the same as an entity. An example of a relation taken from our second example is the Student relation as shown in Figure 8.16.

Student Number	Student Name	Course Code
0156786	Simon Adams	G105
9876455	Jennifer Barker	G105
2341235	James Bull	G106
3493426	Deborah Cameron	G105
.	.	.
.	.	.
4561239	Susan Williams	G108

Figure 8.16 The Student relation

There are several rules that apply to relations, but the main ones are as follows:

- The order of the rows must not be significant.
- The order of the columns must not be significant.
- Each row must be unique.
- Each column must have only one value per row.

By applying normalisation then, we end up with a set of relations. The advantage of organising our data in this way is that we remove data duplication. A Student Name is only stored *once* in the Student relation and is stored alongside the key attribute of that student which is the Student Number. The only time a data item appears more than once is when they act as **links** either as a foreign key or part of a compound key.

By storing a data item once only, we also ensure data integrity. If the Student Name were to appear in more than one place, it would be possible for the same Student to have two different names (possibly due to spelling mistakes). This may sound far-fetched but as far as a computer system is concerned the difference between Williams and Wiliams is the same as between Adam and Kublai Khan.

Basically, we end up with a 'tidy' data set consisting of relations each with their own key and containing attributes that are determined by that key and nothing but that key. The relations are linked via foreign keys and compound keys.

8.5   Normalisation of tables of data

Having noted earlier that humans come into direct contact with data largely via input or output documents or computer screens, we have so far normalised individual documents where each document has a unique key. Documents such as these frequently act as inputs to and outputs from computer systems. However, reports in the form of tables of data are also frequently produced by computer systems and these reports may actually summarise several of the documents that we have just mentioned. We will now have a look at how you normalise such a table of data. We will assume that the table in Figure 8.17 is required as output from our computer system.

Figure 8.17 shows each course, the modules in each course, whether these modules are of type core, optional or elective for each course and details of the module leader for each module. The only real difference between this table and the sorts of documents we have met so far is that the table itself does not have a unique key but is a collection of sets of data that do have a unique key. It is as if several individual documents, one for each course, were combined together. Therefore, we treat the set of course data as our starting point for normalisation and give the un-normalised data a key of Course Code as in the normalisation table shown in Figure 8.18.

Apart from the starting point, this is exactly the same as when we normalised the previous documents. As can be seen in Figure 8.19, however, we now have two more entities to add to our 3NF entity model: Module Type and

Course Code	Course Title	Module Code	Module Title	Lec Code of ML	Lec Name of ML	Mod. Type Code	Module Type Description
G105	BA Business Computing	COM220	Database Systems	SSTI	Sue Stirk	C	Core
		COM221	Systems Analysis	MLEJ	Mark Lejk	C	Core
		COM228	Desk Top Publishing	MMCA	Moira McAllister	O	Option
		COM245	Organisational Study	MLEJ	Mark Lejk	O	Option
G104	HND Computer Studies	COM220	Database Systems	SSTI	Sue Stirk	C	Core
		COM221	Systems Analysis	MLEJ	Mark Lejk	C	Core
		COM228	Desk Top Publishing	MMCA	Moira McAllister	O	Option
		COM245	Organisational Study	MLEJ	Mark Lejk	O	Option
G106	BSc Computing	COM220	Database Systems	SSTI	Sue Stirk	C	Core
		COM221	Systems Analysis	MLEJ	Mark Lejk	O	Option
		COM228	Desk Top Publishing	MMCA	Moira McAllister	E	Elective
		COM245	Organisational Study	MLEJ	Mark Lejk	E	Elective

Figure 8.17 Output required from system

UNF	UNF level	1NF	2NF	3NF
Course Code	1	Course Code	Course Code	Course Code
Course Title	1	Course Title	Course Title	Course Title
Module Code	2			
Module Title	2	Course Code	Course Code	Course Code
Lec Code of ML	2	Module Code	Module Code	Module Code
Name of ML	2	Module Title	Mod Type Code	*Mod Type Code
Mod Type Code	2	Lec Code of ML	Mod Type Desc	
Mod Type Desc	2	Name of ML		Mod Type Code
		Mod Type Code	Module Code	Mod Type Desc
		Mod Type Desc	Module Title	
			Lec Code of ML	Module Code
			Name of ML	Module Title
				*Lec Code of ML
				Lecturer Code
				Lecturer Name

Figure 8.18 The normalised table

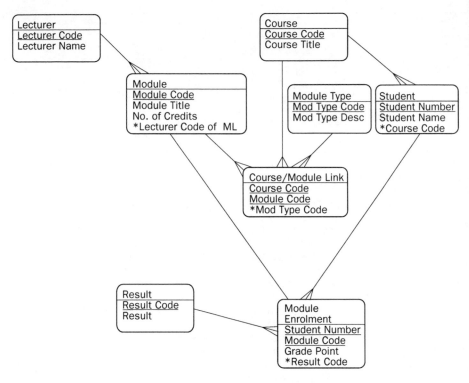

Figure 8.19 The 3NF entity model with entities Module Type and Course/Module Link added

Course/Module Link. You can see our entity model getting bigger and bigger as we normalise more and more data.

8.6 Composite keys

8.6.1 Like a compound key – but not quite

So far, we have met three types of key.

- A **simple** key is a single data item which by itself determines the non-key attributes in an entity. Examples of these are Student Number in the Student entity, Course Code in the Course entity and Module Code in the Module entity.

- A **compound** key contains two or more other keys all of which are needed together to determine the non-key attributes in an entity. Most often these other keys are themselves simple keys. Examples of compound keys are Course Code with Module Code in the Course/Module

Link entity and Student Number with Module Code in the Module Enrolment entity.

- A **foreign** key is not really a key as such. It is a non-key attribute in one entity that is a key attribute in another. Examples of foreign keys are Module Type Code in the Course/Module entity and Lecturer Code (Module Leader) in the Module entity.

There is another type of key that occurs quite frequently and is often confused with a compound key. This type of key is called a **composite** or **hierarchic** key and is subtly different to a compound key. We will introduce this type of key through an example.

8.6.2   The tutor group class list

We have already met modules and module leaders. When a module is actually taught, students are split into tutorial groups, each group having a tutor. The module leader will normally act as tutor for some of these groups but other tutors will take some groups so that the module is taught by a team of tutors led by the module leader.

Tutorial groups are timetabled at different times in different rooms and our computer system is required to produce a class list of students in each tutorial group. The tutor group class list looks like the document in Figure 8.20.

Module Code: COM120	Tutor Group Number: 3
Module Title: Systems Analysis	Day: Wednesday
Lecturer Code (Module Leader): MLEJ	Time: 10.00–11.30
Lecturer Name (Module Leader): Mark Lejk	Room: SP304
	Lecturer Code (Tutor): DDEE
	Lecturer Name (Tutor): David Deeks

Student Number	Student Name
0156786	Simon Adams
9876455	Jennifer Barker
2341235	James Bull
3493426	Deborah Cameron
.	.
.	.
4561239	Susan Williams

Figure 8.20   The tutor group class list

First of all, a word of caution! Documents such as this can be deceptive. One of the problems with normalisation is that it can be too easy to simply follow the rules and not really understand what it is you are doing. Although this document covers only one tutorial group, it is obvious that a module will have more than one tutorial group. In other words, we have a *repeating group* of tutorial groups within a module. On top of that we have a *repeating group* of students within a tutorial group! Hence we have a **nested repeating group** – a repeating group within a repeating group.

That is not all. We are obviously going to have an entity called Tutor Group sometime soon. What is the key of this entity? Tutor Group Number? No, each module is going to have its own Tutor Groups and a Tutor Group Number of 3 is not enough to identify a particular Tutor Group as it may be the third Tutor Group in the Systems Analysis module or the Software Engineering module or any other module. In other words, Tutor Group Number is not unique and needs to be qualified by the Module Code to make it unique. The key of Tutor Group is written as follows:

(Module Code)

(Tutor Group Number)

The brackets mean that the lower level non-unique attribute Tutor Group Number must be qualified by the higher level unique attribute Module Code to make the whole key unique. It looks like a compound key, doesn't it? But it is different.

Consider a compound key we have met already:

Student Number

Module Code

These two keys are put together to determine data associated with both a Student and a Module, that is, the student's grade and result in a module. Both Student Number and Module Code are unique keys in their own right – one Student Number is the key for one and only one Student and one Module Code is the key for one and only one Module. But as already mentioned, in the example we are considering now one Tutor Group Number is not the key for one and only one Tutor Group but for a range of Tutor Groups in different modules – and this is what makes the key a composite rather than a compound. Many students of data analysis find this concept difficult and it is worth taking your time reading this until you understand it.

8.6.3   Normalising the tutor group class list

All of this may well seem complicated. To an extent it is, but to help you get the idea we will show you the fully normalised version of the class list (Figure 8.21) and then demonstrate how we arrived at it. Hopefully it will all become clear.

There is so much of interest here that it is difficult to know where to start – so we will start at the beginning. We have already mentioned the nested repeating groups and you can see how these are written in the UNF column with the different tiers being given increasing UNF Level numbers of 1, 2 and 3.

UNF	UNF level	1NF	2NF	3NF
Module Code	1	Module Code	Module Code	Module Code
Module Title	1	Module Title	Module Title	Module Title
Lec Code of ML	1	Lec Code of ML	Lec Code of ML	*Lec Code of ML
Name of ML	1	Name of ML	Name of ML	
Tutor Group No	2			Lecturer Code
Day	2	(Module Code)	(Module Code)	Lecturer Name
Time	2	(Tutor Group No)	(Tutor Group No)	
Room	2	Day	Day	(Module Code)
Lec Code of Tutor	2	Time	Time	(Tutor Group No)
Name of Tutor	2	Room	Room	Day
Student Number	3	Lec Code of Tutor	Lec Code of Tutor	Time
Student Name	3	Name of Tutor	Name of Tutor	Room
				*Lec Code of Tutor
		(Module Code)	(Module Code)	
		(Tutor Group No)	(Tutor Group No)	(Module Code)
		Student Number	Student Number	(Tutor Group No)
		Student Name		Student Number
			Student Number	
			Student Name	Student Number
				Student Name

Figure 8.21 The normalised class list

When we go to 1NF, we have to remove repeating groups *twice* because they are nested. The first time we end up with details about the Tutor Group with a composite key of

(Module Code)

(Tutor Group No)

and the second time we get details of allocation of students to the tutorial groups with the following key:

(Module Code)

(Tutor Group No)

Student Number

This is starting to look quite complex – but it is really a compound key made up from the composite key and a simple key (Student Number).

In 2NF we examine this last compound key and remove the Student details into another relation. We are left behind with this three-part key on its own with no non-key attributes to determine. However, we cannot and should not get rid of this as it acts as the only link between Student and Tutor Group. It is called a **key-only relation.**

In 3NF, we take out the Lecturer details, but we do it twice, once for the

Module Leader and once for the Tutor. We will end up here with two links from Lecturer, one to the Module and one to the Tutor Group to represent the two different roles of the lecturer as module leader and as tutor.

If we join these relations together, we get the structure in Figure 8.22. The composite keys need a mention here. When linking a composite key to other relations, you mark the top-level unique key (in this case Module Code) as a foreign key and then link it like any other foreign key. You will notice the asterisk to the left of Module Code in the Tutor Group relation marking it as a foreign key. The key of Tutor Group Allocation is really a compound key made up of the composite key and the simple key (Student Number). It is hence linked to the entities that have these two elements as their total key, that is Tutor Group and Student.

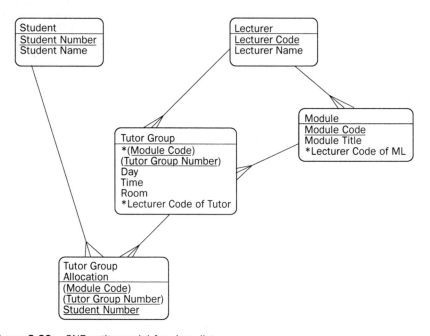

Figure 8.22 3NF entity model for class list

8.7 Combining the 3NF entity models

If we now combine this last entity model with the one we produced at the end of section 8.3, we arrive at the structure shown in Figure 8.23. So as not confuse the overall picture with unnecessary detail, the entity model just contains the names of the relations. By normalising only four different sets of data, it has been possible to produce quite a complicated entity model.

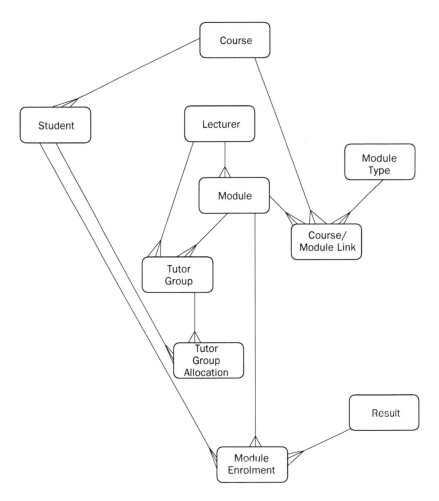

Figure 8.23   Combined 3NF entity model

8.8   Comparing the 3NF entity model with the logical entity model

8.8.1   Aiming for the definitive entity model

You can see how normalisation takes you into the heart of the system. It forces you to take a detailed analytical approach and is invaluable in arriving at a **correct** entity model. You can be pretty sure that normalisation throws up some entities that do not appear in an **intuitive** entity model. However, there are aspects of the intuitive model that are missing here. We do not show optionality or indicate what the relationships actually mean – whereas both of these aspects are included in an 'intuitive' version. We therefore need to combine the two approaches to get the 'best' entity model for the system.

8.8.2 The entity model before normalisation

Imagine that at the end of the entity modelling described in the last chapter, a systems analyst had come up with the model in Figure 8.24. You can see that this is a lot simpler than the 3NF entity model produced at the end of the last section – the analyst has made a number of omissions and mistakes that we can now see that normalisation has brought to light. Normalisation provides the mechanistic framework to sort out the data properly, but the analyst still needs to understand the system in order to make the final entity model realistic.

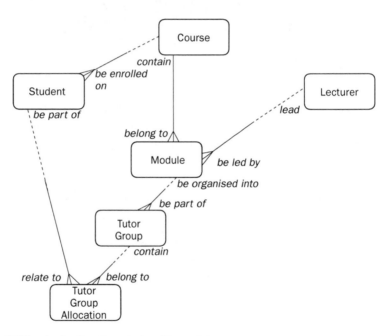

Figure 8.24   Analyst's attempt at entity model

For example, the analyst has assumed that a Module can only belong to one Course whereas we now know it can belong to more than one. The analyst has not realised that the system needs to store the Lecturer Code of the Tutor for a Tutor Group.

The entities Module Type and Result do not appear in the entity model simply because the analyst has not thought of them as entities, even though, strictly speaking, they are.

Finally, the analyst has not linked Student to Module but has tried to be clever and linked them via Tutor Group Allocation. Although this may seem reasonable, the module leader needs to know which Students have been enrolled on the Module *before* Students are allocated to Tutor Groups. So the Student to Module link must still be there, to cater for this time delay. Also, if the number of Students enrolled is not great, there may be only one Tutor Group, in which case the module leader will act as tutor and the Tutor Group and Tutor Group Allocation entities are not really needed.

8.8.3 Combining the two views

Combining the two views may well produce the final entity model in Figure 8.25.

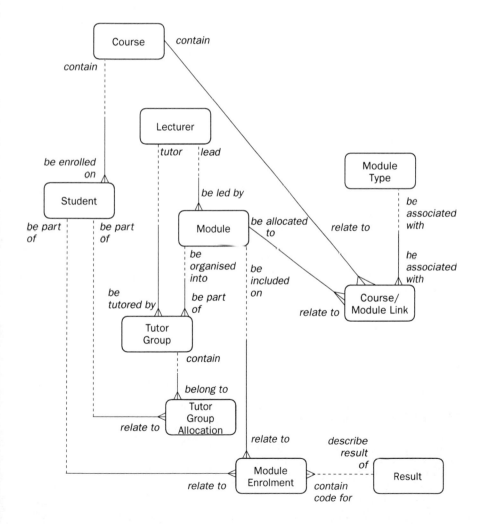

Figure 8.25   Combined entity model

This chapter . . .

. . . began by examining the meaning of a relationship in data analysis. It then introduced the concept of normalisation by slowly introducing you to the three stages: First, Second and Third Normal Forms. We then looked at the Third Normal Form tests and how to construct an entity model from Third Normal Form relations. We then saw how composite or hierarchical keys differ from compound keys and how a Third Normal Form data structure is reconciled with an initial entity model.

You may have realised by now that normalisation and entity modelling are huge subjects and the models can get very complicated. But then, computer systems nowadays *are* complicated and you can only expect them to become more so. Modern databases can be absolutely enormous and it is not unusual to find systems with more than 100 entities. In order to tackle these systems, you need a methodical proven technique that is based on sound theoretical principles. Normalisation is such a technique. Use it correctly and you will not regret it.

A useful exercise

Select at least three documents or computer screen layouts appropriate to your 'own experience' example and including at least some of the same entities as were included in the entity model you created at the end of Chapter 7:

1   Normalise these documents to 3NF.
2   Create a 3NF entity model for each.
3   Create a combined entity model for your 'system'.
4   Compare this entity model with your Chapter 7 one, rationalising any differences.

Further reading

C.J. Date, *An Introduction to Database Systems*, 7th edition, Addison-Wesley, Reading, MA, 1999.

Web addresses worth a visit

www.sum-it.nl/cursus/dbdesign/english
www.tpu.fi~jaalto/5103/normalisation.html
www.doc.mmu.ac.uk/online/SAD

Logicalisation of DFDs   9

9.1 Introduction

9.1.1 Returning to DFDs

Data flow diagrams (DFDs) have been seen to be an extremely useful systems analysis tool. Not only do they allow the analyst to get a structured view of a system, but also they are an excellent communication vehicle between the analyst and user. Because they are pictures, and 'a picture is worth a thousand words', users pretty soon get the hang of them and quite often go away and draw their own versions.

We first met DFDs in Chapter 4 and continued through to Chapter 6, by which time we had expanded to the lowest level the processes that they contain. In Chapter 4, section 4.3.2, we saw that DFDs allowed us to take a physical view or logical view of a situation – but, for good reasons, all the DFDs we saw after that modelled an existing physical system. These were called **current physical DFDs**. We saw that they were extremely useful diagrams as they describe the system as it is and make no attempt to make any improvements or changes to it.

In practice, however, systems evolve over time. It is often the case, for instance, that the people who first started running a system move on and are replaced by new people with different ideas who make changes to the system. Or a company may move into new areas of business. Several such changes can take place over time and a system may be quite different from its original version. If these changes are not co-ordinated, we can end up with a piecemeal set of procedures whose intentions are not particularly clear. Often, when investigating why a particular procedure is undertaken, the answer is 'because it's been done like this since I started working here and I've just carried on in the same way'.

In Chapter 4, section 4.3.3, we saw that the next stage of systems analysis involves logicalising the current physical DFD – and here we explore the transformation that takes place in order to do this, thus creating **current logical DFDs**. You may wonder why we didn't simply continue with DFDs earlier instead of covering data modelling and normalisation in between. The reason is that the logicalisation of DFDs includes the logicalisation of datastores to ensure that data is not duplicated – and we like to use data modelling to show you how to do this. We therefore had to show you data modelling first, and normalisation is of course very closely tied up with it as you have now discovered.

9.1.2   Why logicalise?

So, a system may be in operation that does not fully reflect what the system was originally intended to do, or is intended to do now. As a result, by examining a system and documenting it physically the **policy** behind the system may not be obvious. You often hear the expression 'I can't see the wood for the trees'. This is particularly pertinent in systems analysis. The analyst is confronted with a lot of sometimes detailed procedures, many of which are interlinked, and it is difficult to see the overall picture – what the system is *really* trying to do. The *physical* circumstances are masking what is *logically* going on.

As mentioned above, in Chapter 4 we introduced the idea of being able to take either a physical or a logical view of a situation. It is now time to introduce how DFDs can assist in this. Logicalisation is a very powerful and sophisticated technique for unravelling a physical system and expressing it logically. At the end of the technique, we end up with a **logical DFD** of the **current** system that tells us what the system is doing and reflects the policy behind the current system – as distinct from the current physical DFD, which tells us how that policy is implemented.

Logicalisation is often regarded as difficult by practising systems analysts and some actually avoid doing it. This is a mistake as it often throws light on shortcomings in a system that would have been missed otherwise. It is not a rigid technique, like normalisation for example. It is more a set of guidelines that can be applied with a reasonable amount of flexibility. Not only does it supply a picture of the policy behind the existing system, but also it highlights problem areas, establishes boundaries for future system development, and forms the basis or platform for the specification of the required system. We will see more about this in Chapter 10. In addition, it forces the analyst to start thinking logically and abstractly and to move away from the constraints imposed by the existing system. It is hence an empowering technique and very, very important.

9.1.3   Business Process Re-engineering (BPR)

Before we get on with the subject of logicalisation, we want to pause for a moment and mention a concept that has been widely publicised and that we feel is appropriate at this point. The term Business Process Re-engineering in fact covers three distinctly different management approaches – i.e. process improvement, process re-design and process re-engineering. **Improvement** is the least radical, with improvements tending to be small but ongoing, confined within existing boundaries and focusing on improvements to the existing system. **Redesign** is more fundamental and in reality represents the majority use of the term BPR. It goes beyond improving existing processes, and asks the question 'should we be doing this at all?' **Re-engineering** describes the most radical rethink. It sets targets, aiming for extremely dramatic improvements such as cutting order to delivery times from one month to one day and reducing costs by 70 per cent while at the same time improving service levels by specified amounts. The common thread to all BPR, however, is the attempt to improve, rationalise, replace or simply do away with processes.

You may notice that we introduced BPR by referring to it as a concept. It is our view that it cannot really be described as a method or technique, as it gives no clear instructions for how the analysis necessary for the process improvement (however radical) should be achieved. We are mentioning it here because the analyst who understands processes, who is used to identifying them, describing them, diagramming them, is in a very strong position when it comes to unravelling them, re-organising them, *re-engineering* them.

Processes are of course the fundamental part of the DFD, and the ability to logicalise such a diagram can prove to be extremely valuable to analysts who find themselves in an environment where there is a desire for change but little idea of how to go about it in an organised and efficient fashion. Until recently there was no actual method available for engaging something as 'soft' as a strategic objective into the systems development process. Here at the University of Sunderland, however, we have developed such a method, called Process Improvement for Strategic Objectives (PISO). It has been used with considerable success, not only within failing BPR projects, but also increasingly on its own. We return to PISO in Part 3 of this book.

9.2 Logicalisation step by step

9.2.1 Guidelines

We consider DFD logicalisation to involve four clear steps, using the existing system physical DFD as a basis:

1 **Rationalise data flows**
 • Replace documents with data (documents are a purely physical constraint).

2 **Rationalise datastores**
 • Hold each entity in only one datastore (i.e. get rid of data duplication – it is rarely logical that data should be duplicated).
 • Remove or rename datastores that hold physical documents

3 **Rationalise processes**
 • Remove people and places.
 • Change experts into external entities.
 • Remove processes that simply move data around within themselves.

4 **Re-construct DFD**

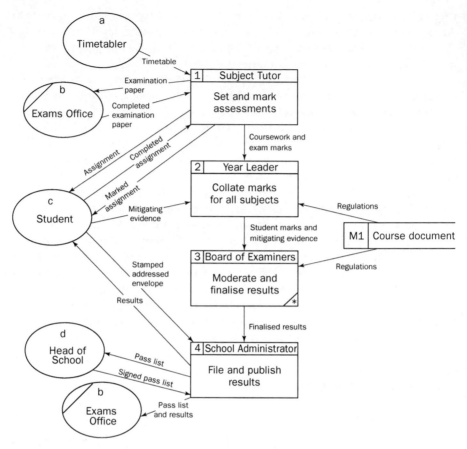

Figure 9.1 Level 1 DFD (current physical) for student assessment system (copy of Figure 5.6)

9.2.2 Example 1 – the student assessment system

The physical system

As usual, we will explain this technique by going through an example. We will return to the student assessment system that was introduced in Chapter 5 (Creating DFDs). That chapter concluded with a complete set of DFDs for the current physical system that incorporated a level 1 DFD and level 2 DFDs for processes 1, 2 and 4. These are reproduced for reference in Figures 9.1, 9.2, 9.3, 9.4 and 9.5. Process 3 in the level 1 DFD was considered unsuitable for expansion into level 2 and so was described in Chapter 6 (Specifying processes) using structured English. You will find an entity model for the current system in Figure 9.5. These diagrams together provide a description of the existing system, expressed physically.

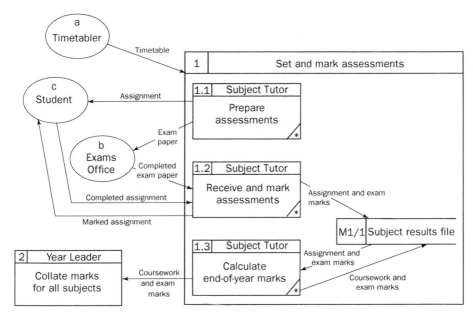

Figure 9.2 Level 2 DFD (current physical) for student assessment system process 1, 'Set and mark assessments' (copy of Figure 5.7)

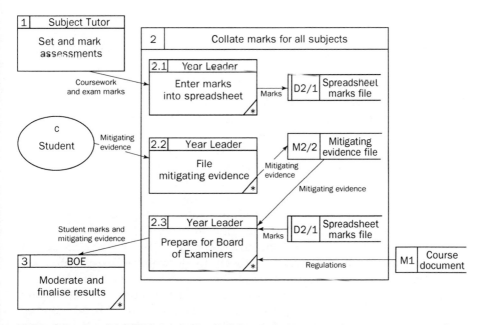

Figure 9.3 Level 2 DFD (current physical) for student assessment system process 2, 'Collate marks for all subjects' (copy of Figure 5.8)

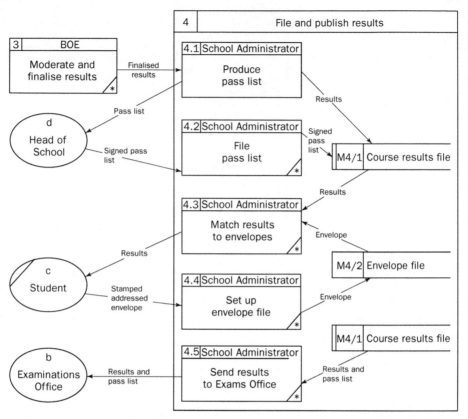

Figure 9.4 Level 2 DFD (current physical) for student assessment system process 4, 'File and publish results' (copy of Figure 5.9)

Step 1 – Rationalisation of data flows

This step is easy. Often, in physical systems, data floats around on pieces of paper – i.e. documents – with names like 'pink top copy' or 'yellow form'. It is common to see data flows on physical DFDs with names such as these. Data can also be sent by email, or transmitted over the telephone by word of mouth, and thus be called, for example, 'emailed spreadsheet' or 'telephoned details'.

Rationalisation of data flows involves replacing the physical data flow name with the data actually flowing. So, for example, the 'pink top copy' may well contain order details and the data flow name should hence become 'order details'.

In the student assessment system, most of the names of data flows are already rational or logical. Student marks are student marks whichever way you look at them. However, a candidate for change is the 'stamped addressed envelope' provided by the student in order that the results can be sent out. When you really think about it, this is a request by the student for results. The stamped addressed envelope is the way this request is physically implemented. Hence the data flow name 'stamped addressed envelope' becomes in the logical system 'request for results'.

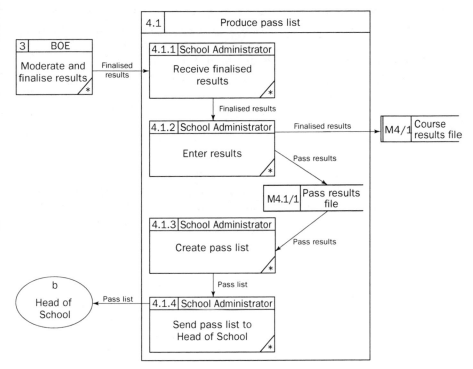

Figure 9.5 Level 3 DFD (current physical) for student assessment system process 4.1, 'Produce pass list' (copy of Figure 5.10)

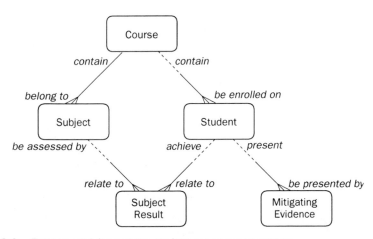

Figure 9.6 Entity model for current student assessment system

Step 2 – Rationalisation of datastores

This is where we come to the stage where an understanding of data modelling is very useful. If you look at Figures 9.1, 9.2, 9.3, 9.4 and 9.5, you can see a number of datastores. All of these contain some of the data that is described in the entity model. For example the datastore M1 is the Course Document and contains the entities Course and Subject. Datastore M1/1 (Subject Results File) will contain parts of the entities Subject, Student and Subject Result.

When we say 'parts' of the entities, we mean that the datastore may not contain all of the data items for each entity. So, for example, it is unlikely that the Subject Results File will contain details of students' addresses as it is really a record of marks gained by students in the different subjects. By looking at the datastores and entities in this way, we can construct a datastore/entity cross-reference and this is shown in Figure 9.7 for the current physical system.

You will see that the various entities are often stored in more than one file. The entity Student, for example, appears in datastores M1/1, D2/1, M4/1, M2/2, M4/2. As already mentioned, each of these datastores will store *some* of the Student details but it may well be that the same data items are stored in more

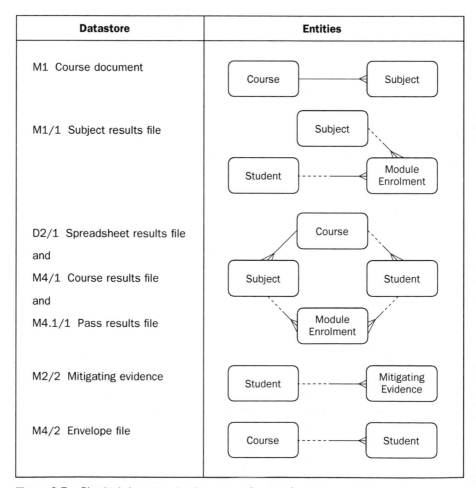

Datastore	Entities
M1 Course document	
M1/1 Subject results file	
D2/1 Spreadsheet results file and M4/1 Course results file and M4.1/1 Pass results file	
M2/2 Mitigating evidence	
M4/2 Envelope file	

Figure 9.7   Physical datastore/entity cross-reference for current physical system

than one datastore. In fact M4/1 (Course Results File) is really the same as D2/1 (Spreadsheet Marks File), and M4.1/1 (Pass Results File) is very similar.

This happens frequently in physical systems. Data is often spread over several files because different people want access to different information. Data is frequently duplicated simply because people find it is easier to have a copy of a file in their office rather than having to go to a central location to look up information.

However, these are *physical* reasons. From a logical point of view, the various parties involved simply need to access data. When we rationalise datastores, we remove this duplication so that an entity resides in *one and only one* datastore. We are really preparing the way for a computerised system here by grouping data into logical groups, storing each logical group once only (a logical database) and allowing anyone who wishes to access this data the ability to do so. In a computer system, this would be achieved by users having access to a central database through terminals. In a logical system, however, we simply say that the users have access to the data. How this is achieved is irrelevant.

It is usual to group the entities in the entity model into logical datastores. This is often quite difficult and, to be quite honest, different analysts do this in different ways. As a result, there is no 'correct' way of doing it and students often find this situation unsatisfactory. As a rule of thumb, entities should be grouped together if they are functionally related – entities that are linked, operated on together, created together or part of the same major inputs or outputs to the system. It is often useful to group them together if they can be described by a single term, such as 'sales ledger'.

Figure 9.8 shows our attempt at grouping the entities. We have decided to have *two* logical datastores. D1 is called *Courses* and contains details of Courses and the Subjects that make them up. D2 is called *Students* and contains details of Students, any Mitigating Evidence and Module Enrolments. It would have

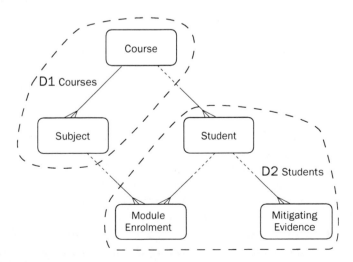

Figure 9.8   Logicalisation of datastores

been equally feasible to include the Module Enrolment entity in the *Courses* file but we feel it belongs more to the Student than to the Course.

These two logical datastores replace all of the datastores on the physical DFD. We have replaced six datastores with two – a considerable achievement. It basically simplifies our view of the system and makes it more accessible and easy to understand. We are saying: 'This system and all of its files is really about Students enrolled on Courses'. It gives us a healthy perspective as to what the policy of the system is.

Before we finish this section, just a word about **transient** datastores. These are datastores that store data temporarily. Examples are in-trays or temporary files that are there simply because data is to be collected and then transferred in a batch at the end of a day, for example. It is usual to remove these datastores in logicalisation because they serve no logical purpose. They exist for a physical reason. However, sometimes they should be kept. This occurs when a subsequent process needs a whole batch of information before it can work effectively. An example would be a set of orders to be loaded onto vans for despatch. The mechanics of loading orders onto vans that may well go to different destinations can only be effectively done when details of all the orders are available. Hence the transient datastore that holds these order details should be carried across to the logical system as it is logically needed.

Step 3 – Rationalisation of bottom level processes

This is the most important step in logicalisation and can often totally transform a system. There are several aspects to this step and we will go through them one at a time with reference to our student assessment system.

1   *As the processes in the logical DFD are meant to be logical rather than physical, all reference to the location of the process or the responsibility for that process should be removed.* Hence the location/responsibility box will be blank.

2   *A logical process should transform or use data simply because the system requires it to do so. How it is implemented is irrelevant.* This applies to processes 4.3 and 4.4 in Figure 9.4 for example which deal with the setting up of an envelope file and subsequent matching of results to the names on the envelope. Process 4.4 'Set up envelope file' should become 'Register request for results' and process 4.3 'Match results to envelopes' should become 'Output results to students'.

3   *If a process is simply re-organising data by sorting or collating then it should be removed.* There are several examples of this in our system. Production and signing of a Pass List is really presenting already existing data in a different form. So, processes 4.1 and 4.2 are no longer needed. Also, the job of a Year Leader is largely one of collation. The Year Leader collects the marks from Subject Tutors and re-organises these marks into a form suitable for the Board of Examiners. Hence processes 2.1 and 2.3 are no longer needed.

4   *Any processes that must remain clerical should be excluded from the DFD and replaced by an external entity.* This does apply in our system. The preparation

and marking of assignments by the module leader is not going to be considered for computerisation. The subject tutor should become an external entity because it is not intended for the computer system to do this part of their job. It would be just about feasible for the subject tutor to set assessments on the computer and for the computer to mark these assessments and store the grades. However, this would be an ambitious and expensive project and it is certainly not intended for this system. The subject tutor sets and marks assessments outside of the logical system and the system then stores the marks.

5   *Where a process involves some subjective decision making or involves an activity that is legally required to be done by a person, then the process should be split. An external entity should be introduced to replace the relevant parts of the process and data flows introduced between the process and the external entity.* This applies to process 3 where the Board of Examiners decides on the final results for students. Automating this process is equivalent to allowing a computer system to issue dismissal notices in a personnel system simply by looking at an employee's details and history. It is, in our opinion, one of the most overlooked aspects of computer systems and can lead to accusations of inhumanity and 'the computer taking over'. In process 3, the Board of Examiners looks at student results, takes into account any mitigating evidence and arrives at a consensus decision. Automating this process is extremely dangerous and, some would argue, immoral.

6   *Where a process is retrieving data only to display or print it, then it should be considered for removal. However, if it is considered to be a major part of the system's functionality, it should be retained.* This applies to the sending of results to students and the Exams Office. We have decided to keep this as it is an important part of the system.

The following aspects should also be considered when rationalising processes but there are no relevant examples in our system:

7   *If a process is simply passing data to another process without transforming it, then it should be removed and replaced by a data flow.*

8   *Where two or more processes are always performed together they should be combined.*

9   *Where two or more processes are performing exactly the same function, they should be combined.*

Step 4 – Reconstruction of DFD

This is where it gets interesting. Several of our lower level processes have been removed. A number of external entities have been introduced to replace part or all of some processes and we have drastically changed our datastores. We now need to re-group our lower level processes into new level 1 processes. This is not easy and requires a combination of applying an overall view with a detailed look at what the lower level processes are actually doing. A level 1 logical DFD of the current system can be found in Figure 9.9.

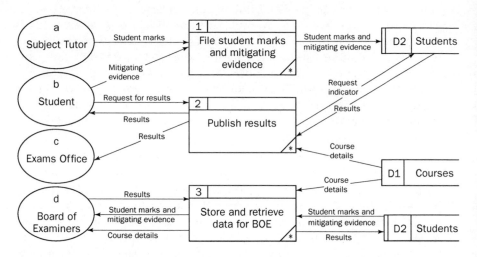

Figure 9.9 Level 1 logical DFD of the current system

The first thing to notice is that the logical DFD is a lot simpler than the physical one. This is as it should be. If the logical DFD is more complicated than the physical, it is likely that you have made a mistake. Basically, the logical DFD is telling us that the system stores student marks and mitigating evidence (process 1), supplies this information to the Board of Examiners and records the Board's decisions (process 3) and then outputs this information to interested parties (process 2). To assist in this processing two logical datastores are used, one of which stores student details and the other course details.

9.2.3 Example 2 – Marine Construction

The physical system

To further help you get the idea of logicalisation we are now going to return to the other example from Chapter 5 – the company called Marine Construction. We will begin by reproducing again in Figures 9.10, 9.11, 9.12 and 9.13 the complete set of DFDs for the current physical system.

The logical system

The level 1 logical DFD for the same system is shown in Figure 9.14. As the original system description is rather sparse, certain assumptions have been made and it is the main thrust of the logicalisation process that we wish to get across. Look at the DFD carefully, and then go through the subsequent explanatory points.

Data flows

The data flows do not now indicate documents – the 'customer specification', for instance, has become 'customer requirements'.

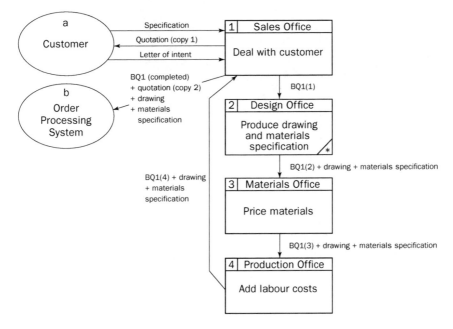

Figure 9.10   Level 1 physical DFD for Marine Construction (copy of Figure 5.2)

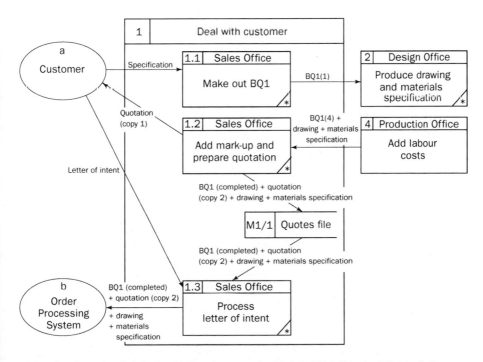

Figure 9.11   Level 2 DFD for Marine Construction Sales Office (copy of Figure 5.3)

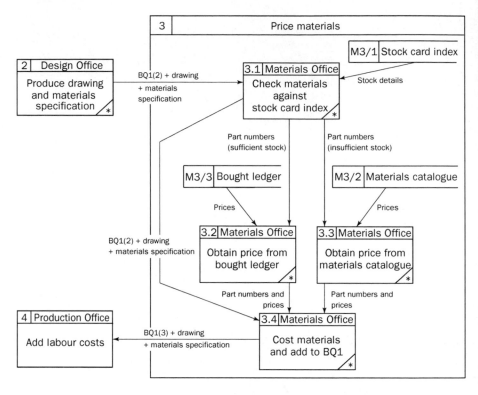

Figure 9.12   Level 2 DFD for Marine Construction Materials Office (copy of Figure 5.4)

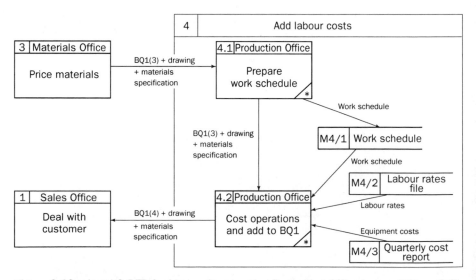

Figure 9.13   Level 2 DFD for Marine Construction Production Office (copy of Figure 5.5)

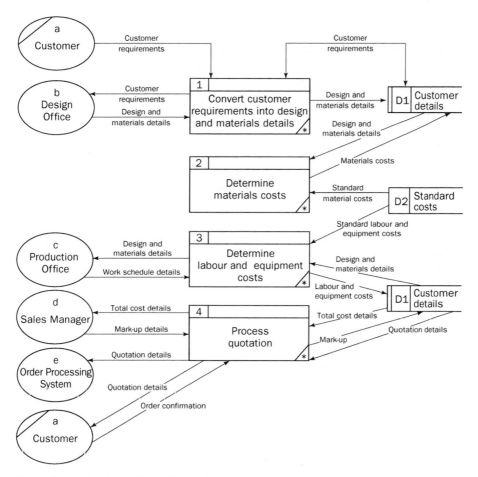

Figure 9.14 Level 1 logical DFD for Marine Construction

Datastores

Datastores now hold pure Data rather than Manual records – and the seven data-stores in the current physical system have been replaced by only two logical ones. D1 is the Customer File and contains details of the specification, the drawing, the materials specification, the work schedule and the overall quotation. D2 is the Costs File and contains all the necessary data for Materials, Labour and Equipment costs. As with other aspects in these notes this was not a 'clear-cut' decision, but as a result of a creative approach to the logic of what was happening – that is, it seemed the most logical way to hold the data.

Processes

- The processes do not indicate who carries them out, or where they take place – simply that they happen.
- The Design Office has become an external entity. Its function is still needed

to produce the design and thus establish the materials details – the system will then store these details. In a computerised system, one can imagine the use of computer-aided design (CAD) to produce the design.

- We have assumed that for the production of quotations, the Materials Office process is not logically required. If the Materials Specification produced by the Design Office is accurate, then the production of material costs is logically done by reference to the Costs file.

- We have assumed that the expertise of the Production Office in producing the Work Schedule is still required and hence it is now an external entity. However, if the Work Schedule is accurate, the calculation of labour and equipment costs can be logically done by reference to the Costs file.

- The addition of the mark-up to the quotation by the Sales Manager is considered to be a subjective process that should not be automated. Hence the Sales Manager has been removed from the system and shown as an external entity.

9.3 Conclusion

As we said at the beginning of the chapter, some people find logicalisation to be difficult and so avoid it like the plague. Others find it intellectually stimulating and very useful. We are strong supporters, even though we agree it can be tricky sometimes. Logicalisation basically sorts things out and is probably the single most important step in the development of a good sound system. It gets you thinking along the right lines and puts the system into its proper perspective. It can be the fundamental turning point between analysis of a current system and design of a worthwhile new one. As we explained, it can also play an important part in the application of a BPR-type of management strategy – and this is increasingly pertinent as companies seek to follow the lead of organisations claiming fundamental efficiency improvements.

Sometimes, the current system is already pretty logical because the physical implementation has been recently and thoroughly thought out and works well. However, particularly if a system has been in place for some time, the process of logicalisation can reveal to the systems analyst underlying themes and policies that would normally escape. It is in situations like these where the technique really shows its worth.

Most of this book is concerned with producing efficient computer systems – systems that greatly improve upon the business and computer systems that may have been in use within a company for years. In Part 3 we return to logicalisation, seeing that it can be pushed further than this. We look at the PISO method, which uses the technique in a more purely business-oriented way in order to produce logical and practical solutions to business problems.

This chapter ...

... began by explaining the background to logicalisation and introduced you to Business Process Re-engineering. Using the student assessment system example, we then went through the four steps of logicalisation: rationalisation of data flows, rationalisation of datastores, rationalisation of bottom level processes and reconstructing the DFD. We then repeated the process using our Marine Construction example.

A useful exercise

Logicalise the 'own experience' level 1 physical DFD that you completed at the end of Chapter 5.

Further reading

J. Peppard and P. Rowland, *The Essence of Business Process Re-engineering*, Prentice Hall, Hemel Hempstead, 1995.

Web addresses worth a visit

www.doc.mmu.ac.uk/online/SAD
www.dcs.bbk.ac.uk/~steve/3_6
www.whatisreality.net

Developing the required system **10**

10.1 Introduction

10.1.1 Learning techniques

This book is mainly about systems analysis **techniques**. We have been introducing you to a range of established and recognised methods of analysing and documenting certain aspects of a system. So, when we wish to describe the processing involved, we use DFDs and structured English. When we wish to describe the data, we use entity models and normalisation.

We have also treated these techniques largely in isolation. Hence, there are separate chapters on data flow diagramming, entity modelling and the like. In reality of course, these techniques are frequently done in parallel and they do overlap. For example, in a data flow diagram, you will find datastores. These datastores contain data, and the relationships within this data are described using an entity model.

The techniques we have introduced in this book are really those that help describe a system. There are several techniques that we have not covered – such as interviewing, handling meetings, preparing and giving presentations – that are all absolutely essential ingredients for a successful systems analyst to master.

10.1.2 Putting techniques into practice

One of the frequent criticisms of textbooks and courses on systems analysis is that because techniques are often presented in isolation, it is difficult for the reader or the student to link them together and to see how the whole development process works. On other occasions attempts are made to overcome this by having only one large scenario – but this inevitably means that some techniques are demonstrated better than others, depending upon the constraints of the scenario. In this book we are trying to present what we feel to be the best compromise – one scenario that gets revisited as often as is appropriate (the student assessment system), and other examples where these describe a technique better. This chapter again uses the student assessment system as its basis.

Note that it is not our intention to go as far as showing how to design the new system – some day we may write a further book about such aspects! Here, we really want to get across the main thrust of how a system is developed up to the point where we know what the required system is meant to do. In order to show how the requirements of a system are established, we will deliberately leave out a lot of detail and strip the system down to a basic skeleton. This will allow you to see the main **principles** involved without being sidetracked and misled by arguments about detail.

So far, you have been exposed to a number of examples concerning the student assessment system. This has been used to illustrate various techniques such as data flow diagrams, structured English, decision tables and normalisation. The separate examples in the different chapters are not really intended to be consistent with one another – we have simply used the system as a good way of illustrating certain concepts. For example, in the chapter on normalisation (Chapter 8) we got really carried away and actually allocated students to tutor groups and tutor groups to tutors. We did this because it was a good way of teaching you about composite or hierarchic keys. The example on data flow diagramming (Chapter 5) did not mention tutor groups at all, and concentrated on the assessment side of things.

You are by now used to this system and probably have a good basic understanding of many of its features. You will find that in this chapter the processing example is similar to the one in Chapter 5 but that the entity modelling one is deliberately simplified to aid understanding.

10.2 The existing student assessment system

10.2.1 The scenario

You may remember that the scenario is based on Year 2 of a degree course, but the procedures are the same for each year. Some time ago our university changed from this system to a modular one and we will show how the changes would be handled using the techniques with which you are now becoming familiar.

The following is taken directly from Chapter 5 (Drawing DFDs):

In the second year of the BA Business Computing course, students study six subjects:

Quantitative Methods
Systems Analysis & Design
Computer Systems
Software Engineering
Business Studies
Behavioural Studies

They are assessed in each subject by coursework and an end-of-year examination. The following description of the system is based around the roles of the various 'players'.

The subject tutor
Subject tutors first get involved when they are allocated to a subject by the timetabler. Subject tutors are responsible for setting courseworks (assignments) and giving them to students. The student completes the assignment and returns it to the subject tutor. They are then marked, the marks recorded and the assignments returned to the students with

feedback. There may be a number of assignments per subject each with a different weighting (i.e. some assignments may be worth 50% of the coursework mark while others only 20%). Tutors record the marks in a variety of ways. Most use a spreadsheet while some still record them on paper. At the end of the year the subject tutor must calculate a final coursework mark for each student and pass a copy of these to the Year Leader.

Subject tutors are also responsible for setting an end-of-year examination. Once the paper is written and moderated (we shall ignore the moderation process for simplicity) the paper is sent to the Examinations Office who organise the time and place of the examination, arrange for the exam to be invigilated and then return the completed scripts to the subject tutor. The subject tutor then marks the scripts, records the mark and sends a copy to the Year Leader along with the coursework marks.

The Year Leader

The Year Leader is responsible for the final collation of marks for presentation to the Board of Examiners. The Year Leader produces a spreadsheet that shows, for each student, the coursework mark and the examination mark for each subject and the weighted average of these two marks (courseworks and examinations normally have a 20/80% weighting). Any fails are highlighted on the spreadsheet and the Year Leader brings copies of the spreadsheet to the Board of Examiners, together with any mitigating evidence received from the student.

The Board of Examiners

The Board is made up of all the subject tutors, the Year Leader (who is almost always a subject tutor as well), at least one external examiner and is chaired by the Director of School. The School Administrator is also in attendance to record decisions and take minutes. The Board looks at each student's marks carefully, takes into consideration any mitigating evidence and decides on the results for each student by applying a set of regulations. The regulations are complicated and will not be described here but basically students may be required to do extra work in some subjects or, in extreme cases, may have to repeat the whole year or even withdraw from the course.

The School Administrator

When the School Administrator receives the results from the Board of Examiners, he/she produces a Pass List which is passed to the Head of School. The results are then filed in a Course Results File. The Head of School signs the Pass List and returns it to the School Administrator who files it with the results. When all the results from all of the Boards of Examiners have been processed in this way, the School Administrator sends a copy of the results and Pass List to the Examinations Office.

Students who wish to have a copy of the results must submit a stamped addressed envelope to the School Administrator who sets up a file of such envelopes. A little while after the Board of Examiners, the School Administrator matches the results to the names on the envelopes and sends the results to the students.

First, then, we will describe the above system using the techniques introduced in this book.

10.2.2 Current physical DFDs

As we have already seen, these describe the system exactly as it is, warts and all. The processes reflect what is actually done and the participants are the real individuals, groups of people or departments. The datastores are the actual files used. A physical DFD describes exactly what is *physically* going on.

The level 1 and level 2 current physical DFDs for this system taken from Chapter 5 are shown in Figures 10.1, 10.2, 10.3 and 10.4. A detailed description of the procedures involved in process 3 (Moderate and finalise results) is shown in Figure 10.5 and is taken from Chapter 6, Specifying Processes. As you may remember, this description was written using a combination of structured English and decision tables.

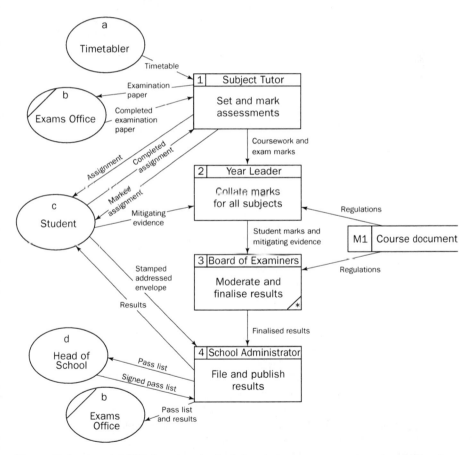

Figure 10.1   Level 1 DFD (current physical) for student assessment system (copy of Figure 5.6)

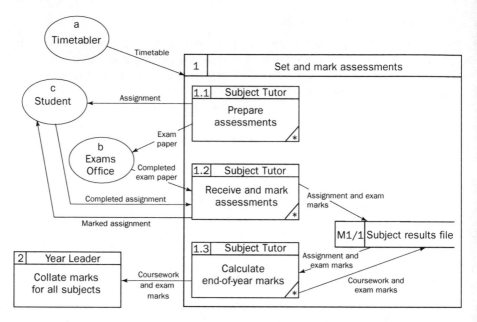

Figure 10.2 Level 2 DFD (current physical) for student assessment system process 1, 'Set and mark assessments' (copy of Figure 5.7)

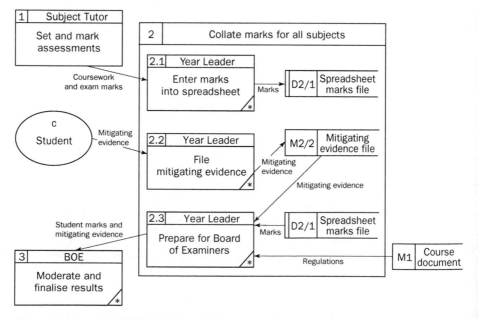

Figure 10.3 Level 2 DFD (current physical) for student assessment system process 2, 'Collate marks for all subjects' (copy of Figure 5.8)

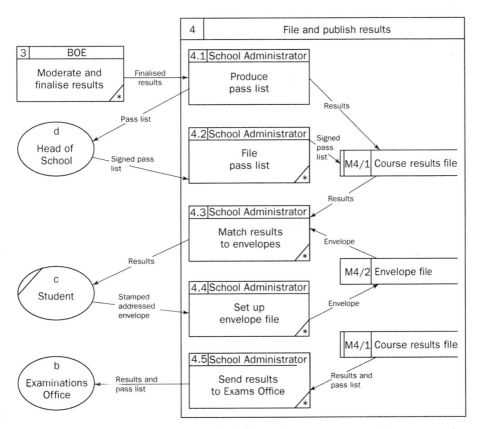

Figure 10.4   Level 2 DFD (current physical) for student assessment system process 4, 'File and publish results' (copy of Figure 5.9)

Do the following for each student:
    Step 1   Determine the number of failed subjects:
                    A subject is failed if any of the following are asterisked:
                    – Course-mark
                    – Exam-mark
                    – Subject-mark
    Step 2   Determine student results:
                    CASE 1   (Number of subjects failed = 0)
                                    Student has passed the year
                    CASE 2   (Number of subjects failed = 1 or 2)
                                    For each subject determine the result according
                                    to the following decision table:

Course-mark <40	Y	N	N	**E**
Exam-mark <35%	N	Y	N	**L**
Subject-mark <40%	N	N	N	**S**
				E
Redo coursework	X			X
Resit exam		X		X
Subject passed			X	

                    CASE 3   (Number of subjects failed > 2)
                                    Determine result according to the following
                                    decision table:

Repeat student?	Y	N	N	N
Any Course-mark <40%	–	Y	N	N
Any Subject-mark < 40%	–	–	Y	N
Leave course	X			
Internal repeat		X	X	
Internal or external repeat				X

Figure 10.5   Process description for process 3, 'Moderate and finalise results' (copy of
Figure 6.14)

10.2.3 Current entity model

For the sake of simplicity, we will only consider the entities Course, Subject, Student, Subject Result and Mitigating Evidence. We first saw the entity model of the current system in Chapter 9, Logicalisation of DFDs, and for convenience it is shown in Figure 10.6.

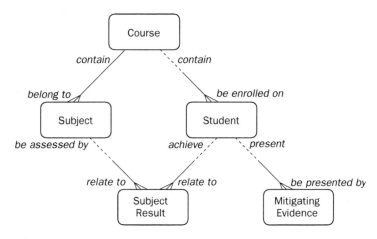

Figure 10.6   Entity model of current system (copy of Figure 9.6)

10.2.4 Current logical DFD

Also in Chapter 9 we saw how the current physical system was stripped of all its physical constraints to reveal the underlying policy behind the system. The level 1 logical DFD for the system that was used for the illustration is shown again in Figure 10.7.

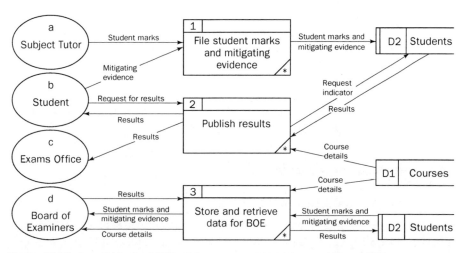

Figure 10.7   Level 1 logical DFD of the current system (copy of Figure 9.9)

10.3 The requirements of the new student assessment system

Changing from the existing system to a modular one is a huge endeavour. We will simply describe some of the major changes involved.

1   In the existing system, a course contains a number of subjects in each year, and each subject only belongs to one course. In the modular system this is totally changed. A subject is now called a Module, each module being appropriate to a particular level of study. The levels are 1, 2 and 3 which are equivalent to Years 1, 2 and Final Year in the existing system. However, a Module can be part of several Courses. So, students from several courses could all be studying the same module. A Course is hence made up from a number of Modules, some of which are **core** (or compulsory) for a course and some of which may be **optional.**

2   Instead of one Board of Examiners for a course, there will now be two. Each Module will have a Board that will examine that module's results. When all the Module Boards are complete, each Course will have a Board that will look at the complete set of module results for each student and decide on progression. The rules and regulations for this Course Board are too complicated to describe here.

3   The computer system will hold full details of Students, Courses, Modules and Module Enrolments. Details of members of staff will not be held in this computer system. Module leaders and course leaders will be held in a parallel manual system. In the current system, the Course and Subject details are held in a Course Document that describes the course in detail, the subjects that make it up and the regulations that apply to the course. In the new system, the relationships between Course and Module must be stored in the computer to allow students to study the correct modules on their chosen course.

4   The Year Leader does not appear in the new system. It is the responsibility of the module leader to provide student results to the School Administrator for entry into the computer system before the Module Boards. Any changes to the results arising from the Board will be entered by the School Administrator before the Course Board.

The above is a limited set of requirements, but they all impact upon either the entity model, or DFDs, or both.

10.4 The required system

10.4.1 The required entity model

The only really major change to the current entity model is due to the change in nature of a Subject. It is now called a Module and its relationship to a Course is now many-to-many instead of one-to-many. Normalisation of data also throws up two new entities called Result and Module Type (which are really look-up tables – refer to Chapter 8, section 8.3, subsection on Third Normal Form, and section 8.5, where these two entities are described in more detail). Hence the required entity model is shown in Figure 10.8.

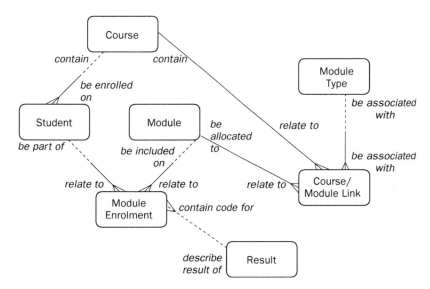

Figure 10.8   Entity model for required student assessment system

10.4.2 The required DFD

Requirements 2 and 4 in section 10.2 force changes to the data flow diagram. A level 1 required data flow diagram is shown in Figure 10.9.

You can see that this diagram shows the person or persons interacting with the system. In this case, the only person entering data is the School Adminstrator who will actually have a number of clerks to help. Attentive readers will note one new aspect of DFD notation – i.e. the dotted data flows between external entities. This is a useful piece of DFD notation that we introduced in Chapter 4, section 4.5, although this is the first time that we have actually shown an example. *Any data transferred between external entities that is necessary to the functioning of the system* may be shown in this way – it helps in the design of clerical procedures later on in the system development.

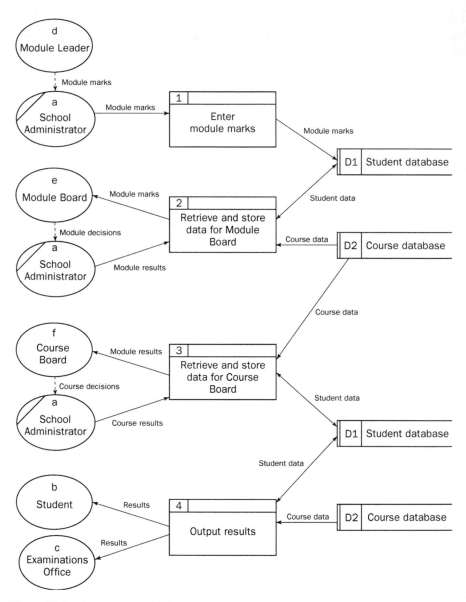

Figure 10.9   Level 1 logical DFD for required system

10.5 What is missing?

10.5.1 No maintenance

The answer to the above question is ... a great deal! You may have thought that this chapter has been straightforward enough, but we have deliberately missed out several important things simply to show the general direction in which systems analysis proceeds.

If the system modelled in the required data flow diagram were implemented as it stands, the system would soon fall flat on its face. Have you noticed for instance that there is *no maintenance*? How does a student get onto the system in the first place, where do courses come from and where do we allocate modules to courses? What happens when a student changes address or when a module becomes defunct? All of these considerations are looked upon as standard 'maintenance' questions that any self-respecting systems analyst usually considers as a matter of course.

This will be explored more fully in the next chapter when we look at such things as entity life histories and (briefly) state transition diagrams, which make sure that we have thought of everything. In fact, the system will be **maintained** by the School Administrator who will enter new students, courses and modules into the system.

When starting out in systems analysis, you will have to watch out for such things. During your systems investigation it is obvious that you will be exposed to the day-to-day operations and may not witness or be told about the procedures that are only done now and again. In our example, new courses will only appear once every two years or so and you must get into the habit of questioning how every entity begins its life and meets its end. As already mentioned, the next chapter includes techniques that make sure you do this, and so the final version of the required data flow diagram is left until then.

10.5.2 No alternatives

Our 'required' system seems to have just come together of its own accord. In practice, there may be several ways of implementing requirements and, usually, several options are considered that implement the requirements in different ways and to different extents. Some of these will be cheaper than others and cost will be a prime consideration for the user.

In addition to these different approaches to functionality there will be different approaches to hardware configuration. Some options may involve a stand-alone machine, others a network configuration and others a central processor linked to users through terminals. In practice, however, most computer systems are designed for computer configurations that already exist. We have only looked at functional requirements in this book.

The implementation of those requirements is not the subject of systems analysis but the province of systems design, which as explained earlier is beyond the scope of this book.

This chapter ...

... began by drawing together most of the techniques taught in this book. It looked at the student assessment case study and brought together all the diagrams drawn up to this point. It then introduced you to some requirements for this case study and showed how these could be implemented by changes to the entity model and data flow diagrams. It finished by raising the question of completeness.

A useful exercise

Revisit your 'own experience' analysis and, using the content of this chapter for guidance, develop your previous diagrams to incorporate features that you feel would improve your 'system'.

Further reading

G. Cutts, *Structured Systems Analysis and Design Methodology*, Blackwell, Oxford, 1991.
L. Maciaszek, *Requirements Analysis and Systems Design*, Addison-Wesley, Harlow, 2001.

Web address worth a visit

www.analysttool.com/require.html

The effect of time

11

11.1 Introduction

So far in this book we have looked at two main aspects of a system – processing and data. The processing view will be the foundation of the computer programs and the data view will be the basis of the computer files or databases. They interact to a great extent because processing affects data by reading it, updating it or deleting it. These two views are extremely important and fundamental to the development of a system but do not give the complete picture. What is missing is the concept of time.

Time considerations can be thought of as the glue that holds the system together. By considering this extra dimension, we can control the sequence of processes and make sure that a system does not do anything that it should not do at a particular point. The techniques involved also force us to consider the complete life of a system and its constituent parts and therefore help considerably in ensuring that the system is as complete as possible.

In methods like SSADM the technique that models time (strictly speaking it models **events** and we consider this later in section 11.5) is so fundamental that it is used as the major plank for developing process specifications in preference to the DFDs, which are considered too imprecise to be of much further use.

The main part of this chapter is concerned with the processing aspects of a system, but we begin by considering how time can affect the data model.

11.2 Time and the data model

11.2.1 The possible effects

Over what period of *time* do we need the system to hold the information? Will the system need to hold just one simple record for a minute or an hour, or a large number over a long period of time – with all the relationship variations that this might entail? The doctor–patient relationship that we first saw in Chapter 7 is used in Figure 11.1 to demonstrate how time considerations can transform both degree and optionality.

Example 1 shows a system where a record of the doctor and patient is to be

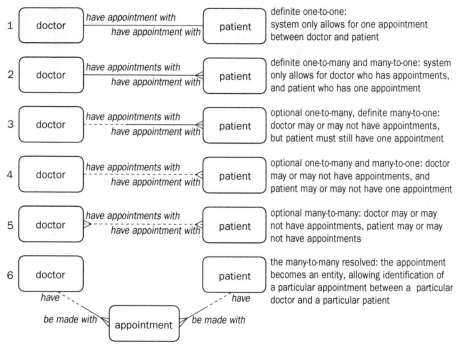

Figure 11.1   Developing the doctor–patient relationship by applying time aspects

held for only a short period – that is, while they have their appointment. Subsequent examples illustrate systems that will be able to retain doctor and patient details over increasing periods of time, with example 6 indicating a system that can steadily accept more and more doctor and patient records, while still being able to identify a particular appointment,

11.2.2 The vehicle breakdown and rescue system

We will now revisit the description of a vehicle breakdown and rescue system that we first met in Chapter 7.

Each engineer is allocated one van (which is driven up to a certain mileage and then replaced). Each member has only one address but perhaps many vehicles. Each visit is to deal with only one vehicle. A member can be visited more than once on any given date, and there may be many visits to a member on different dates. A member may only be covered for some of the vehicles they own and not for others.

When we looked at this we decided that Engineer and Van (among others) were probably entities in the system. Let us look at the relationship between these two entities. We will assume that one Engineer is allocated one Van and that the Van belongs to only one Engineer and is not shared. The Engineers may even be allowed to keep their Vans at their houses overnight. The system is only required to keep track of existing Engineers and their current Vans. This is obviously a one-to-one relationship that can be expressed as follows.

One Engineer *must* be allocated *only one* Van and one Van *may* be allocated to *only one* Engineer. By using the word 'may' in the second half of the sentence we have allowed for spare Vans that are only used if an allocated Van breaks down. A diagrammatic representation of the relationship is shown in Figure 11.2.

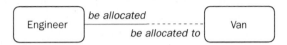

Figure 11.2   Representation of relationship between Engineer and Van

However, what if we wanted to keep a historical record of Engineers and their Vans? Vans will eventually become unreliable and need to be replaced. They can also become involved in accidents. The managers of the company might well wish to check which Engineers looked after their Vans reasonably and also look at the history of a particular Van.

Simply by introducing **history** into the system, we make the entity model more complex. The relationship between Engineer and Van now becomes many-to-many as an Engineer can be allocated more than one Van over the period of his or her employment and a Van can be allocated to more than one Engineer over its lifespan.

The entity model now changes quite dramatically and, if we wish to differentiate between current and previous allocations, is represented by the diagram in Figure 11.3.

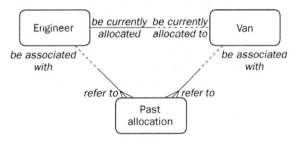

Figure 11.3   Introducing **history** into the relationship

This situation happens frequently. For example, in a library system, a Book can only be on loan to one Borrower at a time and this **current loan** relationship is one-to-one. However, the library may well wish to keep records of loans once the books have been returned for statistical purposes. For example, they may wish to find out the most popular and least popular books. This makes the relationship between Book and Borrower many-to-many in the same way as Engineer and Van. It is well worth watching out for this when investigating a system as it is a common feature of several systems.

We trust that you are getting the idea and are beginning to appreciate that time is a key consideration in the design of an entity model.

11.3 Time and the DFD

It might be worth your while having a quick look back at Chapters 4 and 5 – where we first met physical DFDs. DFDs can cause a lot of trouble because their purpose is often misinterpreted. We want to return to a point first made in Chapter 4, section 4.5.2. We commonly find that students (and sometimes practising systems analysts) try to impose time sequencing onto a DFD when it is really not one of its purposes. Before DFDs became such a popular and powerful technique, system processes were often shown using various forms of **flowchart**. Flowcharts are often taught in schools as part of mathematics or computer studies courses and they *do* show the sequencing of operations. Because DFDs and flowcharts can *look* so similar and because a lot of people meet flowcharts before DFDs, they often confuse the two and it is often hard to adapt to the principles of the DFD.

A good example of this occurred in Chapter 5 when we looked at the processes involved in producing quotations for the company called Marine Construction. You may remember we started off by following a form called a BQ1 around the system in a sequential manner and discovered that it started off in the Sales Office, went round a couple of departments and then returned to the Sales Office. We drew this sequential set of operations as a Level 1 DFD and then **redrew** it by grouping together all the operations for one department and making each department one process box on the DFD.

A DFD does not really consider time at all and is not intended to. It simply shows the data flowing into and out of a system, where the data comes from and where it goes to, what processes act on the data flows and which datastores are affected by these processes. It does not address the sequencing of the processes and several mistakes are made when people assume that it does.

Of course, in reality, some processes cannot start before other processes have finished. Some processes will only start if a certain set of conditions have been satisfied in other processes. The only circumstance where a DFD shows this is when one process sends data directly to another, rather than first sending it elsewhere.

We now need to consider **events**.

11.4 Events

11.4.1 What is an event?

An event is something that happens in the real world that changes one or more of the entities in the system under consideration. It is the trigger that brings one or more of the processes in the DFDs into action.

This is the secret behind the sequencing of operations. Although it is the **process** that updates an entity, it is the **event** that triggers this process. Hence the control of processes is really about the ways in which events affect the system.

11.4.2 Finding events in DFDs

It is very useful to think of an event as just something that happens and this 'something' has an effect on one or more entities in the system. As an event *always* triggers a process, there is a strong link between events and DFDs. The most obvious events are obtained by looking at the data flows on a DFD. We will demonstrate this by referring again to the level 1 required system DFD for the Student Assessment System that we first met in Chapter 10, section 10.4.2. See Figure 11.4, which is simply a copy of Figure 10.9.

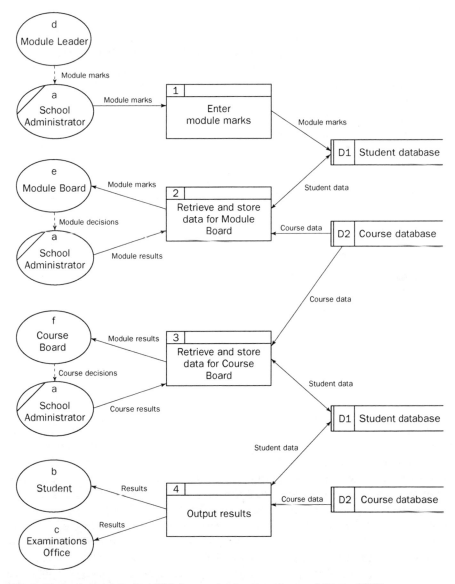

Figure 11.4 Level 1 logical DFD for required system (copy of Figure 10.9)

11.4.3 Types of event

Externally generated events

Process 1 is called *Enter module marks* and is performed by the School Administrator. The event that triggers this process is the arrival of the module marks from the module leader. This is the thing that happens that gets the School Administrator to enter the marks. This event would be probably described as *Receipt of module marks* or something similar. This is an example of an **externally generated** event and is shown as a data flow across the system boundary.

Internally recognised events

This occurs when something happens within the system that causes a subsequent event to occur. For example, within process 2 (File retrieval and storage for Module Board), students who fail a module will be highlighted. This would be shown in a Level 2 DFD and the associated process descriptions. Recognising a 'fail' is an event that will cause that student's module record to be updated. This is an **internally recognised** event.

Time-based events

This occurs when a process is triggered simply because a particular time has been reached. An example might be the automatic deletion of records that have been inactive for over a year. The event is the arrival of a particular time. This is a **time-based** event.

11.5 Entity life histories (ELHs)

11.5.1 What an ELH is

An entity life history (ELH) is a diagram that looks at all of the possible events that can affect an entity. Within SSADM these diagrams are absolutely crucial as they form the basis for process specification using Jackson-type structures (Jackson Structured Programming – JSP – was referred to briefly in Chapter 1, section 1.2.4) to show the sequence in which these events can occur. In SSADM, this transition from ELHs and entity models through an effect correspondence diagram to a Jackson program structure is complete, concise and intellectually beautiful. However, it does pre-judge that you are going to design your processes using Jackson structures and this is far from true in most system development nowadays. Also, we have found that ELHs are sometimes difficult to 'get right' when there are several events that can affect an entity and the sequencing requirements are a little complex. As a result, we are going to show you a slightly 'watered down' version of ELHs that misses out some of the complexities that occur. We will also introduce you to a simple 'home-grown' procedure that some students have found helpful in drawing ELHs.

While ELHs are widespread within organisations and university/college courses and most of the remainder of this chapter is subsequently devoted to them, there are other techniques that serve the same purpose. We will introduce you to one of these at the end of the chapter.

11.5.2 Drawing an ELH

The example

Figure 11.5 (a copy of Figure 10.8) shows the entity model for the required student record system that we last discussed in Chapter 10. The point to note is that each entity in the system has a life history, so in this system there should be seven ELHs – one for each of the entities Student, Course, Module, Module Type, Course/Module Link, Module Enrolment and Result. Let us look at the life history of the entity Student.

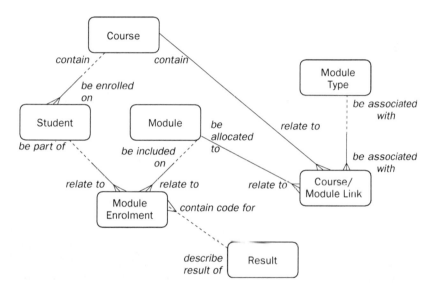

Figure 11.5 Entity model for required student record system (copy of Figure 10.8)

Creation and deletion events

These should always be the first events to be considered when drawing an ELH. What causes a Student record to be placed on the system in the first place? When students arrive, they are required to register and this event triggers the creation of a Student record on the database. Hence the creation event is *Student Registration*.

What causes a Student record to be deleted from the system? We will assume that a Student record is kept on the system until a year after they have left the university. Their records are then removed to another Archive File which, for the sake of simplicity, is part of another system. Hence the deletion event is time-based and we will call it *One Year After Student Departure*. This event will obviously depend upon the system having recorded the date of student departure and so cannot take place until the previous event *Student Departure* has taken place.

We hence have a strict sequence of events. For every occurrence of the Student entity, the above three events *must* occur in the following sequence.

Student Registration followed by

Student Departure followed by

One Year After Student Departure

The second event cannot occur without the first event having taken place and the third event cannot occur without the second. In ELH notation this is drawn as shown in Figure 11.6.

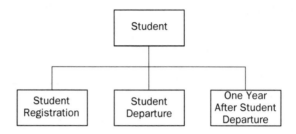

Figure 11.6 ELH for Student entity

This is a '**sequence** construct'. The sequence progresses from left to right. The name of the entity is always shown in a rectangular box at the top of the diagram.

Mid-life events

What can happen to a Student between arriving and leaving? Obviously all sorts of things, but we are only interested in events that change the entity. The most common occurrence that happens to all entities in all systems is an **amendment** or change to one of the data items in the Student record. For example, a Student might change address or there might have been a mistake when the Student details were first entered. We will assume that these amendments or changes can only take place between *Student Registration* and *Student Departure*. Also, you will

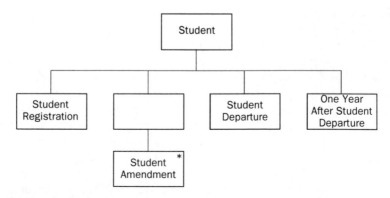

Figure 11.7 ELH for Student entity, including Student Amendment event

realise that the event Student Amendment can take place more than once for a particular Student. It is hence an iterative event. Inclusion of this event changes the ELH as shown in Figure 11.7.

Notice the asterisk in the top right-hand corner of the new event, which indicates an '**iteration** construct'. An iteration can occur zero, one or many times and so this allows for there being no amendments to a particular Student record throughout its life. Also note that the new event is a level below the other sequenced events with a 'dummy' box above it. This is because you are not allowed to mix different constructs at the same level in an ELH.

What else can happen to a Student in their life? They will enrol on modules. However, does enrolment on a module affect the Student entity? If you look at the entity model, enrolment on a module will create a new entity Module Enrolment that is linked to the entity Student.

In a relational database there is no processing as such which forms this link – it is simply a relationship between keys. Nevertheless it is normal practice to show the formation of this link on the ELHs of both the entities involved in the link, as in other database management systems some processing takes place in establishing the link.

Hence we have another event called *Module Enrolment* that will happen several times and is therefore an iteration. However, if we now draw the ELH as in Figure 11.8, we cause problems.

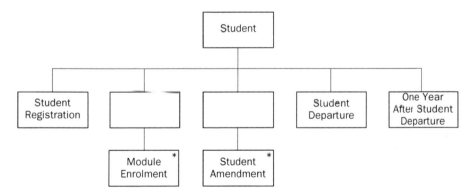

Figure 11.8   ELH for Student entity, including Module Enrolment event

The above diagram is wrong as it implies that all of the Module Enrolments have to be done before all of the Student Amendments which is obviously incorrect. The two events are interspersed and can occur in parallel with each other.

Some texts actually describe a special construct for parallel events, but there is an alternative that uses more 'standard' constructs and we prefer it because we feel it keeps things simple. This sort of situation happens in several systems and we would show it as in Figure 11.9.

The circles in the top right-hand corner of the middle boxes are selection symbols, and we now have a '**selection** construct'. Basically, the diagram is saying that after Student Registration, there is an iteration, each occurrence of

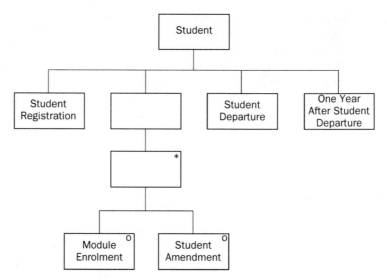

Figure 11.9 ELH for Student entity including Module Enrolment and Student Amendment events, utilising 'selection'

which is *either* a Student Amendment *or* a Module Enrolment. These diagrams get very complex very quickly. Students are allowed to withdraw from Modules and we would have to show Module Withdrawal as a separate event as this removes the link between Student and Module Enrolment.

In addition, we may wish to update the Student record differently depending upon the nature of Student Departure. If a Student were to leave the university prematurely as opposed to leaving when the course was completed, the processing involved may well be different. The event Student Departure now becomes qualified as follows into two sub-events.

Student Departure (Premature)

Student Departure (Course Completed)

The items in brackets are called **effect qualifiers**. The final ELH for the Student entity is now shown in Figure 11.10. Included are two new events: Yearly Course Result which updates the Student's course status decided at the Course Board and Course Completed which occurs after the Final Course Board for a Student. The fact that a Student cannot complete their course until they have gained a certain number of credits is not governed by this ELH. The Course Board decides whether a Student qualifies for an Award after looking at the profile of each Student.

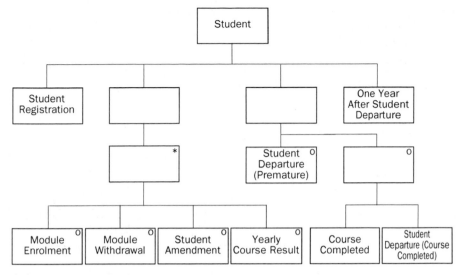

Figure 11.10   ELH for Student entity, final version

The ELH for the entity Module Enrolment would be constructed in a similar fashion, and is shown in Figure 11.11. Note the inclusion of a 'null' box (indicated by a line instead of an event – indicating a 'non-event'), which indicates that a module withdrawal may not happen.

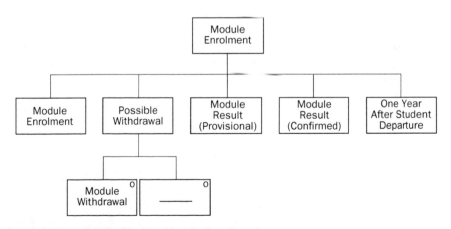

Figure 11.11   ELH for Student Module Result entity

11.5.3 The entity/event matrix

The entity/event matrix is a very useful grid that is often constructed before the ELHs are drawn. We have developed our own extension of this approach that many students have found of great assistance in the creation of a correctly drawn ELH. This is described fully in section 11.5.4.

To begin with, the partially completed matrix for our system as shown in

Figure 11.12 shows the events for the two entities which have already been discussed. The entries C, M and D stand for Create, Modify and Delete respectively and are known as 'effects'.

Event \ Entity	Student	Module Enrlmt	Course	Module	Course/ Module	Result	Module Type
Student Registration	C						
Student Departure (Premature)	M						
Student Departure (Course Cmplt)	M						
One Year After Student Departure	D	D					
Student Amendment	M						
Module Enrolment	M	C					
Module Withdrawal	M	M					
Module Result (Provisional)		M					
Module Result (Confirmed)		M					
Course Completed	M						
Yearly Course Result	M						

Figure 11.12   Partially completed entity/event matrix showing Student and Module Enrolment entities

This matrix is very useful. Firstly, it acts as a check that every entity has a Create and Delete event. You may remember that our required DFD did not consider the processing associated with these events. Secondly, it makes you think very carefully about all the things that can happen to a particular entity. This entity/event approach is crucial because thinking in this way ensures that as much of the required processing as possible is considered. It provides an extra perspective to the systems analysis that has so far been missing and, in our view, this is the main benefit of the technique – it is an aid to ensuring the analysis is complete. Thirdly, it ensures that all the entities that are affected by one event are considered together. You will notice that a number of the events in the matrix affect both of the entities Student and Module Enrolment.

The columns of the matrix form the basis of the ELHs and the rows form the basis of an SSADM diagramming technique called the **effect correspondence diagram** (ECD). Use of ECDs eventually leads to the JSP process structure mentioned earlier. However, this book does not consider these latter techniques and interested readers should refer to SSADM textbooks – a favourite of ours is mentioned at the end of the chapter.

11.5.4 Creating an ELH by further analysis of the entity/event matrix

An almost(!) foolproof method

Some students take quite easily to the concepts of entity life histories and how to draw them. If you are not one of these, do not despair. Instead, read on. In teaching ELH diagramming we have developed our own simple extension of the above approach that many students have found helpful. It uses further analysis of the entity/event matrix to first create the variety of constructs that it describes, and then put these constructs together to create the final diagram. We have found it to provide a fairly foolproof means of coming up with a practical ELH. Before we leave entity/event matrices we will therefore give an example of how this approach can be applied. To do so, we will consider the following scenario that describes a simple hotel booking system.

The hotel booking system

A reservation request is received and a reservation is then entered into the system. However, a reservation is not always made – guests sometimes turn up in the hope of finding a free room. In some cases, a deposit is received after the reservation has been made and this is entered into the system. On the day a guest is to check in, a room is allocated to the reservation. When the guest arrives the reservation becomes a booking or, if a reservation has not been made, a booking is created. Chargeable items are entered into the system as and when they arise and a running total is kept on the Reservation/Booking entity. When the guest departs an invoice is produced. At the end of each month paid bookings are removed to the Booking History file.

Before reading further you may like to go over the above description carefully again, and try to produce an ELH for the entity Reservation/Booking based upon what you have seen so far – either by attempting to draw an ELH directly from the description, or by first creating an entity/event matrix. To keep things simple, ignore the possibility of a Reservation/Booking being cancelled or amended.

The hotel booking system ELH – first attempt

The ELH in Figure 11.13 is a typical answer. Whether or not you have had a go at drawing your own, you should check the one in this figure against the scenario. You should be able to confirm that it meets all the requirements of the scenario, and is a perfectly proper solution.

One obvious feature, however, is the very complicated Creation stage. This makes the system look rather 'front heavy' and it is possible to produce a simpler version using a methodical approach rather than the semi-intuitive one used so far. This time we will carefully decide upon the best constructs by using the entity/event matrix to the full.

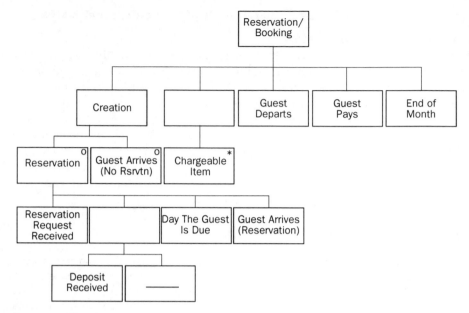

Figure 11.13 Completed ELH for Reservation/Booking (version 1)

Quits and Resumes

Before we do so, it is time to mention an added refinement – the use of Quits and Resumes. These allow you to skip events that are unnecessary under certain conditions. They are often frowned upon by purists but can lead to a simpler, more practical solution. For those who have experience of an appropriate programming language, it is helpful to think of these in terms of 'bypassing a sub-routine'.

As stated, we will begin by creating the entity/event matrix, but this time we will add selection (either this event or that one) and iteration (an event that can happen repeatedly) notations to the right of each appropriate create/modify/delete effect. Those without either of these 'special' notations must by default be a simple sequence. By using Quits and Resumes we will also add any instances where, following a certain action, any other events may be 'skipped'. These are always numbered. Q1 leads to R1, Q2 to R2 etc. If there is a Quit, there must of course be a corresponding Resume. In the example we are considering, there is only one instance of a Q–R. This may all sound somewhat confusing at present, but we will go through the process step by step and everything should then become clear.

Adding annotations to the entity/event matrix

Re-read the scenario and compare it with the entity/event matrix in Figure 11.14, which you will see includes (to the right of some of the C/M/D effects):

- the ELH select, iteration and null annotations that we saw earlier on the ELHs;
- a Quit and Resume as described above.

Event \ Entity	Resrvtn/ Booking
Reservation Request Received	C o
Deposit Received	M o –
Day Arrives When Guest Is Due	M
Guest Arrives (Reservation)	M
Guest Arrives (No Reservation)	C o (**Q1**)
Chargeable Item Arises	M*(**R1**)
Guest Departs	M
Guest Pays	M
End of Month	D

Figure 11.14   Entity/event matrix for Reservation/Booking

We will now show step by step how the above was derived. Having listed the **events**, the process that leads to the allocation of the **effects** and **ELH notations** is fairly straightforward, and is in three stages:

1   *Identify/analyse Creation event(s)*. A sensible interpretation of the scenario is that there is a choice of *two* events which can do this. These are Reservation Request Received, or Guest Arrives (No Reservation). A **C** is therefore entered alongside each of these, and 'o' added to indicate selection. It is also noted that if Guest Arrives (No Reservation) is the event that occurs, then other events are not applicable (i.e. Deposit Received, Day Arrives When Guest Is Due, Guest Arrives (Reservation)). A (**Q1**) is therefore shown alongside the Guest Arrives (No Reservation) event. We now need to identify the next event that could possibly take place after the skipped ones are passed over. It is obvious that this is Chargeable Item Arises, and so (**R1**) is entered to indicate where the Resume occurs.

2   *Identify/analyse Deletion event(s)*. It is obvious from the scenario that this occurs only with the End of Month event. A **D** is therefore entered alongside this. No alternative event is involved, so no further notation is entered.

3   *Identify and analyse Modification event(s)*. Having identified all events appropriate to creation and deletion, all other events must by default be modification ones – so an **M** is placed alongside these. Taking each in turn, we now use the scenario to identify whether any are 'selected' ones. This can either be because some *other* event may alternatively take place (as happened with the Create effect), or because *no* event may alternatively take place – that is,

an alternate 'null' as introduced at the end of the section 'Mid-life events' in sub-section 11.5.2. In this case we see that the 'Deposit Received' event may or may not occur, so **o-** is entered beside the **M**. A little more analysis of the scenario establishes that there are no further 'select' events.

We therefore turn to the final ELH notation – that of **iteration**. This was ignored when we were considering Creates and Deletes, because each of these can of course only happen once. But does the scenario describe any Modify events that can take place more than once during the life of the entity? We see that there is one – 'Chargeable Item Arises'. The '*' symbol is therefore entered alongside this one.

Drawing the 'non-sequence' constructs

With the matrix thus annotated as described, it is time to draw the identified **non-sequence** constructs, as shown in Figure 11.15. Each of these complete constructs will be in some sort of sequence within the life of the Reservation/ Booking, as will all the remaining events on the matrix. It is now simply a case of putting them together. If we have a pre-drawn construct that includes the event, we use this construct. If not, we simply enter the event in a box of its own.

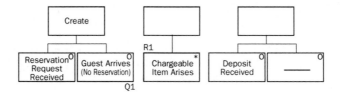

Figure 11.15   Reservation/Booking ELH constructs for Create, Chargeable Item Arises and Deposit Received

Completing the ELH

The 'creation' obviously comes first, and the 'end of month' represents the delete, which comes last. We have a pre-drawn construct that includes the Creation event, so we use it to begin the ELH. We don't have one for End of Month, so we simply draw an End of Month box at the end of the ELH. See Figure 11.16.

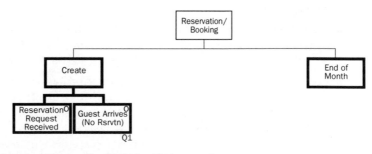

Figure 11.16   Reservation/Booking ELH stage 1

We have said that every other construct comes in between, in sequence, so we now need to add these. But creation consists of two possible events here. Which do we begin with in order to identify the subsequent event? It should be fairly evident that we choose the one that has no Quit – 'Reservation Request Received' – because if it has no Quit the next possible event *has* to follow it. We note from the scenario that the next possible event to this would be Deposit Received. We have a pre-drawn construct with 'deposit received' within it, so we simply add this whole construct to the sequence. See Figure 11.17.

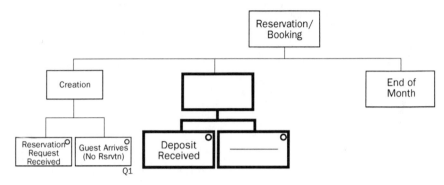

Figure 11.17 Reservation/Booking ELH stage 2

We then do the same to all other events that happen sequentially following the reservation request. If we have a pre-drawn construct, we include it; if not, we simply enter the event in a box of its own.

First, two events without a pre-drawn construct (Figure 11.18) are followed by the next pre-drawn one (Figure 11.19) and then the last two, which again are not pre-drawn and are therefore simply shown in single boxes (Figure 11.20).

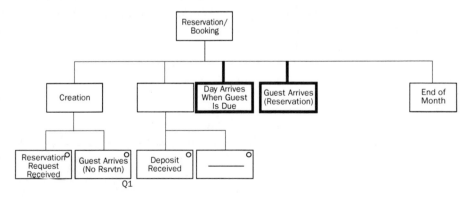

Figure 11.18 Reservation/Booking ELH stage 3

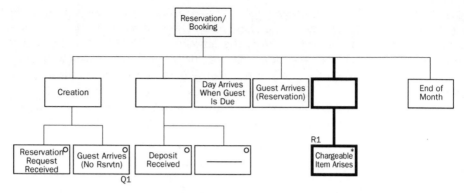

Figure 11.19   Reservation/Booking ELH stage 4

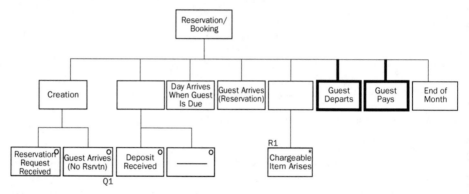

Figure 11.20   Completed ELH for Reservation/Booking (version 2)

It can be seen that by blindly following our annotated entity/event matrix together with the pre-drawn constructs where appropriate, our Quit–Resume feature has automatically been taken care of; that is, if the event Guest Arrives (No Reservation) takes place, Q1 jumps directly to R1 at Chargeable Item Arises.

A quick comparison with version 1 of the ELH (Figure 11.13) shows that we have created a diagram with a far simpler creation stage – and we have done so using a step-by-step approach that is probably more reliable than the partially intuitive one. Many texts seem to expect an ELH to be put together in some intuitive way. Perhaps with experience it is possible to do so – but we hope that at least for the present the above approach will help you create diagrams that are reliable and practical.

11.5.5 The process/event matrix

This matrix maps events to DFD processes. Each event *must* trigger a process or processes and the main benefit of this matrix is that it sometimes traps missing processes. A sample matrix for our student record system is shown in Figure 11.21. The matrix contains only the events we have met so far – that is, the ones that affect the entities Student and Module Enrolment.

Process / Event	Enter Module Marks	File Retrieval & Storage for Module Board	File Retrieval & Storage for Course Board	Output Results	No process present for this event
Student Registration					X
Student Departure (Premature)					X
Student Departure (Course Cmplt)					X
One Year After Student Departure					X
Student Amendment					X
Module Enrolment					X
Module Withdrawal					X
Module Result (Provisional)	X				
Module Result (Confirmed)		X			
Course Completed			X		
Yearly Course Result			X		

Figure 11.21 Partially completed process/event matrix showing events that affect Student and Module Enrolment entities

The first thing to note is that the process Output Results does not have an associated event. This is because the process does not actually update anything but simply retrieves data and prints it out. However, the most striking feature of this matrix is that all of the events that trigger simple maintenance processing do not have a process present on the DFD.

Please note that this example is rather extreme and it is very unlikely that such a situation would have been allowed to go unnoticed up to this point. Nevertheless, it is important to note that unless you undertake some event modelling, it is possible for processes to be missed. Even so, there is no guarantee that construction of ELHs will discover everything.

If the fact finding and general observation are not thorough enough, certain **events** may well be missed. A revised level 1 DFD of the required system incorporating missing maintenance functions is now shown in Figure 11.22, and a level 2 DFD for the maintenance functions is shown in Figure 11.23.

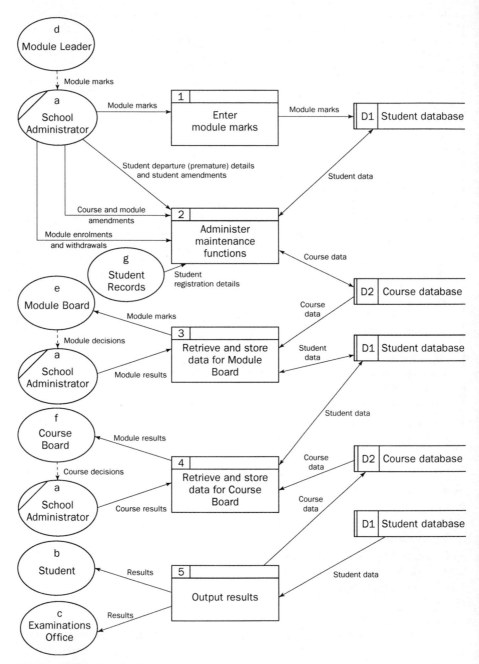

Figure 11.22 Revised level 1 logical DFD of the required system, incorporating missing maintenance functions

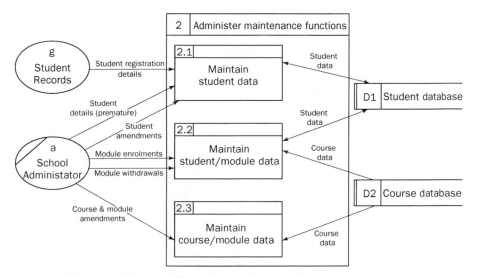

Figure 11.23   Level 2 logical DFD for the maintenance functions

11.5.6 State indicators and the control of processes

ELHs provide a framework that shows the systems analyst in which sequence events should be allowed to affect an entity. How do we make sure that the processing triggered by an event happens at the right time and does not take place 'illegally'? For example, in the Student entity, we have to make sure that the event One Year After Student Departure takes place after the event Student Departure has taken place. How do we prevent a Student record being deleted before a Student leaves? One very attractive and simple way of doing this is to have a **state indicator** associated with each event on an ELH. A state indicator is simply an extra data item in the entity that changes to a unique value after each event. So, after the create event Student Registration, the Student state indicator would be set to 1. Each subsequent event would then change it to a new value. State indicators are often shown on the ELH as in Figure 11.24. The number(s) before the '/' symbol are the allowable values of the state indicator before the event can take place. The number after the '/' is the value to which the state indicator is set after the processing triggered by the event has taken place.

It is easy to see that this can be used as an effective means of stopping processing taking place out of sequence. A simple check of the state indicator at the start of a process would make sure that its value would allow the process to continue. If the state indicator was not one of the allowable values, an error message would be displayed and the process abandoned.

State indicators can enforce a sequence which is difficult to show using the Jackson structures and you often come across ELHs where the state indicators show the correct sequencing whereas the ELH structure is either incorrect or misleading.

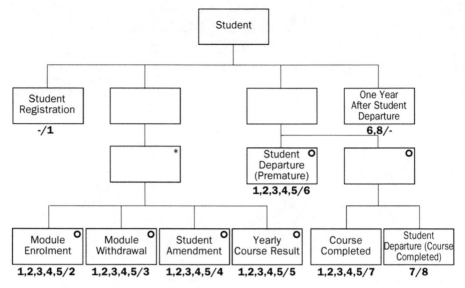

Figure 11.24 ELH for Student entity, showing state indicators

11.6 State transition diagrams

Another way of showing the same principles as the ELH is a technique called the state transition diagram. There are variations on the way these diagrams are drawn but our favourite representation is the so-called **fence diagram**. A fence diagram for the life of the Student entity is shown in Figure 11.25.

You will notice in this diagram that **states** are shown as *vertical* lines, joined by the occurrence of **events** which are labelled *horizontal* lines. We have not distinguished between the mid-life states produced by the four events Module Enrolment, Module Withdrawal, Student Amendment and Yearly Course Result. This is because it is of little or no use to the system to know which of these transactions was the last to affect the Student entity.

This sort of diagram provides greater flexibility than an ELH as you can really go from any state to any other state quite easily. In an ELH it is sometimes quite difficult, often requiring the liberal use of Quits and Resumes.

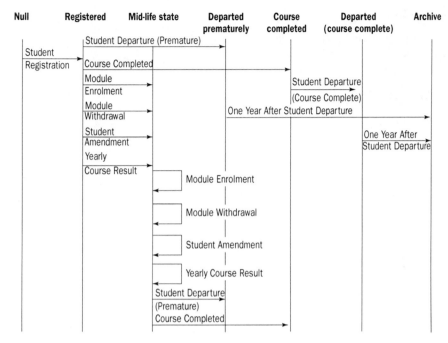

Figure 11.25   Fence diagram for the life of the Student entity

11.7 Conclusion

Consideration of data and processing alone in the development of a system is not enough. It is easy to miss things out, particularly processing that occurs on an infrequent basis. By considering all the changes that can occur to each entity over the period of its life, we often find additional functions that were missed the first time around. Construction of ELHs or state transition diagrams adds completeness to the systems analysis and provides an extra important view that can then be taken into the design phase.

This chapter ...

... began by looking at how time can affect the entity model and then went on to introduce the concept of events. Different types of events were described and you were introduced to a diagram called an entity life history (ELH) which looks at the ways events affect an entity. Through an example, the three constructs of sequence, selection and iteration were described. The entity/event matrix was introduced as a valuable aid in the construction of an ELH and the process/event matrix was mentioned as a valuable way of spotting missing processes. The chapter finished with a description of state indicators and state transition diagrams.

A useful exercise

Draw an entity life history for at least two of the key entities in your 'own experience' system.

Further reading

M. Goodland and C. Slater, *SSADM Version 4: A Practical Approach*, McGraw-Hill, London, 1995.

Web address worth a visit

www.doc.mmu.ac.uk/online/SAD

Part 3

Process Improvement for Strategic Objectives (PISO®)

Introducing PISO® 　　　12

12.1 A new development

12.1.1 Origins

As first explained back in Chapter 1, we authors have seen our interests in systems analysis develop in two clear ways in recent years. Here we introduce you to the first of these – a new business-oriented method that has become called Process Improvement for Strategic Objectives (PISO).

PISO was originally designed to help part-time business students appreciate how useful structured computer systems analysis techniques can be in sorting out problems and inefficiencies in their day-to-day work. PISO heavily depends upon being able to represent graphically both physical and logical views of a circumstance and because DFDs are very appropriate for this purpose, these have been adopted. Don't dismiss this part of the book as simply 'more about DFDs', however. To do so will miss the point entirely. PISO uses them to allow the strategic objectives of an organisation to engage with the logicalisation process, and certainly does not assume that the outcome will be a computer system.

12.1.2 Like BPR, but . . .

If your first reaction is that this sounds somewhat vague or esoteric, be assured that this is not the case. Our purposes are practical rather than academic. PISO provides a rapid means of bringing about real change in the workplace. In Chapter 1, section 1.2.4, and Chapter 9, section 9.1.3, we referred to a concept called Business Process Re-engineering (BPR). BPR has largely fallen out of favour, providing unpredictable results – but on a minority of occasions it works well. Those familiar with BPR have found it useful to consider PISO to be a stripped-down, method-based, 'do-it-yourself' ('diy') version of it. The 'method-based' aspect refers to its clearly defined framework, with specified stages and steps. The 'diy' aspect refers to the fact that the PISO approach is easy to learn and intended to be used by the employees who actually carry out the functions that are being re-engineered – with no prior knowledge of systems analysis techniques required. Unlike BPR, PISO has been found to have a high success rate – and as well as being used on its own to improve a wide range of business and manufacturing processes, it has provided bogged-down BPR projects with radically positive outcomes. PISO's use of DFDs closely parallels their use within conventional structured systems analysis as first explained in Chapter 4, section 4.3.1. The PISO framework is shown in Figure 12.1, with the DFD steps highlighted.

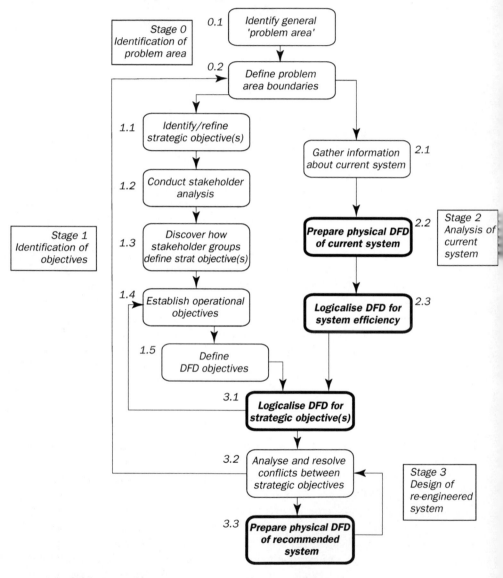

Figure 12.1   The PISO framework, with DFD steps highlighted

At the time of writing, well over three hundred students from HND to Masters level have undertaken PISO projects, many based upon their own place of work, with extremely positive results. Seminars are now being provided direct to large and small organisations, and the reported proportion of successful PISO projects continues to be far greater than with other approaches. At the last count, 92 per cent have said that the project produced a worthwhile and usable outcome whereas a number of recently published statistics for 'conventional' BPR have reported only 15 to 18 per cent considering their project a worthwhile and cost-effective exercise. A PISO business unit has been created, with the mission statement 'Workplace creativity driven by strategy'.

We have been somewhat bemused by PISO's success and have concluded that there appear to be three key reasons for this. While none of these is new in its own right, it would seem that PISO puts them together for the first time, in a way that is attractive to organisations seeking to harness the creativity of their workforce in solving business problems.

- It uses already proven computer systems analysis techniques – i.e. DFDs.
- It brings a new rationale to these techniques – i.e. the strategic objective.
- It makes these techniques directly accessible to those affected by the changes – i.e. the stakeholders.

12.1.3 Views, objectives and stakeholders

In Chapter 4, section 4.1, we saw that there can be many ways of logically viewing a situation. The key to how someone does so is the information they consider relevant or most important – and you may remember that in that chapter we used bus travel to illustrate this. The level of relevance or importance may not simply depend upon the type of factual examples used in that scenario, however. It can also depend upon a person's **vested interests** or **preferences** – and this is a very important aspect for the systems analyst to be aware of.

To consider this further, let us return to the bus travel example. Perhaps you tend to prefer to travel on the back seat of buses, and see that a back seat is empty. You are on your way to it when you see a friend already seated in the middle of the bus, with a vacant space beside her – and choose to sit there instead. Or perhaps you suddenly realise that one of the back seats is occupied by someone you'd prefer not to have to talk to, so pretend you haven't seen him and sit near the front.

If our logical views of physical circumstances were not coloured in this way, there would be no such thing as debates or disagreements, racial discontent or political parties. In employment, people react to work situations and colleagues in a whole variety of ways.

Every person in every circumstance that involves them can be considered a **stakeholder**. Their 'interests' in this stakeholding may be obvious (e.g. you select the bus that will get you home), or not immediately apparent to those around (e.g. your choice of seat) – and this obviously extends into the workplace. All **information gathering**, for whatever purpose, does well to take this into account and address it appropriately. PISO clearly acknowledges this and recognises **stakeholder consensus** as a key basis for success.

12.1.4 A new rationale for DFD logicalisation

In Chapter 9 we were introduced to DFD logicalisation – stripping away all physical constraints so that we got a very efficient view of what a system was achieving, and an insight into the policy behind it. The relevant information that was being applied in this case was implied rather than stated – that is, what was relevant was the objective to come up with as efficient a computer system as possible. In Chapter 10 we saw how such insight became capitalised in the development of a 'new logical' DFD, indicating the required computer system.

PISO brings a new slant to this second logicalisation stage. It recognises that there is a **strategic objective** to almost everything we do. In structured systems analysis this objective is usually to *create an efficient computer system* to support the business. PISO does not make the same assumption. It raises the profile of the strategic objective. Instead of assuming that it is to create a computer system that will efficiently carry out the current way of going on, PISO gives the opportunity to ask not only 'is the current way the right way?' but 'are we fundamentally doing the right thing?' PISO demands that a strategic objective to improve the business in some way, meet a need, solve a problem, is clearly defined before the second logicalisation stage. It then allows the knowledge and creativity of typical employees to engage directly with the strategic objective, to solve the identified business problem – and note again that PISO makes no assumptions even as to whether a computer system forms part of the re-engineered solution.

If you are finding it a little difficult to get your mind around this at the moment, don't worry – read on! It is time to see practical 'before and after' examples taken from real PISO projects. Here they are simply intended to illustrate the kind of effect that is achievable using the PISO method. In the next chapter, we will return to them and see how they came about.

12.2 'Before and after' PISO examples

12.2.1 The effect of the strategic objective

The application of PISO can have a radical effect upon the *shape* of an organisation – even when the overall aims of that organisation remain fairly static. In broad terms, a strategic objective that emphasises efficiency aspects (achieve what we do now, but more quickly/cheaply) will tend to reduce the processes and complexity of an organisation's systems. One that emphasises 'quality' aspects (achieve what we do now, but to a higher standard) may well have the opposite effect.

Because PISO includes a general **systems efficiency** approach first (step 2.3), and then introduces the strategic objective (step 3.1), in practice most PISO projects provide some efficiency gains – even if the strategic objective has also introduced quality ones. For those organisations that wish to explore the possible outcomes of doing something entirely different (such as expand into new markets, or a completely new area of business), PISO can come up with even more radical solutions.

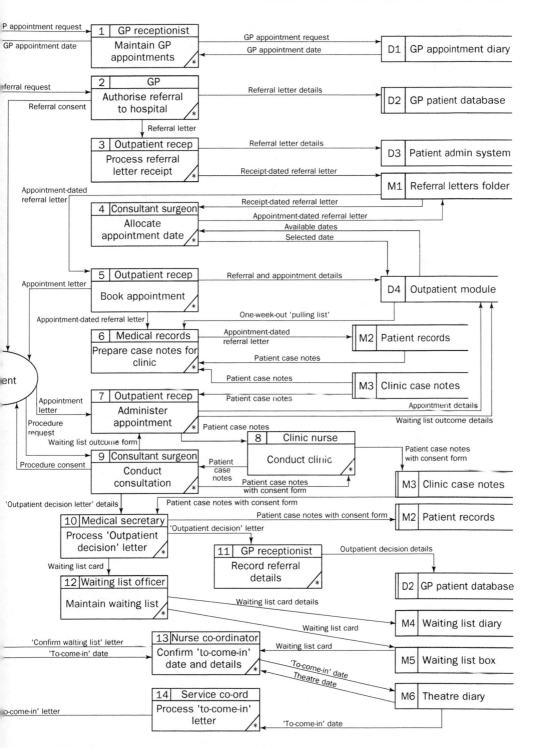

Figure 12.2 Pontefract General Infirmary system *before* PISO

12.2.2 The Pontefract General Infirmary example

Figure 12.2 shows a system in use by Pontefract General Infirmary at the beginning of the PISO analysis (step 2.2 – see Figure 12.1), and Figure 12.3 shows the re-engineered outcome (step 3.3). Note that these are *both* level 1 physical DFDs – the second is in no way simply a higher-level view of the first, but represents a significantly simpler way of achieving the same outcome. This is because the strategic objective was to do just this – that is, achieve the same outcome but much more efficiently.

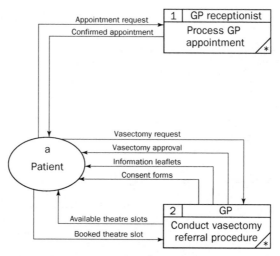

Figure 12.3   Pontefract General Infirmary system *after* PISO

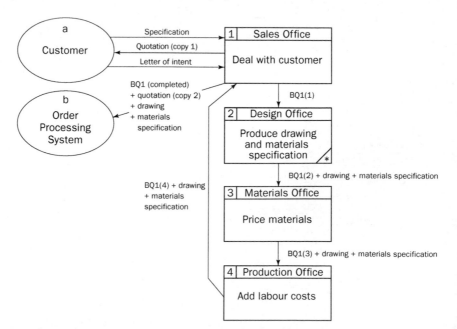

Figure 12.4   Marine Construction system *before* PISO (copy of Figure 5.2)

12.2.3 The Marine Construction example

As already noted, not all strategic objectives are such purely 'efficiency' ones as the Pontefract example. There may instead be a predominant need for more 'quality' in a system. To illustrate this we return to the Marine Construction example last seen in Chapter 5.

Figure 12.4 is a repeat of the level 1 **current physical** DFD for that company, and Figure 12.5 shows the PISO solution to meet the strategic objective, which in this case emphasises a need for significant improvements in service to the customer. When we return to this example in Chapter 13 we see the analysis that took place in order to produce this outcome. For now, simply note the marked change in the 'shape' of the organisation brought about by the **PISO effect** – with the introduction of new customer liaison and estimating processes.

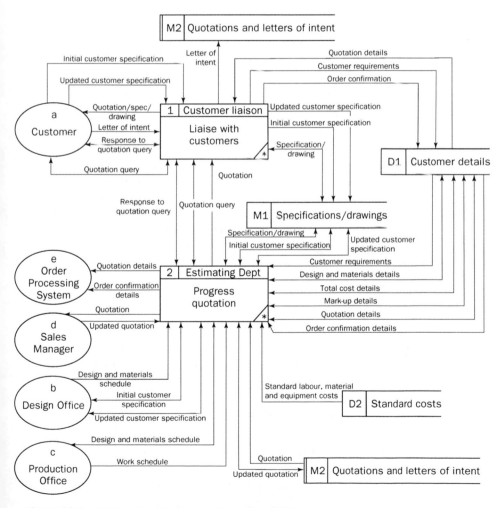

Figure 12.5 Marine Construction system *after* PISO

12.3 The PISO stages and steps

We trust that you are beginning to get the idea and are looking forward to discovering how PISO can bring about such transformations. As explained at the beginning of this chapter, *any* equivalent analysis method that includes logicalisation could be incorporated within the overall PISO approach, but we have chosen to use DFDs.

The intention in this book is to focus upon PISO's use of *logicalisation* using DFDs; this differs somewhat from the structured analysis approach seen so far. Before we continue with this, however, a more complete view of the method is in order. Refer again to the framework in Figure 12.1 and relate it to the details below.

PISO stage 0 – identification of problem area

Step 0.1   *Identify a general problem area* within the organisation, where it is suspected that there is room for improvement. A specific problem does not have to have been identified, only recognition that there is one.

Step 0.2   *Define problem area boundaries* – this may vary as analysis takes place.

PISO stage 1 – identification of objectives (in parallel with stage 2)

Step 1.1   *Identify and refine strategic objectives.* These can be objectives that operate at a business level but must be relevant to the specific problem area chosen (for example, in the NHS – 'patient care').

Step 1.2   *Conduct stakeholder analysis.* Using 2.1 (Analyse Current Process Structure) and 2.2 (Construct Physical Data Flow Diagram) as a basis, identify stakeholders (for example, external entities and those operating within processes) for the chosen problem area. Use other approaches to evaluate relative importance of stakeholders. **Weighted matrices** have been used to good effect, although this aspect of PISO is still subject to research and development at the time of writing. (See Chapter 1, section 1.5.)

Step 1.3   *Discover how stakeholder groups define strategic objectives* in operational terms – possibly use approaches such as SSM, producing rich pictures to clarify/gain agreement (refer to Chapter 1, section 1.3.6). Each stakeholder group to prioritise objectives. Note danger of tactical objectives confusing strategic objectives. (For example, an NHS example could have strategic objective of 'improved patient care'.)

Step 1.4   *Establish operational objectives* by synthesising a single set of operational objectives that satisfies the greatest number of/most significant stakeholders.

Operational goals identified for achieving the above strategic objective could be:

- Reduce number of different types of staff coming into contact with patients.

- Improve information available to patients.
- Question demarcation of roles.
- Make better use of skills – e.g. enriching jobs of suitably qualified nurses.
- Use unskilled support workers to do tasks that do not require specific training.

Step 1.5 *Define data flow diagram (DFD) objectives* by specifying the operational objectives in terms appropriate to DFD notation.

These DFD objectives could be described as follows:

- Processes that involve contact with patients, to be reduced in number.
- Processes that provide information to patients, to be improved/introduced.
- Data flows to and from patients, to be reduced/improved/introduced as appropriate.

PISO stage 2 – analysis of current system (in parallel with stage 1)

Step 2.1 *Gather information about current system* using standard systems analysis techniques to capture current 'system' operating in identified problem area – interviews, document examination, 'walkthroughs' etc.

Step 2.2 *Prepare a physical DFD of the current system* as covered in Chapter 5, ensuring final diagram has only 'one process per functional area' as this significantly aids subsequent logicalisation.

Step 2.3 *Logicalise the DFD for system efficiency,* by following standard 'structured analysis logicalisation' process as covered in Chapter 9. By stripping away all physical constraints, this provides a view of the current system potentially operating as efficiently as possible.

PISO stage 3 – design of re-engineered system

Step 3.1 *Logicalise DFD to meet strategic objective(s).* Using DFD objectives derived in step 1.5, enhance DFD created in 2.3 to create strategically logicalised DFD for analysis/negotiation. Iterate to step 1.4 until acceptable convergence is achieved.

Step 3.2 *Analyse and resolve conflicts between strategic objectives.* Where conflict arises between strategic objectives, return to a previous step. Return to step 0.2 if a need to reconsider the boundaries of the process, and to step 1.1 if necessary to reconsider importance of different strategic objectives.

Step 3.3 *Prepare one or more physical DFD(s) of new system* demonstrating recommended physical implementation(s) of strategically modified logical DFD. If more than one physical outcome prepared, gain consensus among stakeholders as to chosen outcome.

So, there is much more to PISO than DFDs. The framework shows clearly that PISO emphasises the need for stakeholder involvement in a re-engineering project, with stakeholder consensus being emphasised as crucial at every stage. But DFD logicalisation is at the core of what makes PISO a successful approach, and as this is a book about systems analysis techniques it is this aspect that we will focus upon here.

12.4 The PISO steps that use DFDs

PISO's use of DFDs begins by following the standard approach seen in Chapters 4, 5 and 9, using them to show both physical and logical views of the current system. Although elementary process descriptions as covered in Chapter 6 are also a part of conventional 'current system' DFD analysis, it is rare for a PISO project to use these. PISO's purpose is to emphasise the strategic objective, and this usually implies analysis that takes place at a higher level than is necessary for working out the detail of how a system carries out its processing.

The relationships between the PISO steps and DFDs are as follows:

- PISO step 2.2, *Prepare physical DFD of current system*. We saw how to prepare current system physical DFDs in Chapters 4 and 5.
- PISO step 2.3, *Logicalise DFD for systems efficiency*. In Chapter 9 we saw how to logicalise current system physical DFDs so that they became current system logical DFDs. But why does PISO add the words '... for systems efficiency'? This is done to emphasise that while the implied objective at this stage of logicalisation is usually to transform a currently out-of-date inefficient system into a new, efficient computer-based one, PISO is about to logicalise for a different reason, that is:
- PISO step 3.1, *Logicalise DFD for strategic objective(s)*. This is where the 'PISO difference' takes effect – where the method deviates from the standard structured systems analysis approach. As we saw in Chapter 10 when we considered the development of the required computer system, the standard approach assumes that the objective is simply to consider any further features that may be needed in the intended system. Instead, PISO users apply their own knowledge and creativity to correct system weaknesses, with the potential to come up with fundamental re-engineering – or at least show that the current system is as good as it can be.
- PISO step 3.3, *Prepare physical DFD of new system*. This is again the same as in conventional structured analysis, but this new DFD is being derived from a strategically logicalised DFD and so may well represent a whole new approach to managing the system – and there is no assumption that a computer system is involved.

In the next chapter we see how the Pontefract and Marine Construction 'before and after' examples came about. Before we do so, however, there is one last aspect of PISO to mention.

12.5 PISO and 'green field' systems development

The large majority of PISO projects involve the re-engineering of existing systems as already described. But what if the strategic objective is to establish, say, a completely new business? Or what if the brief within an existing organisation is to completely scrap an existing system and start again? What if there are literally no constraints upon the shape of the organisation, no existing model that is worth starting with – in other words, nothing for which a current physical DFD could be prepared?

In Chapter 1, section 1.3, in the subsection entitled 'the soft systems approach' we saw two examples of SSM rich pictures, and we would suggest that an initial analysis of this type would be appropriate in a completely 'green field' situation. Although in such a circumstance there are no direct **existing system stakeholders** to provide input, it is of course strongly advisable to endeavour to elicit advice from a range of people with appropriate experience – with the aim of obtaining *their* consensus as to how the new project should be approached. These may be potential business partners with a bright new idea, or simply friends with relevant backgrounds. The rich picture could be derived based upon everyone's ideas as to what the 'system' should involve.

One approach to the DFD analysis could then be to miss out steps 2.2 and 2.3, and jump straight to step 3.1 – preparing a logical DFD that already fulfils the requirements of the strategic objective. In such a case, the rich picture is being used to replace the need for the current physical and current logical DFDs. Alternatively (and more thoroughly), physical and logical DFDs equivalent to steps 2.2 and 2.3 could first be prepared to represent the 'initial thinking' arising out of the rich picture, before progressing to step 3.1. Stakeholder consensus supported by rich pictures and strategically logicalised DFDs as described leaves little room for something important being overlooked in such a 'new system' situation.

Detailed instruction in the preparation of rich pictures is beyond the scope of this book (we have to draw the line somewhere!) but for readers interested in exploring the use of PISO for such new systems development, we would recommend further study of the Soft Systems Methodology. One text that we like in particular is noted below.

This chapter . . .

. . . began by explaining that the Process Improvement for Strategic Objectives (PISO) method could be considered as a 'diy', method-based approach to Business Process Re-engineering. It explained that PISO incorporated a new rationale for DFD logicalisation – the strategic objective. It introduced a couple of examples of PISO in action, and looked in detail at the stages and steps of the PISO method. It ended by considering the use of PISO in the development of 'green field' systems.

A useful exercise

Reconsider the 'own workplace' scenario that you have been using for exercises, and begin your own PISO project by identifying some area of difficulty within the 'system' that you have been analysing. If necessary, interview others who work there. Express this in terms of a *strategic objective* and identify whether it is primarily an *efficiency* one or a *quality* one.

Further reading

A. Berztiss, *Software Methods for Business Re-engineering*, Springer-Verlag, New York, 1996.

P. Checkland and P. Scholes, *Soft Systems Methodology in Action*, Wiley, Chichester, 1999.

Web address worth a visit

www.cet.sunderland.ac.uk/webedit/CET/reachout/piso.htm

PISO® and DFDs

13

13.1 Reminders

13.1.1 The PISO steps that use DFDs

In Chapter 12 we were introduced to the PISO framework and saw that there are four PISO steps that use DFDs – steps 2.2, 2.3, 3.1 and 3.3. For convenience, the framework is again reproduced in Figure 13.1 – and again, these DFD steps are highlighted.

In order to illustrate the kinds of transformation typical of PISO projects, Chapter 12 then introduced us to 'before and after' physical DFDs taken from PISO projects for Pontefract General Infirmary and Marine Construction – representing steps 2.2 and 3.3 in each case.

We are about to see the analysis that brought about these transformations, by going through all four DFD steps for each system. The first two (steps 2.2 and 2.3) use DFDs in exactly the same way as standard structured systems analysis, as already covered in Chapters 4, 5 and 9.

13.1.2 People doing it for themselves

While the mechanics of preparing these DFDs are identical to structured systems analysis, however, in a properly conducted PISO project there will be one key aspect that is very different – and that is the person who carries out the analysis. The whole ethos of PISO is based upon the 'people doing it for themselves' approach. The person preparing the DFDs will not be a systems analyst, but an expert in the area of work that is being analysed. The people identified as stakeholders in the system will not be presented with a completed diagram, but consulted on an ongoing basis and invited to contribute directly to the result. The intention is that the project is undertaken by a committed team of people who feel ownership for the outcome.

We are going to explore the Marine Construction scenario first, because we are most familiar with it – firstly from Chapter 5 when we drew physical DFDs of the current system, and then in Chapter 9 when we tackled DFD logicalisation.

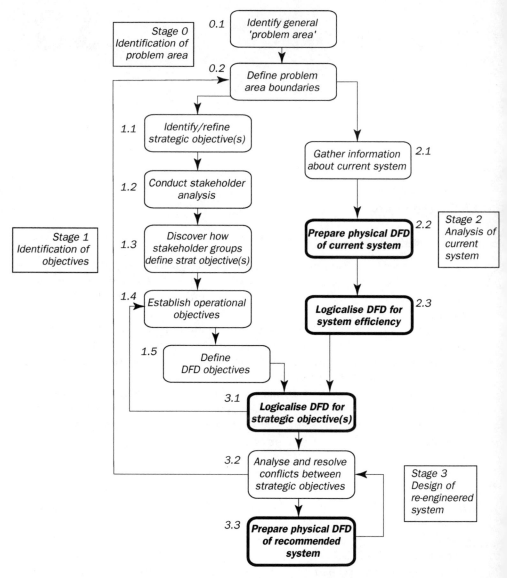

Figure 13.1   The PISO framework (a copy of Figure 12.1)

13.2 The Marine Construction PISO analysis

13.2.1 Marine Construction step 2.2 – Preparing current system physical DFDs

The outcome of step 2.2 is the creation of physical DFDs to an acceptable level of detail appropriate to the PISO project. As we said above, these are done in exactly the same way as for a conventional structured systems analysis project.

The ones in Figures 13.2 to 13.6 are therefore copies of those we first saw in Chapter 5.

You will remember that the first level 1 physical DFD (Figure 13.2) is a 'walk-through' type – perfectly acceptable as a first attempt, but then refined (Figure 13.3) so that it is presented as 'one process per functional area'. The level 2 DFDs (Figures 13.4 to 13.6) then expand those processes where more detail is considered necessary.

Look through the DFDs and if you are finding your memory a bit hazy regarding how they were developed, it may be worth revising Chapter 5 before you continue.

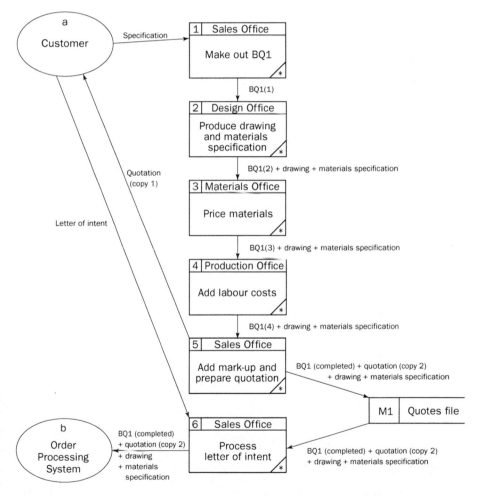

Figure 13.2 Level 1 DFD for Marine Construction ('walk-through' approach) (a copy of Figure 5.1)

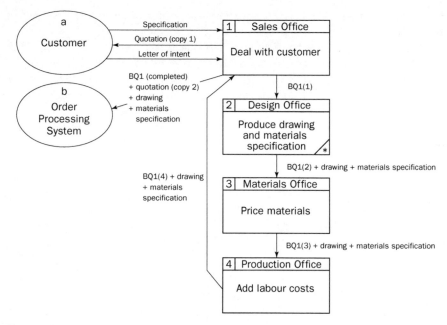

Figure 13.3 Level 1 DFD for Marine Construction (one process per functional area) (a copy of Figure 5.2)

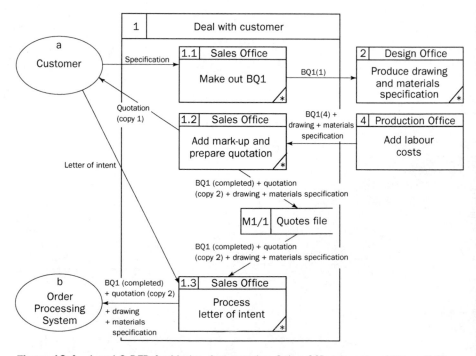

Figure 13.4 Level 2 DFD for Marine Construction Sales Office (a copy of Figure 5.3)

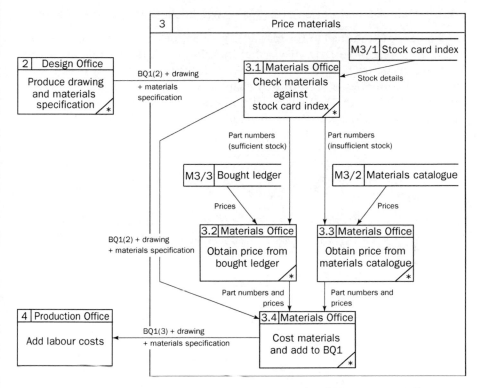

Figure 13.5   Level 2 DFD for Marine Construction Materials Office (a copy of Figure 5.4)

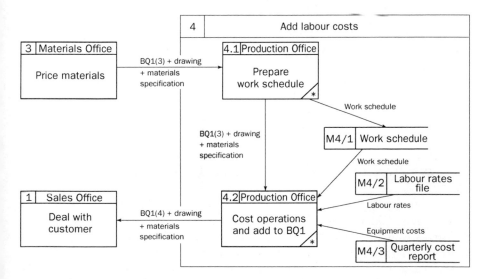

Figure 13.6   Level 2 DFD for Marine Construction Production Office (a copy of Figure 5.5)

13.2.2 Marine Construction step 2.3 – Logicalising for systems efficiency

In Chapter 9 we returned to the Marine Construction system, this time seeing it evolve to a logicalised DFD view – that is, stripped of all physical constraints, exposing the policy behind the system. As with the 'current physical' DFDs, the 'current logical' ones as seen in that chapter would be developed in the same way in a PISO project. The logical DFD for Marine Construction that was developed in Chapter 9 (Figure 9.14) is therefore reproduced in Figure 13.7.

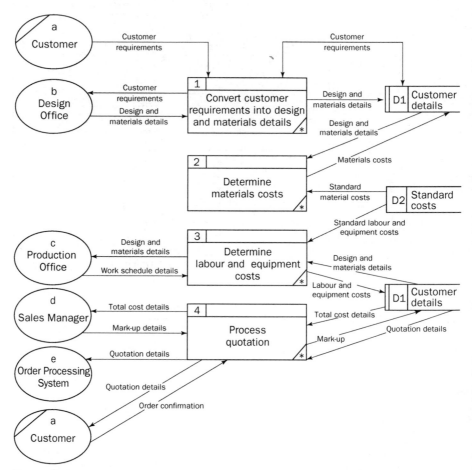

Figure 13.7 Level 1 'systems efficiency' logical DFD for Marine Construction (copy of Figure 9.14)

The eagle-eyed among you may notice there is one slight difference between Figure 13.7 and the version seen in Chapter 9, Figure 9.14 – and that is the caption. PISO refers to this logicalisation as being for 'systems efficiency' purposes. There is no reason for conventional systems analysis to include this phrase because it is assumed that this is *always* the purpose of logicalisation – or in other words, the strategic objective is *always* to come up with an efficient computer solution. In PISO terms, if we had no strategic objective other than for the system to do what it does already but as efficiently as possible, this logical DFD would give us the answer. The result is a **logical DFD** of the **current** system that exposes the **policy** behind the current system, unconstrained by physical limitations such as documents and people – the current **physical DFD** of course tells us how that policy is currently implemented.

It may be worth looking back at Chapter 9 as a reminder of how this logicalisation took place. There is one respect, however, in which the typical PISO project takes a less structured approach than described in Chapter 9 – that is, when determining the datastores for the logicalised version. In that chapter it is seen that the full rationalisation of these is done by using data modelling techniques. PISO does not incorporate such techniques, as it is considered more important to keep the method simple and accessible by people who have no experience of computer systems analysis. But remember that the typical PISO user *does* have an in-depth knowledge of the system – so is able to have a pretty good stab at deciding the datastores logically needed to support the processes.

To those more used to a precise, step-by-step approach to computer systems development this may seem a little 'loose' – but the strategic, 'business-oriented' nature of the PISO method deliberately emphasises a more 'holistic', creative stance. The typical PISO user would be encouraged not to be too concerned whether they could work out exactly why the Marine Construction datastores have been reorganised the way they have, and to feel free to apply their own knowledge and creativity to their own PISO project. A logical view depends upon applying the relevant information, and typical PISO practitioners and their identified stakeholders are well placed to decide what is relevant. As a reader of this book, you have the best of both worlds at your disposal – that is, knowledge of data modelling, and our permission to do without it if you wish!

It is important to note that some projects (be they for PISO or conventional structured systems analysis purposes) simply demonstrate at this stage of the analysis that *the current system is already fairly logical* – possibly because the physical implementation has recently been thought through, or circumstances have changed little even though some time may have passed. In situations like these, it is clear that less radical changes will take place at this 'systems efficiency' logicalisation stage. The logic of the system has at least been proven.

But has the strategy behind what the system *should* be doing been recently considered? That is, have changes in outside or less obvious influences been taken into account? Should objectives be revisited because of updates in legislation, changing market forces, or even the arrival of a member of staff with usable extra skills that could be capitalised upon? It is at this stage that the PISO approach addresses such issues and can make a radical difference. It is the next step in the PISO structured analysis process, step 3.1, where stakeholder consensus about the problem area is applied to further logicalisation in order to meet the 'strategic objective'. This is the point at which PISO deviates from standard structured analysis, by introducing a new rationale to the logicalisation process.

13.2.3 Marine Construction step 3.1 – Logicalising for strategic objectives

Establishing the strategic objective

As we saw in Chapter 10, the conventional use of structured analysis takes the current system logical DFD and goes on to add requirements into it in order to come up with one that incorporates all the features of the intended new system. Instead, PISO now allows strategic objectives to engage with the analysis. As can be seen by the framework in Figure 13.1, this is the point, step 3.1, at which the two parallel stages of the framework come together.

The logicalisation that we saw in Chapter 9 was achieved through a set of guidelines that could be applied with a reasonable amount of flexibility. PISO logicalisation to meet the strategic objective is again achieved by following guidelines but these allow, if anything, even more flexibility and creativity. An important precursor to this logicalisation is the development of the objectives from strategic, to operational, to DFD objectives – i.e. steps 1.3, 1.4, 1.5.

In order to demonstrate this, we will continue with Marine Construction but first need some background as to why the company has embarked upon this PISO project – and what the strategic objective is. Consider the following scenario.

The company has had an increasing number of customers complain that completed boats do not meet expectations in terms of specification, and this is causing Marine Construction considerable costs in partial refits/rebuilds – as well as lost custom. The management team is aware that as modern technology allows customers ever-increasing choice, the specification and ordering methods that have served the company well for over fifty years are in need of a rethink. It has been decided to come up with some means of having the customer more involved in the whole process of preparing the quotation, so that any misunderstandings regarding the specification are fully thrashed out prior to the order being confirmed.

Some department heads are concerned that such involvement may get in the way of what they consider to be the efficient preparation of quotations, but there is general agreement that something needs to be done. They have all been involved in the creation of the original physical DFD and are now agreed that the 'systems efficiency' logicalised version shows the essence of how the system currently works. It seems simple enough – the customer specifies his/her requirements, and each department involved works out its costs so that the final quotation can be prepared and sent to the customer.

So, 'strategic objective' logicalisation means re-logicalising the 'systems efficiency' logicalised DFD. To do so, it is necessary to have at least one carefully agreed strategic objective.

Strategic objective (step 1.3)

The initial strategic objective is specified as 'To produce boats that meet the customers' expectations first time, without modification'. After discussions between the management team and heads of department, and canvassing of existing customers (i.e. stakeholders identified from the original physical DFD) this strategic objective is refined to include a clear indication of how it may be achieved operationally. It becomes 'To allow customers ongoing involvement with the quotation process'.

Establishing operational and DFD objectives

Before the DFD can be strategically relogicalised it is necessary to convert the overall strategic objective into operational objectives and then DFD objectives.

Operational objectives (step 1.4)

The individual managers express concerns about the number of direct enquiries that they may have to deal with in order to meet the strategic objective, and it has been agreed that a customer liaison function be considered. Three operational objectives have therefore been established as follows:

- Create new customer liaison function.
- Automatically provide customer liaison function with up-to-date information regarding quotation progress.
- All customer enquiries to be dealt with by customer liaison function.

DFD objectives (step 1.5)

The above operational objectives are converted into DFD objectives as follows:

- Data flows to and from customers to be improved/increased.
- Data flows to and from customers to contact only the new customer liaison function.
- Datastores of up-to-date quotation details to be maintained by all stages of quotation process and accessible by customer liaison function.
- Datastores of up-to-date customer queries/responses to be maintained by customer liaison function and accessible by all stages of quotation process.
- Process(es) that make up the new customer liaison function to have direct data flows to all datastores maintained by the quotation process.

In the same way as Chapter 9 gave guidelines for what we are now describing as 'systems efficiency' logicalisation, PISO provides guidelines for strategic objective logicalisation. These can be viewed two ways – they both have the same effect, and which you adopt is down to personal preference. See Figure 13.8.

From the **objective** viewpoint . . .

. . . taking each DFD objective in turn:

1 Might this DFD objective have implications for any **existing** DFD component?
- If YES, **modify or delete** the component to meet the objective.

2 Might this DFD objective require a **new** DFD component?
- If YES, **introduce** the new component to meet the objective.

OR from the **component** viewpoint . . .

. . . taking each DFD component in turn:

1 Does this DFD component **completely obstruct** any of the DFD objectives?
- If YES, **delete** the component.

2 Does this DFD component **need to be modified** to meet any of the DFD objectives?
- If YES, **modify** the component.

3 Is a **new** component necessary to achieve any of the DFD objectives?
- If YES, **add** the component.

Figure 13.8   Guidelines for logicalising to meet strategic objectives (note: DFD objectives first need to be derived from strategic objectives, as explained in the text)

A level 1 'strategic objective' logicalised DFD for the same system is shown in Figure 13.9, derived from the above objectives. Note that, as stated earlier, this logicalisation stage is very much based upon the creativity of the individual carrying out the analysis. Do not be too concerned if you cannot see exactly why the DFD has been derived in this way – it would be surprising if you could! The aim here is to simply feel comfortable with the fact that a DFD can be reorganised or modified in a fairly radical fashion as a result of introducing a strategic view of what should be happening.

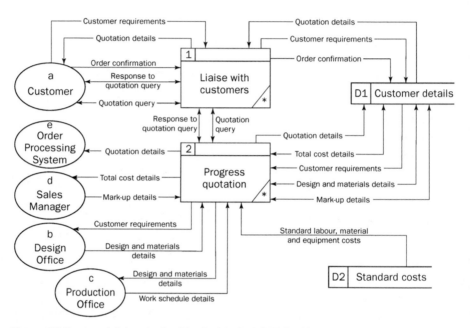

Figure 13.9   Level 1 'strategic objective' logical DFD for Marine Construction

It will be noted that both of the new processes are 'busy' ones – that is, they are connected with a number of data flows. Indeed, there are more data flows than on the previous DFD. We were first introduced to these different kinds of 'strategic logicalisation' effect in Chapter 12. The strategic objective in this Marine Construction example emphasises a need for improvements in **quality** rather than **efficiency**, and strategic relogicalisation will therefore tend to introduce elements rather than remove them. The Marine Construction objective involves engaging the customer in the quotation process – so it is understandable that

- the data flows labelled 'quotation query' and 'response to quotation query' have been introduced (and note, incidentally, that these are 'two-way' – indicating queries backwards and forwards between the company and the customer);
- the new processes represent the introduction of a complete customer support

approach, changing the major players in the original system into external entities and therefore requiring data flows between them and the new 'progress quotation' process.

It is pretty obvious in a situation like this – i.e. with so many data flows connecting each level 1 process – that a number of sub-processes are taking place within each. A level 2 DFD for each process may therefore be thought useful. While there would certainly be no harm in preparing such DFDs, when logicalising for strategic purposes it is commonly acceptable to leave such details until the final stage of the PISO structured analysis – that is, the creation of a new physical data flow diagram showing how the strategic changes will be physically implemented.

13.2.4 Marine Construction step 3.3 – Physical DFD of recommended system

To create the recommended system physical DFD it is necessary to study carefully the strategically logicalised DFD and ask two fundamental *organisational* questions of each process:

- Which person/department will do this?
- How will it physically be made to happen?

It is often helpful to 'put yourself in the place' of each of the processes. Imagine it was *your* job to make it happen. What outputs are demanded of you? What do you need as inputs?

These questions typically translate into the following DFD questions:

- Will existing functions/departments undertake the identified processes – or does the diagram indicate that one or more new ones are needed?
- Have any existing functions/departments become unnecessary?
- Is it necessary to reintroduce any physical documents/Manual datastores (particularly appropriate to 'official' documents, or ones that have to be hand-completed by people outside the organisation)?
- Do computer Datastores indicate the need for extensions to an existing computer system – or a whole new one?
- Do any external entities that were removed from the system need to be reinstated? (For example, experts whose authority and/or subjective judgement is, after all, considered necessary within the system.)

Bearing the above in mind, refer to Figure 13.10 which shows the 'new system' physical DFD for Marine Construction that we first saw in Figure 12.5.

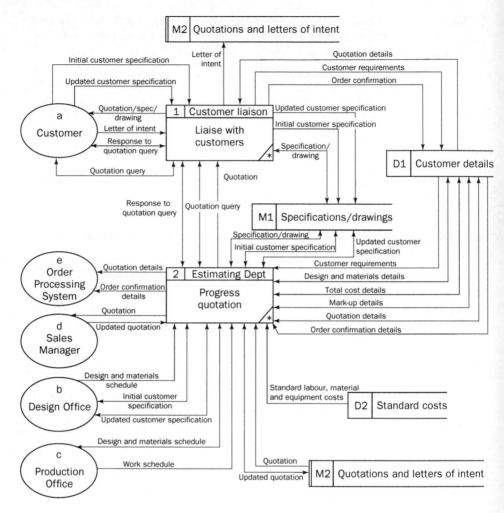

Figure 13.10 Level 1 recommended physical DFD for Marine Construction (copy of Figure 12.5)

- The presence of computer Datastores in the final solution indicates a decision to install a computer system.

- Manual datastores are for 'official' documents that must remain 'paper-based' – with some logical data flows (e.g. 'Customer requirements', 'Order confirmation') becoming physical ones (in these examples, 'Initial/updated customer specification', 'Letter of intent').

- Overall, there has been a significant reduction in the number of datastores needed to support the system (the asterisks in the bottom corner of the processes indicate that no more datastores are 'hidden' at a lower level) – with the new Estimating Department having access to overall Standard Costs for the purpose of calculating the cost of a specification.

As mentioned at the end of sub-section 13.2.3, it would be usual now to create a set of level 2 DFDs equivalent to the ones for the current system seen in Chapter 4, so that the precise mechanics of the system are worked through – including, perhaps, the discovery of one or two additional datastores. It is the main thrust of PISO's use of DFDs that we are endeavouring to put over here, however; we will see such further analysis when we consider the Pontefract example.

13.2.5 Marine Construction – what has been achieved?

We already saw the above diagram as the second of the before-and-after diagrams for Marine Construction in Chapter 12. Even a cursory comparison then showed the radical change that had taken place. The extra features introduced are typical of those PISO projects where the prime thrust of the strategic objective is to **improve quality** rather than **enhance efficiency**.

You will recall that we were told that the company had been experiencing significant difficulties with completed boats not being as the customers intended. This was resulting in having to make adjustments, causing subsequent orders to go late, and generally causing unrest among customers with the possible loss of future business. Something obviously had to be done. The agreed strategic objective was 'Allow customers to have ongoing involvement with the quotation process'.

The most obvious way to do this would have been to have customers dealing direct with all of the departments involved in the quotation process as it originally worked – that is, with the BQ1 circulating around the factory. Managers were understandably concerned about the interruptions to their normal work that this would cause, however – and in any case, how would the customer know who to contact?

The basis of the solution has been to introduce the new Customer Liaison and Estimating functions, thus protecting the factory from direct customer contact while providing customers and factory with a dedicated information service. This approach introduces another level, separating customers from the factory; and solutions involving such separation of communication should always be treated with care. The shared datastores will mean consistency of information, however, and everyone should gain from a lack of communication discrepancies. Efficiency gains will be made by the factory because of lack of interruptions and no reworking of completed boats, while customers will be better served by having their boats built exactly as they want them.

So, we have seen our Marine Construction example used to illustrate how PISO manipulates DFDs to achieve a solution to a problem described in terms of a strategic objective. What about the before-and-after DFDs for the *other* example we saw in Chapter 12 – the one for Pontefract General Infirmary? If anything, these seemed to show an even more remarkable transformation – certainly a radical efficiency gain. We end this chapter by showing you the full set of DFDs produced by the Pontefract project.

13.3 Pontefract General Infirmary PISO analysis

13.3.1 Pontefract step 2.2 – Preparing current system physical DFDs

This project began in the same way as the Marine Construction one – by preparing the 'walkthrough' level 1 physical DFD seen in Figure 13.11, being the equivalent of the Marine Construction one in Figure 13.2. The 'one process per functional area' DFD in Figure 13.12 was then prepared, equivalent to the Marine Construction one in Figure 13.3. For this project, however, there was considered no need to create level 2 DFDs at this stage. The rule when using DFDs is always to continue until an appropriate level of detail has been reached, and level 1 was considered appropriate in this case.

13.3.2 Pontefract step 2.3 – Logicalising for systems efficiency

By comparing the current physical DFD in Figure 13.12 with the 'systems efficiency' logicalised DFD in Figure 13.13, it can be seen that the recommended logicalisation guidelines from Chapter 9 have again been followed, that is:

- data flows now indicate data rather than documents;
- datastores have been rationalised (a less radical change than in the Marine Construction example, but carefully done based upon the changed data flows, and knowledege of what was required);
- datastores now hold pure Data rather than Manual records;
- processes do not indicate who carries out the process, or where it takes place – simply that it happens;
- experts (Consultant, GP) have become external entities;
- processes with a purely manual data management function (e.g. 'File referral letter') have been deleted.

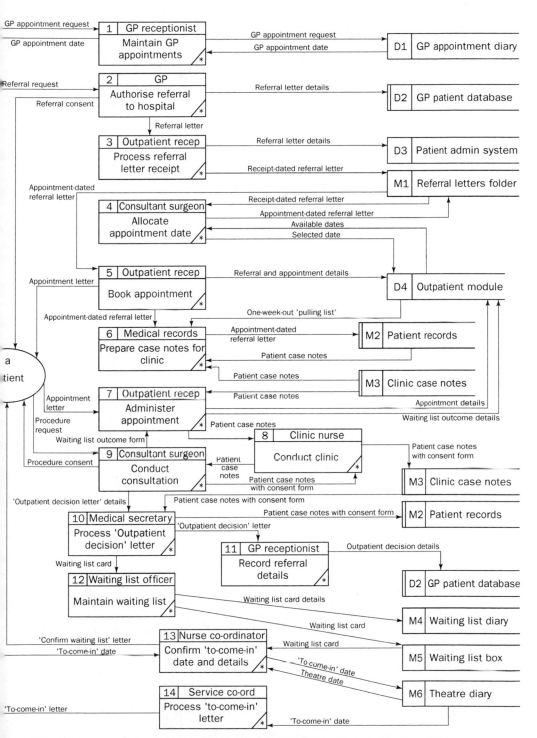

Figure 13.11 Level 1 original 'walkthrough' physical DFD for Pontefract (copy of Figure 12.2)

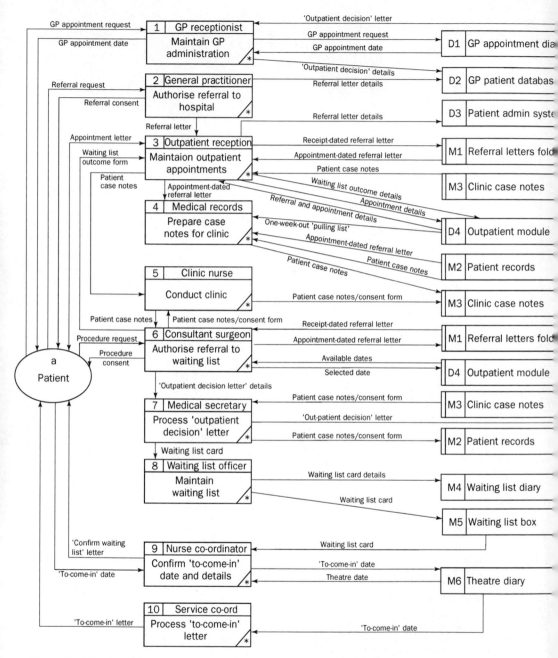

Figure 13.12   Level 1 original 'one process per functional area' physical DFD for Pontefract

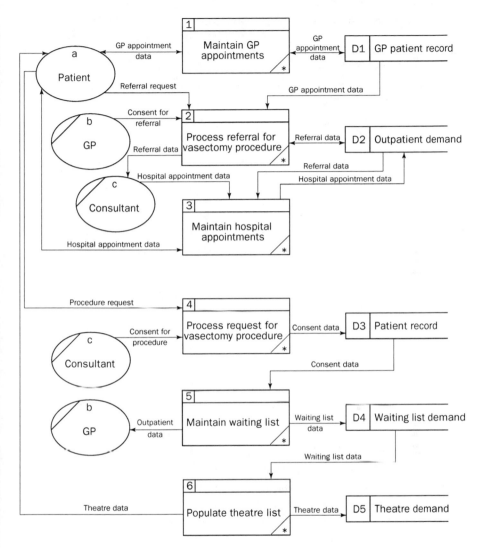

Figure 13.13 Level 1 'systems efficiency' logical DFD for Pontefract

13.3.3 Pontefract step 3.1 – Logicalising for strategic objectives

Introducing the strategic objective

Strategic objective (step 1.3)
After much discussion, this was agreed as 'To improve patient access to a theatre slot for a vasectomy under local anaesthetic by way of a direct booked admission'.

Establishing operational and DFD objectives

Operational objectives (step 1.4)

The agreed operational objectives became:

- To provide a one stop visit to the GP surgery with a successful outcome of a booked date and time on a theatre slot.

- To reduce the number of non-attenders at surgery.

- To reduce the waiting time for surgery.

- To produce up-to-date patient information documentation to be distributed at the time of booking.

DFD objectives (step 1.5)

The above operational objectives were then translated into DFD objectives as follows:

- Processes that involved contact with patients should be reduced in number.

- Data flows to and from patients should be reduced in number.

- Availability of theatre slots should have a degree of flexibility and be available at the visit to the GP surgery.

- The patient information documentation had to be available at source.

With these objectives identified, and with much discussion and consensus among stakeholders, the strategically logicalised DFD was prepared. Note that this foundational work is extremely important to any PISO project, for two fundamental reasons.

- The sometimes widely differing views of stakeholders can provide unexpected insights into what a strategic objective should be.
- It is vital that stakeholders should feel early ownership of the PISO project; the best solution in the world may be rejected by stakeholders who feel it is being imposed upon them without their involvement and agreement.

In Figure 13.14 then, we see how the 'systems efficiency' logical DFD has been transformed into the 'strategic objectives' one. As with the Marine Construction example, do not expect to fully appreciate how the shape of the 'strategic objectives' DFD came about – again, the creativity and knowledge of the person undertaking the project contributes significantly to this. We can gain some useful insights, however. Note processes 2 and 4 in the 'systems efficiency' logical DFD. We can see that these processes have been found to represent largely duplicated effort, and that the consultant's part in the system has been made redundant. Again with reference to the logicalisation guidelines in Figure 13.8, it is possible to appreciate why it is that

- the strategically logicalised DFD shows only the GP and the Patient, with the processes rationalised to fit the new approach, and

- this in turn has resulted in a further reduction in the datastores necessary to support the new processes.

Unlike Marine Construction therefore (where the strategic objective was largely driven by a need for improved 'quality' in the system), in the Pontefract example the strategically logicalised DFD is continuing the trend to fewer elements, begun with the 'systems efficiency' DFD. Indeed, because of the large amount of duplicated effort found in the original system, it shows more of a transformation than commonly occurs after the 'systems efficiency' logicalisation. With predominantly efficiency-based strategic objectives, systems efficiency logicalisation often, unsurprisingly, comes close to a final solution.

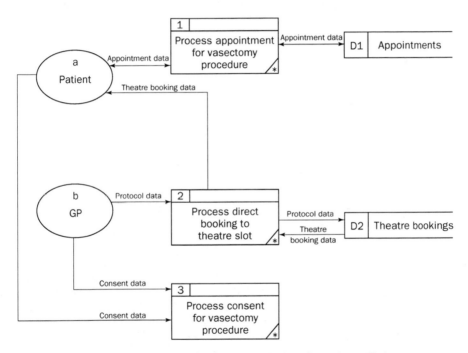

Figure 13.14   Level 1 'strategic objective' logical DFD for Pontefract: 'To improve patient access to a theatre slot for a vasectomy under local anaesthetic by way of a direct booked admission'

13.3.4 Pontefract step 3.3 – Physical DFDs of recommended system

Now refer to Figures 13.15, 13.16 and 13.17. Here we see level 1 and 2 DFDs showing the physical implementation of the re-engineered system. It is of course the level 1 DFD in Figure 13.15 that should be directly compared with the original ones in Figures 13.10 and 13.11 – but unlike Marine Construction it has been felt useful here to drop to level 2 to show the detail of how the higher level processes are being maintained.

It will be noted that the GP has returned as a key player in the system, rather than an external entity. The GP Receptionist has re-appeared. The Appointments and Theatre Bookings have been kept as computer Datastores, indicating a computerised system. Manual datastores for Consent Forms and Information Leaflets have been introduced. These should probably have appeared on the original physical DFD in Figure 13.11, but must have been overlooked at that time and the rigorous analysis conducted since has unearthed them as a formal part of the system – this is typical of PISO projects.

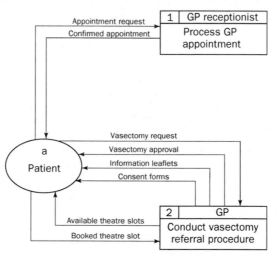

Figure 13.15   Level 1 physical DFD for re-engineered procedure – Pontefract (copy of Figure 12.3)

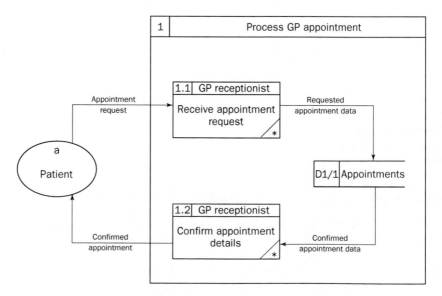

Figure 13.16   Level 2 physical DFD for process 1 of re-engineered procedure – Pontefract

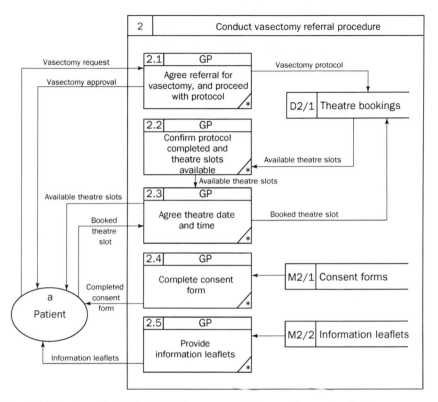

Figure 13.17 Level 2 physical DFD for process 2 of re-engineered procedure – Pontefract

13.3.5 Pontefract – what has been achieved?

The strategic objective in this case aimed to improve efficiency while maintaining service. The two people in the improved system are now achieving the same outcome as the ten identified in the original physical DFDs seen in Figures 13.11 and 13.12 – with the strategic objective of a 'direct booked admission' now clearly achieved. The Pontefract example thus gives a startling illustration of how far things can go when 'logicalising out' system inefficiencies.

There is a final point to note. We saw earlier that the strategic objective of the Marine Construction example emphasised a quality improvement but that the solution resulted in 'spin off' efficiency gains. In the same way, while the Pontefract strategic objective emphasised efficiency gains the solution not only clearly achieves this but also provides a better quality service to the patient. This is because of the 'two stage' logicalisation that PISO uses – that is, no matter what the strategic objective, a system is first logicalised for efficiency purposes.

We hope that you have found these two PISO chapters interesting and useful.

This chapter . . .

. . . used two case studies to demonstrate how PISO utilises DFDs in order to re-engineer systems to meet strategic objectives. The Marine Construction objective was primarily a quality one and resulted in a system with newly introduced processes. The Pontefract objective was clearly efficiency-based, and gave a solution that incorporated a marked reduction in data and process duplication.

A useful exercise

Continue the 'own experience' project that you began at the end of Chapter 12, by following the steps described in the Marine Construction and Pontefract case studies.

Further reading

A. Berztiss, *Software Methods for Business Re-engineering*, Springer-Verlag, New York, 1996.

Web address worth a visit

www.piso.org.uk

Part 4

Object-oriented analysis techniques

Introducing objects

14

14.1 Background

14.1.1 Structured analysis

As explained earlier, it is relatively recently that we authors have become interested in the object-oriented view of systems. You are aware by now that in the structured analysis approach such as used within SSADM, emphasis is placed on three fundamental views – processes, data and events – and that each of these is modelled using separate diagrams – that is, data flow diagrams, entity models and entity life histories respectively. These diagrams of course interact and cross-reference one with the other – we saw this happening as Part 3 of the book developed – but they are still separate diagrams and concepts. In particular, structured analysis separates the data stored from the processes which act upon the data; and this is the way that most systems nowadays are designed – a set of programs accessing a set of data stored in files or databases. These two things are viewed as separate and independent of each other.

However, this separation of processes and data has led to a number of problems which fundamentally boil down to three aspects:

* Software re-use
* Software maintenance and testing
* The ever-increasing complexity of systems

14.1.2 Software re-use

Software re-use has long been a goal of software developers. In general engineering, it makes sense to re-use components. Why have several varieties of spark plugs for different cars, if one type would do without much effort? It is much more cost-effective. The same argument could be applied to information systems. There is a lot of common processing that goes in different information systems, but these pieces of processing are most often developed from scratch each time. The reasons for this are complex, but part of the problem is to do with the separation of process from data. The piece of software that can potentially be re-used will have references to other pieces of software and other items of data which may not apply to the problem in hand. Programmers are reluctant to tinker with code in this way as small changes can sometimes have unpredictable consequences and lead to further problems.

Traditional programming methods have attempted to deal with this problem by applying proper modular programming principles but this has been only partially successful. Object-orientation attempts to deal with this problem because an object is a self-contained package which is, by and large, closed to the outside world and independent of other objects. Software re-use then becomes a natural part of its philosophy.

14.1.3 Software maintenance and testing

This separation of processes and data also leads to problems with the maintenance and testing of software. Most software running nowadays has been designed using functional decomposition – the structure of the program is based on its function. In the main, changes to a system are to do with changes to the functionality of the system. Changes to the structure of the data stored are much less common. As a result, software, which was originally designed according to proper modular design principles, gets changed and tinkered with, leading to a lack of coherence in the result – the software loses its shape and becomes more and more difficult to follow and understand. Although modular design is intended to lead to independent modules, these changes in functionality lead to a dilution of this principle and the result is sometimes 'spaghetti code'. This obviously leads on to problems with software testing as well. In object-orientation, software objects are produced which are independent and self-contained and are therefore more straightforward to maintain and test. They are not solely based on functionality, they are complete packages in their own right.

14.1.4 Dealing with today's complex systems

As computer systems have become larger and more complex, new approaches to systems development have been introduced to cope with the inadequacies of the previous approaches. Object-orientation is seen as one of the latest answers to the development of today's complex systems. It is the next generation of systems development approaches and is viewed as a successor to the structured approach.

The structured approach is very good at producing systems based on a menu structure. The idea of levelling and functional decomposition lends itself to a menu-based design. Nowadays, most systems need some sort of graphical user interface (GUI). It is becoming expected by the increasingly sophisticated user community. People who would not have touched a computer a few years ago are now hooked up to the Web and expect the latest approaches in their interfaces. Although the structured approach can be adapted to deal with these demands, it is becoming increasingly regarded as old-fashioned and object-oriented approaches lend themselves in a more natural way to the development of such systems.

14.2 Objects and object classes

So what is object-orientation? How is it different? Well, as we hope to show you, it is very different and, at the same time, very similar to structured approaches. Let us explore object-orientation. As we do so, we will keep looking over our shoulder at the structured approach and bring out similarities and differences as we go along.

Let us start with an **object**. This seems the most sensible place to begin. Here are three definitions from various authors:

> A software unit packaging together data and methods to manipulate that data (Britton and Doake, 2000)

> An abstraction of something in a problem domain, reflecting the capabilities of the system to keep information about it, interact with it, or both (Coad and Yourdon,1990)

> A concept, abstraction, or thing with crisp boundaries and meaning for the problem at hand. Objects serve two purposes: they promote understanding of the real world and provide a practical basis for computer implementation (Rumbaugh *et al.*, 1991)

These three definitions are rather different, aren't they? The first one talks about an object as something present in a final computerised system – it's a piece of software. The second one talks about an object as a thing in the area under investigation about which we may wish to keep information and with which the system will interact. The third one seems, in some sense, to combine the two – it's something in the real world and it's also a piece of software. These definitions are all correct in their own way but it is still not that clear what an object is.

When we as authors were first introduced to objects, we found it confusing, as we were analysts who belonged very much to the structured analysis tradition. We practised structured analysis and we taught structured analysis to our students. Perhaps it would be best if we told you how we came to understand about objects. We shall take a few liberties and no doubt offend a few purists, but this is how our understanding developed.

14.3 Objects, entities and class diagrams

14.3.1 The 'object' concept

When we first met the idea of objects, we thought that they were not a million miles away from the concept of entities. In fact objects serve exactly the same purpose as entities but they also do a lot more. Let us return to the definition of an entity which was introduced in Chapter 7:

> An entity is a thing of interest to the system about which data is kept.

Well, believe it or not, an object is also a thing of interest to the system about which data is kept. But it is also other things as well. The nature of an object actually changes as the systems development progresses but it is always about the same thing. In the early stages of development, an object is something that exists independently in the problem domain.

So in the student assessment example which we examined in the early chapters, Course, Student and Module are all examples of objects. They are things that exist in the real world. Later on, in the analysis stage, they become examples of **object classes**. Paul Green and Wendy Gould are objects in the object class Student – they are particular instances or particular objects in the object class.

These object classes would be shown as in Figure 14.1. We have shown only two attributes for each of the object classes for the sake of clarity. The empty rectangle at the bottom of each of the class boxes is for something else, which we shall introduce later in this chapter. It is the contents of this rectangle that make objects very different from entities.

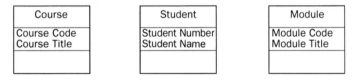

Figure 14.1   Initial object classes in the student assessment system

You should note that the diagram conventions and the overall object-oriented philosophy used in this textbook are those of the Unified Modelling Language or UML for short. This is becoming the *de facto* standard for object modelling.

14.3.2 Association

Objects can be **associated** with each other. You may remember the initial entity model for the student assessment system (Figure 8.6). It is reproduced in Figure 14.2.

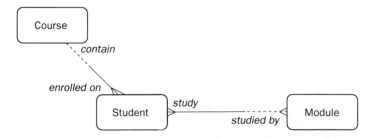

Figure 14.2   Initial entity model for student assessment system (copy of Figure 8.6)

In object-oriented analysis, the equivalent diagram is called a **class diagram**. It is shown in Figure 14.3. Although this diagram is different to Figure 14.2, it is only different in the way symbols are used. It is fundamentally the same. Let us compare the two.

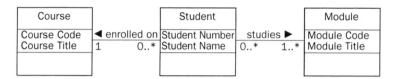

Figure 14.3   Initial class diagram for the student assessment system

The **degree** of the relationship in the entity model (whether it is one or many) is called the **multiplicity** of the relationship in the class diagram. Whereas in the entity model, a 'many' is shown by a crow's foot, in the class diagram it is shown by actual numbers. In addition, **optionality**, which is shown by a dotted line in the entity model, is shown by a zero in the class diagram.

Figure 14.3 says that one Student is associated with only one Course and one Course is associated with zero, one or many Students. One Student is associated with one or more Modules and one Module is associated with zero, one or many Students. These are one-to-many and many-to-many associations respectively. In object-orientation they are called **associations**, not **relationships**.

The nature of the association is shown by writing it along the line joining the two objects. Again there is a difference between the entity model and the class diagram. The entity model shows a relationship name at each end of the relationship whereas in the class diagram, the association is shown only once with the direction of the association shown by an arrowhead (◄ or ►). Hence a Student is enrolled on only one Course and a Student studies one or more Modules. The reverse associations are simply assumed – a Module being studied by zero, one or more Students is an obvious association as the reverse association is quite explicit. A full list of the type of associations is given in Figure 14.4.

Multiplicity	*Shown as*
One or more	1..*
Zero, one or more	0..* or just *
Zero or one	0..1
Precisely one	1 (or omitted)
Precisely a number	e.g. 2 or 5 or 19
Range of numbers	e.g. 3..7, 4..*

Figure 14.4   Symbols for multiplicities of associations

Careful readers may be now wondering about the many-to-many relationship in Figure 14.2 and its equivalent many-to-many association in Figure 14.3. You will remember that in structured approaches, the many-to-many relationship is resolved to provide a link entity. The link entity in the entity model was shown in Figure 8.7 and is reproduced in Figure 14.5.

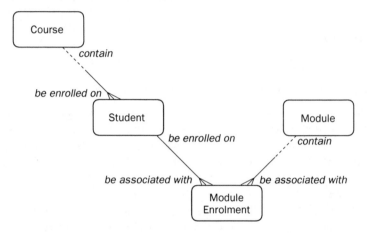

Figure 14.5 Data model for student records system, with many-to-many resolved (copy of Figure 8.7)

The link entity Module Enrolment contains data which belongs to both the Student and the Module. This data is the Grade obtained by the Student for the Module. Obviously, the Grade needs to be stored somewhere in the class diagram as well. This is done by the introduction of an **association class** called Module Enrolment and it is shown in Figure 14.6.

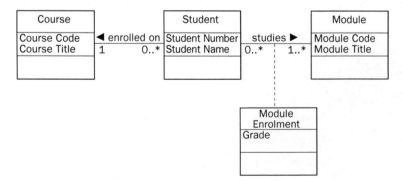

Figure 14.6 Introduction of an association class into the class diagram

This association class might well have been discovered by applying normalisation (see Chapter 8) to the system. However, class diagrams are allowed to contain unnormalised 'relations' if they correspond to the user's view of the system. Students who have studied entity modelling will probably not find this sort of overlap between entity modelling and object modelling confusing. They will hopefully find it surprisingly similar and straightforward.

14.3.3 Inheritance

In structured analysis, it is possible to have an entity that is a supertype and entities that are subtypes. We mentioned this in Chapter 7. The example we used was between two types of students – those who study courses at the university campus and those who study the courses at a distance learning centre. In an entity model, this would be shown as in Figure 14.7.

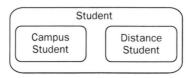

Figure 14.7 Supertype and subtype entities (copy of Figure 7.22)

The supertype entity, Student, has subtype entities Campus Student and Distance Student. Most of the attributes of the two subtypes will be the same: Student Number, Student Name etc., but the Distance Students will also have the name of their Study Centre stored with the student details. In object-oriented analysis, this is called **inheritance**, and the classes are called **super-classes** and **sub-classes**. The sub-class inherits the attributes of the super-class. The class diagram is in Figure 14.8.

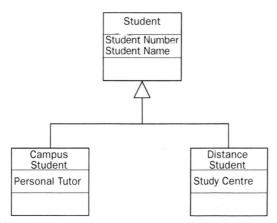

Figure 14.8 Class diagram for inheritance

Notice that the arrow in Figure 14.8 is not filled in like the arrows in Figure 14.6 as they have totally different meanings. The sub-classes Campus Student and Distance Student **inherit** the attributes of the super-class Student, but the Campus Student has an extra attribute called Personal Tutor which the Distance Student does not have and the Distance Student has an extra attribute called Study Centre which the Campus Student does not have. The inherited attributes are not repeated in the boxes for sub-classes.

Inheritance can go down to many levels. For example, campus students can be divided into students from the European Community (EC) and non-EC students. Non-EC students contain the same details as EC students but also include their passport number and visa expiry date if applicable. This would be shown as in Figure 14.9.

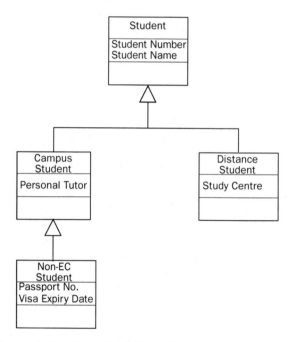

Figure 14.9   Class diagram for multi-level inheritance

14.3.4 Aggregation and composition

Aggregation is quite a difficult concept and does not have an exact equivalent in structured analysis. It occurs when one class is 'made up of' or 'consists of' more than one instance of another class. Looking from the other direction, it occurs when a class is 'part of' another class. Aggregation and association are often confused with each other – and the reason is that aggregation *is* association! It is worth remembering this. Aggregation implies that the aggregate is the sum of its parts, but the distinction between aggregation and association is often a matter of interpretation and not something to get worked up about. In fact the UML Language Reference Manual encourages readers to think of aggregation as a 'modelling placebo'!

To give an example from the student assessment system, a Module will consist of a number of Lectures and a number of Tutorials. All Modules will have Lectures but not all Modules will have Tutorials. This can be viewed in two ways – as **associations** between Module and Lecture, and Module and Tutorial, or as an **aggregation** in which a Module is made up of Lectures and Tutorials. The two versions are shown in Figure 14.10.

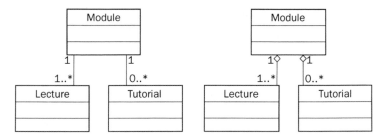

Figure 14.10   Association (left) and aggregation (right) between Module, Lecture and Tutorial

The diamond shape goes at the aggregate end of the line. Figure 14.10 implies that a lecture and a tutorial can only be part of one module. It is feasible for the same lecture and tutorial material to be used in more than one module. For example, a lecture on project management could quite easily be used in a module on systems analysis or a module on software engineering. In this case, Figure 14.10 would be modified slightly to show a one or more multiplicity or, alternatively, an aggregation at the Module end. This is shown in Figure 14.11.

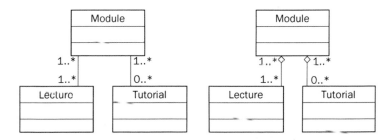

Figure 14.11   Association (left) and aggregation (right) between Module, Lecture and Tutorial incorporating many-to-many aggregations

Although aggregation is not a particularly precise concept, one of its variants is. This is **composition**. According to the UML Reference Manual, composition is 'a form of aggregation with strong ownership and coincident lifetime of parts by the whole'. What this actually means is that when the composite dies (is deleted), its constituent parts go with it. This implies that an object can only be part of *one* composite at a time. This is different to general aggregation where an object can be part of more than one aggregate, for example in Figure 14.11.

It is difficult to find an example of composition in the student assessment system but a good example is provided by part of a sales order processing system. Figure 7.19 showed the relationship between an order and a stock item and this is reproduced in Figure 14.12.

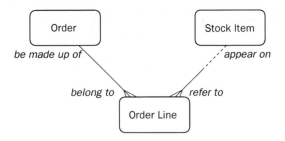

Figure 14.12   Relationship between Order and Stock item (copy of Figure 7.19)

Now an Order can be thought of as being **composed of** a set of Order Lines. An Order Line can only belong to one Order and when an Order is deleted, so will all the Order Lines. This seems to obey all the conditions for a composite association and the class diagram equivalent to the entity model is shown in Figure 14.13. The composition is shown in a similar manner to aggregation but with the diamond box filled in.

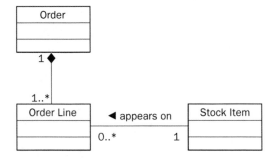

Figure 14.13   Class diagram with composition

14.4 Operations and class diagrams

We now arrive at what makes objects different from entities. You may remember that in section 14.1.1, we said that one of the problems with the structured approach is the separation between processes and data. Well, in object-oriented analysis, they are not separated, they are *together*, wedded, joined for life. This is called **encapsulation** – the packaging together of data and operations into objects. An operation is equivalent to a procedure or function. An object **encapsulates** not only the data associated with it, but also the operations that act upon that data. Think about it – this is a fundamental shift in computer science. Object-orientation is a *new and different* approach.

We will look at how operations are identified in the next chapter but, for now, let us look at an example from the student assessment system. In Figure 14.14, we have redrawn the class diagram with some of the operations included.

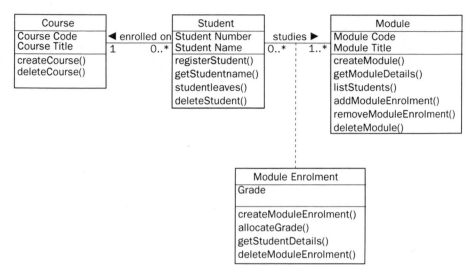

Figure 14.14   Class diagram including operations

The exact nature of the operations will become clear in the next chapter. The names are meant to be self-explanatory. It is the responsibility of each class to execute each of their operations when called upon to do so.

This chapter ..

... serves as an introduction to object-oriented analysis. It started by examining the perceived problems inherent in a structured approach to analysis and suggested that an object-oriented approach can go some way towards solving these problems. Objects were introduced and compared to entities. Simple class diagrams for part of the student assessment system were constructed and compared to entity models. The similarities and differences were discussed. Finally, operations were introduced to produce a completed class diagram.

A useful exercise

Return to the scenario you developed in the earlier chapters of this book and construct a class diagram for the system. Use the entity model as the basis for your objects and try to tease out some of the operations from your required system.

Further reading

C. Britton and J. Doake, *Object-oriented Systems Development – a Gentle Introduction*, McGraw-Hill, Maidenhead, 2000.

P. Coad and E. Yourdon, *Object-Oriented Design*, Yourdon Press; Prentice Hall, Englewood Cliffs, NJ, 1991.

J. Rumbaugh, M. Blaha, W. Premerlani, E. Eddy and W. Lorensen, *Object-Oriented Modeling and Design*, Prentice Hall International, Englewood Cliffs, NJ, 1991.

Web address worth a visit

www.cyberdyne-object-sys.com/oofaq2/

Modelling object behaviour

15

15.1 Use cases

At the end of the last chapter, we introduced you to the idea of operations which are part of the class diagram. They are obviously equivalent to processes – they create, amend or delete attributes and/or objects. But where do we find out about these operations? In the 1990s a number of techniques were developed which involved the user at the centre of the technique. One of these is the **use case**.

Use cases look at what the system will do from the users' point of view. They are free of technical jargon and look at how the users will interact with the system from their viewpoint, that is, what they will expect to have to tell the system and what the system will then do. They can be thought of as equivalent to tasks that a user will be expected to perform with the system – a little job of work such as 'enter an order', 'change an order', 'print out an invoice' etc.

Let us take an example from the student assessment system. When module tutors mark the work of students studying their module, they record the marks in a variety of ways. At the end of the module, the tutors use the marks for all the pieces of work for the module to calculate a final grade for each student. They pass these on to the School Administrator for entry into the system. The use case is shown in Figure 15.1.

The matchstick figure is called an actor. In fact, the student assessment system only has one actor as all the inputs and outputs go through the School Administrator. The module tutor, the student etc., all interface with the system through the School Administrator.

Each use case is accompanied by a description, which is a generic description of the functionality required. It does not go into the ins and outs of the function

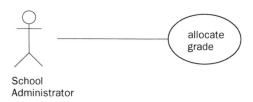

School Administrator

allocate grade

Figure 15.1   Use case for 'allocate grade'

but shows the general purpose of the use case and the normal expected inputs and outputs. A possible description is as follows.

The School Administrator wishes to enter the module grades for a student on a module. This information has been obtained from the module leader. The School Administrator enters the student code and the module code. The system prompts for the module grade, which is then entered. The system confirms the grade.

Although use cases are associated with object-oriented development, their use is obviously not restricted to this approach. They are perfectly relevant to other methods such as the structured approach covered earlier in this book.

15.2 Scenarios

The use case just described is very general and does not give much detail. What happens when things do not go according to plan? For example, what happens if the student is not registered against that module, or there are students on the module who have not attended and so there is no grade for them? This is where **scenarios** come in.

Scenarios are really a way of eliciting requirements and the analyst's skills are needed to a large extent here. If we go back to the example use case 'allocate grade', what we need to find out is exactly how the grade is allocated, and what happens if things do not go according to plan. This is only possible by sitting down with the user and talking to them. As use cases are not in general huge functions, it is quite possible to look at *all* the alternative paths through them. Each of these paths is a scenario.

There is always a **normal** scenario where things go according to plan. It reflects what usually happens. This is sometimes called a 'happy day' scenario – or perhaps better described as a 'no hiccups' scenario (this one is our own invention!). An initial 'no hiccups' scenario for allocate grade could be as follows:

- the School Administrator receives the module results for a particular module;
- the School Administrator enters the module code and student code for each student;
- the system presents the module name and student name for confirmation;
- the School Administrator enters the grade for each student.

When the analyst and the School Administrator discuss this scenario and 'act it out', they find it is very inefficient and time-consuming. The normal situation is for the School Administrator to receive a list from the module leader in alphabetical order of all the students on the module together with their grades. As all the students on the list are on the same module, the analyst and School Administrator question why they need to enter the module code for every student. The system by this time has a module list which was produced by the application of the operation createModuleEnrolment() in the object Module Enrolment (see Figure 14.14). They modify the 'no hiccups' scenario as follows:

- the School Administrator receives the module results for a particular module;
- the School Administrator enters the module code;
- the system displays a list of students enrolled on the module in alphabetical order with a space to enter the grade;
- the School Administrator goes down the list and enters each grade.

Once the normal 'no hiccups' scenario has been constructed, the user and analyst can then look at things which can disrupt the smooth flow of the operation. For example, what happens when a student on the list from the module leader is not recognised by the system as being on that particular module? The scenario for this scenario (!! – that's how it got its name) is as follows:

- the School Administrator receives the module results for a particular module;
- the School Administrator enters the module code;
- the system displays the module details;
- the School Administrator confirms that this is the correct module;
- the system displays a list of students enrolled on the module in alphabetical order with a space to enter the grade;
- the School Administrator goes down the list and enters each grade;
- a name is found on the module leader's list which is not on the system's list;
- the School Administrator marks it in pencil on the module leader's list;
- the School Administrator carries on down the list until finished;
- a module enrolment is created for each pencilled student on the module leader's list;
- the grade is entered for each of these students.

Now, enrolling a student on a module is another job that the School Administrator does at the start of a module. This is shown in Figure 15.2.

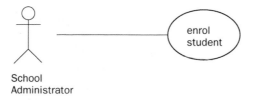

Figure 15.2   Use case for enrol student

As this piece of processing already exists, it makes sense for the use case 'allocate grade' to use the use case 'enrol student'. The correct terminology is that the use case 'enrol student' **extends** the use case 'allocate grade'. It is shown as in Figure 15.3.

A final example of a scenario could be when there is a name on the system's list which is not on the module leader's list. The School Administrator says that in this case, the name should *not* be deleted from the list but it needs further investigation and a special marker should be put against this student's grade. The scenario for this is below:

- the School Administrator receives the module results for a particular module;
- the School Administrator enters the module code;
- the system displays the module details;
- the School Administrator confirms that this is the correct module;
- the system displays a list of students enrolled on the module in alphabetical order with a space to enter the grade;
- the School Administrator goes down the list and enters each grade;
- a name is found on the system's list which is not on the module leader's list;
- a special marker is put in the grade for this student;
- the School Administrator carries on down the list until finished.

This might well lead to the creation of another use case which prints out all these marked students for subsequent investigation. This investigation could then lead to the use case 'allocate grade' again or alternatively it could lead to a use case called 'delete module enrolment'.

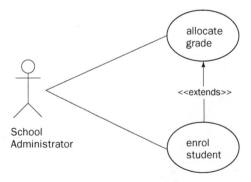

Figure 15.3   Use case using <<extends>>

15.3 CRC cards

Use cases are useful in helping to identify classes and also operations. However, operations are at quite a low and detailed level and it is sometimes useful to look at a higher level to consider the **purpose** or **responsibilities** of a class. CRC

(Class Responsibility Collaboration) cards are used for this purpose. They can be used at any stage of the system development process but are especially useful in the analysis phase when developers are getting bogged down in too much detail and need a clear overall grasp of the functionality of the system.

The construction of CRC cards is an interesting exercise in group work and dialogue between the members of a group who role play the various objects involved in a particular use case. The idea is for each object to do as little as possible by persuading other objects that the responsibility for a particular job is theirs. All members of the team pick the most appropriate object for a particular responsibility and the aim is to minimise the number of messages which pass between objects.

Let us consider the scenario in the use case illustrated in Figure 15.3. The CRC cards for this use case could look like Figure 15.4.

Figure 15.4 may require some explanation. The responsibilities are equivalent to jobs or tasks that the system will be expected to perform. If we take the

Module	
Responsibility	*Collaborators*
Provide module details	
Provide list of students on the module	Module Enrolment provides student codes and fetches student names
Enrol a student on the module	Module Enrolment constructs new object

Module Enrolment	
Responsibility	*Collaborators*
Provide list of student codes and names	Student provides student names
Store grade for student	

Student	
Responsibility	*Collaborators*
Provide student name	

Figure 15.4   Example of CRC cards

example task of 'Provide list of students on the module', the CRC card shows that the responsibility for this task lies with the Module object class. However, in order to perform this task data is needed from other object classes – these are called collaborators. So the Module Enrolment class collaborates by supplying the student codes for the students on the module. This in turn invokes another collaboration with the Student class which supplies the names of the students on the module.

15.4 Sequence diagrams

Sequence diagrams are very much linked to scenarios. A scenario is a specific instance of a use case. In order to achieve the functionality that the scenario sets out to achieve, objects and actors need to **interact** with each other and send messages to each other. Sequence diagrams show this interaction. In the early stages of analysis, sequence diagrams are not particularly stylised and are meant to help the analyst and the user figure out what messages must be passed to and fro between objects and actors in order for the scenario to achieve its purpose.

Let us look at the sequence diagram for the 'no hiccups' scenario for the use case 'allocate grade'. It is shown in Figure 15.5.

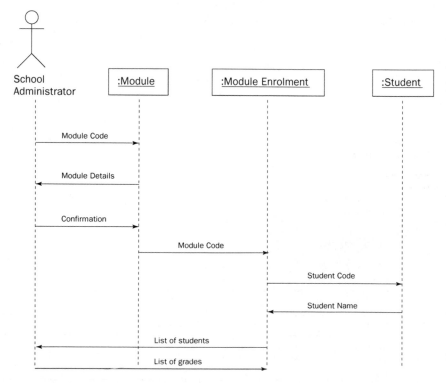

Figure 15.5   Sequence diagram for 'no hiccups' scenario for 'allocate grade'

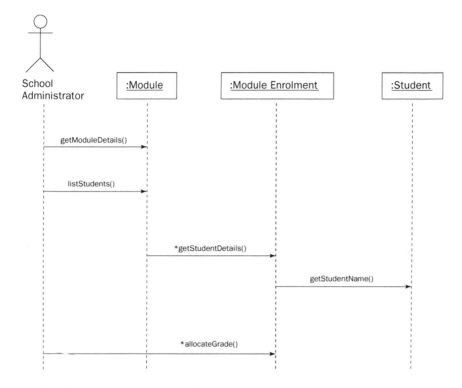

Figure 15.6 Sequence diagram including message signatures

As we move from analysis to design, the sequence diagram becomes more specific and incorporates message signatures as in Figure 15.6. These are the same as the operations in the class diagram at the end of the last chapter (Figure 14.14) and you should have another look at this diagram.

Notice that in Figure 15.6, returns of data are omitted. They can be included and are shown as a dotted line, but they tend to clutter up the diagram. It is important to note that *control always returns to the object that sent the message*. Also note the iteration indicated by a preceding asterisk in *getStudentDetails() and *allocateGrade(). The use of brackets is a convention in UML. They will eventually contain the parameters which are passed to the receiving object. If the brackets are empty, this means that there are no parameters or they are not yet defined.

Conditions can also be placed on the sequence diagram. For example, the condition for continuing the iteration *getStudentDetails can be shown as follows:

[For all students on module] *getStudentDetails().

A 'belt and braces' version of Figure 15.6 is shown in Figure 15.7.

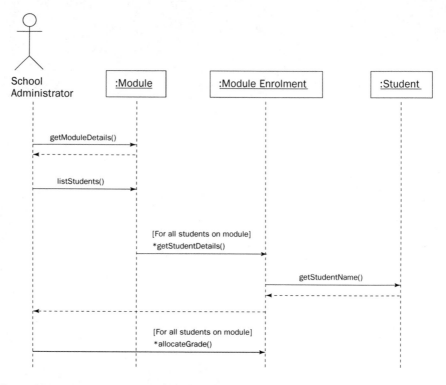

Figure 15.7   Sequence diagram including returns and conditions

Creation and deletion of objects can be shown on sequence diagrams. For example, the various scenarios for the use case 'allocate grade' include the creation and deletion of a module enrolment. These are shown in Figures 15.8 and 15.9.

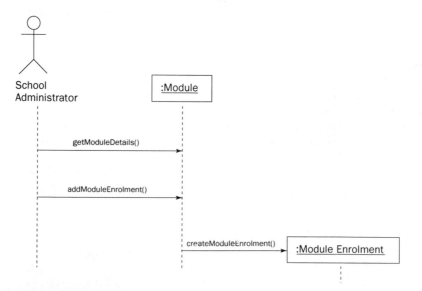

Figure 15.8   Object creation

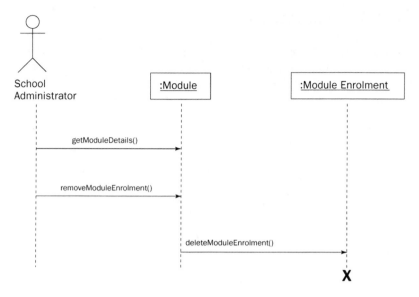

Figure 15.9   Object deletion

Combining Figure 15.8 and Figure 15.6 gives the sequence diagram for the second scenario described earlier and illustrated in Figure 15.3. The combined diagram is shown in Figure 15.10.

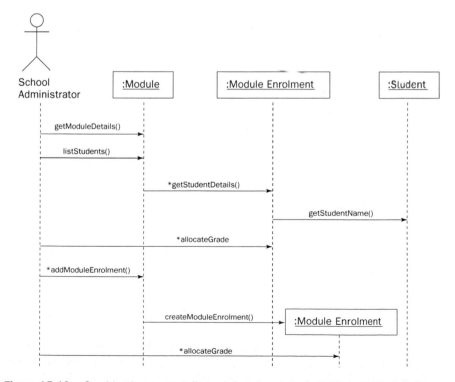

Figure 15.10   Combined sequence diagram for when not all students are enrolled

15.5 Collaboration diagrams

Collaboration diagrams are an alternative to sequence diagrams. Together they are classed as interaction diagrams. Basically the interaction is shown on part of the class diagram and the diagram actually shows the links between objects. The collaboration diagram which is equivalent to the sequence diagram in Figure 15.10 is shown in Figure 15.11.

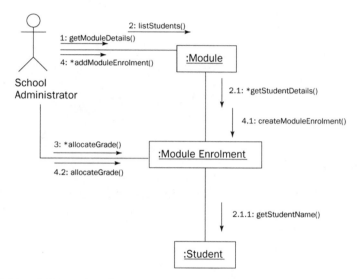

Figure 15.11   Collaboration diagram for the same scenario as Figure 15.10

The difference between the two types of interaction diagrams is quite apparent. In the collaboration diagram, there is no real consideration of time. The sequence of events is shown by the sequence numbers before the operations. Some sequence numbers are nested. For example, 2.1 is nested inside 2 to show the iteration which is being performed and then 2.1.1 is nested inside 2.1.

15.6 State diagrams

When we looked at structured analysis techniques earlier in this book, we introduced the technique of entity life histories. Basically, each entity has a life history which shows the events which affect it in diagrammatic form. Object-oriented analysis has an exactly equivalent technique called the state diagram. These are sometimes called statechart diagrams or state transition diagrams. In fact, we saw a state transition diagram in section 11.6. For simplicity we shall just call them state diagrams.

In object-oriented analysis, each **class** can have a state diagram. We use the word *can* here because some classes have such simple lives that they do not warrant a separate state diagram. In the same way, an entity in structured analysis may not really need an entity life history because the only things that happen to it are creation, followed by a few amendments followed by deletion.

In Chapter 11, section 11.6, we illustrated a particular version of the state transition diagram called a fence diagram. The entity we used was Student and the fence diagram is reproduced in Figure 15.12.

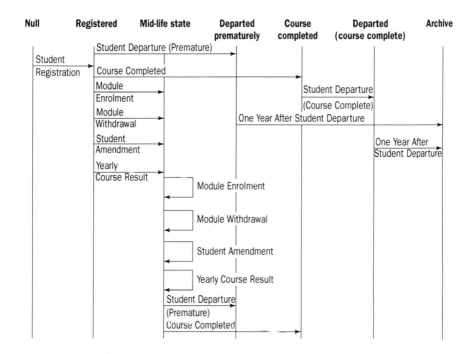

Figure 15.12 Fence diagram for the life of the Student entity (copy of Figure 11.25)

We have already seen that in the object-oriented version of the student assessment system, the Student **entity** has an equivalent Student **class**. The state diagram for the Student class is shown in Figure 15.13.

The diagram starts with a black circle, called the start state, and ends with a bulls-eye, called the stop state. Each box represents a state that the class is in at a point in time. The arrowed lines are quite complicated. The text alongside the line is split into three parts. The first part shows the event that causes the change in state. This is optionally followed by a guard, written in square brackets, which specifies a condition which will allow the transition to take place from one state to the other. The last part is the action which the event triggers. This is an operation or operations and is preceded by a slash /. For the sake of simplicity the diagram does not show the events Module Withdrawal, Student Amendment and Yearly Course Result. These would be shown in the same way as the event Module Enrolment as a loop on the Registered state.

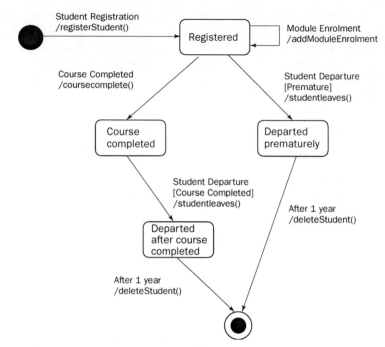

Figure 15.13   State diagram for Student class

This chapter . . .

. . . looked at different techniques for modelling the behaviour of objects. It started by looking at use cases, which are stylised diagrams of jobs that the user will wish to undertake in the new system. Use cases are explored and described by means of scenarios. CRC cards were introduced as a simple but effective technique for allocating responsibilities to classes. Sequence and collaboration diagrams were then described. These are both types of interaction diagrams that illustrate the passing of messages between the various object classes. The chapter finished with an examination of state diagrams, which are very similar to the entity life histories present in the structured approach (as covered in Chapter 11).

A useful exercise

Using the scenario you have developed, devise one use case, one sequence diagram, one collaboration diagram and one state diagram.

Further reading

S. Bennett, S. McRobb and R. Farmer, *Object-oriented Systems Analysis and Design Using UML*, McGraw-Hill, 1999.

J. Rumbaugh, I. Jacobson and G. Booch, *The Unified Modeling Language Reference Manual*, Addison-Wesley, 1999.

Web address worth a visit

www.smartdraw.com/index2.htm

Part 5

And finally . . .

Drawing it all together   **16**

16.1 Some principles of systems analysis

At the beginning of this book we were aware that it would cover a lot of ground. In Chapter 1 we endeavoured to prepare you, by describing aspects of the environment in which systems analysis finds itself. As we start this last chapter it is in the hope that you have found the book useful, and can now much more fully appreciate how the techniques we have described fit within the wider context of systems development as a whole. We want to leave you with a few 'parting shots'. To begin with, we are going to return to the list of systems analysis 'principles' we introduced at the end of Chapter 1, and expand briefly on each. Hopefully, these will now make a lot of sense.

   1. Systems analysis is problem solving.

The more we have become involved in systems analysis as teachers and practitioners, the more we have become convinced that systems analysis is simply a type of problem solving. This book has shown you a number of diagrammatic (and other) techniques that help in this problem-solving process. Part of the key to solving problems that involve a number of people is to get everyone to participate in the process. There is a saying: 'a problem shared is a problem halved'. If the owners of the problem also own the solution to the problem, then this solution is likely to be successful. If the owners of the problem feel left out, then they are unlikely and/or unwilling to help the solution along. This is the basis for PISO's emphasis upon the involvement of 'stakeholders'.

   2. Systems analysis involves research.

If you undertake a project in the final year of an undergraduate degree course, you are normally expected to do a fair amount of research. If you do a higher degree such as a Master of Philosophy or a PhD, you are expected to do a very large amount of research. This research will involve you in literature reviews and applying some well-established research techniques. These include interviewing, designing questionnaires, designing and undertaking experiments, measuring things, sampling populations, participating in systems and many others. All of these are activities that can be and are used in systems analysis. One of us has recently completed a PhD in educational research and found that educational research methods were so similar to conducting a systems analysis that the whole project could be treated in very much the same way as a systems investigation. Educational research methods are mirrored in systems analysis.

3. Systems analysis is about communication.

Systems analysts can be regarded as facilitators. They should not work in isolation – if they do so they are not doing their job properly. In order for the users to own the solutions to their problems, it is obvious that there has to be a good deal of communication between the users themselves and between the users and the analyst. The techniques presented in this book will not make you a good communicator, but they will help. Most of them are diagrammatic and relatively easy for users to understand.

4. Systems analysis is different to systems design.

This book is almost all about systems analysis – pretty well the only part that strays into systems design is where the PISO method introduces the strategic objective, ending with a physical DFD that shows how the objective might practically be implemented. But with most PISO projects even this end-product represents only the very first part of the design process. The design phase of a project is often constrictive. The designer often has to design the system so that it will be implemented in a particular environment, using a particular programming language and using a particular operating system and hardware environment. If this is the case, then the analysis phase can be very much influenced by the design phase and techniques can be used which enable the analysis to 'slot in' to the design phase. This is a very common occurrence. For example, if a system is to be written using an object-oriented language then it does make sense to use object-oriented analysis and design techniques.

However, in this book, we have deliberately avoided this link between analysis and design because we wanted to show the power of systems analysis *on its own*. In particular the chapters on PISO show how powerful systems analysis can be when solving business problems. We also wanted to divorce systems analysis from *computer* systems analysis as we feel that computers are sometimes used for the sake of using computers or in an attempt to mask an inefficient system, rather than for the sake of solving a particular problem in the best way.

5. Systems analysis is about using techniques appropriate to the problem.

This is an almost self-evident principle but it is surprising how often it is not adhered to. You often find that a system has a predominant feature – it may be very data-centred or it may have lots of processes going on with not much data. Some techniques will be more appropriate to one system than another. It is useful to have a cynical attitude towards techniques and not to regard them with a biblical faith because 'that is what I've been taught' or 'that is what this particular book says'. We have seen students trying to design web pages using data flow diagrams! They have run into trouble and think it is their fault. It is not – they are simply using an inappropriate technique.

If something is going wrong or gives you an uneasy feeling, you should ask the question 'Is this technique really the one I should be using?' Sometimes, we see new techniques appear which are really variations of old techniques. In object-oriented analysis, for example, there is a technique called an activity diagram – not covered in this book. To us, it looks very much like the old-fashioned flowchart.

6. Systems analysis is about attention to detail.

This is so important. Getting the detail wrong can lead to disaster. Imagine, for example, a system that should calculate interest on customer accounts and you get the calculation wrong because you were not concentrating when you asked the user. It is useful to be pernickety (a Scottish word: origin unknown!) but pernicketiness can be irritating to other people. So . . . be privately pernickety.

7. Systems analysis is broader than computer systems analysis.

We already implied this and have really tried to hammer home this point throughout the book. Often, when you are working as an analyst, you are asked to modify or add to an already existing computer system. There is no argument about it and so you will be using techniques that lead to a computerised solution.

However, as illustrated by the chapters on PISO, for example, systems can be improved without necessarily resorting to computers or with only partial use of computerisation. It is a much broader view. It could be termed 'business systems analysis' but we prefer just plain simple 'systems analysis', because we feel the same principles can be applied to organising your music collection or arranging your holiday.

16.2 Maintenance and use – information systems and motor cars

The majority of people these days are familiar with the ups and downs of car ownership – perhaps their own, or at least one belonging to a family member or friend. Let us now compare maintaining and using information systems with maintaining and using a motor car. The similarities are there but so are the differences.

16.2.1 Maintaining

Firstly, let us look at the person who looks after the information system or motor car – the person who maintains it, and fixes it when it goes wrong. Sometimes, the owner of the motor car is capable of looking after it but, for most of us, we rely upon the services of a garage. A car mechanic will have to deal with all sorts of cars – the latest ones with computerised guidance systems right through to the 'old banger' that takes half an hour to start in the morning. It is pretty similar with information systems. A company may have completely new systems. But you may work as an analyst or programmer in an organisation that has had computer systems for a number of years and/or has perhaps bought up other companies with systems of their own (these are commonly referred to as 'legacy systems'). If so, you will find all sorts of different approaches, computer languages, interfaces and so on. The process of replacing tried and tested systems with newer ones incorporating new technology and new designs is very expensive and often risky. As an analyst you will find systems that were designed using systems flowcharts, structured methods, maybe object-oriented methods and systems that were not 'designed' at all but sketched out on a piece of scrap paper! You have to be adaptable. You will be amazed at how imperfect things really are.

16.2.2 Using

Now let us look at what happens when you want to replace an information system or a motor car. This is where the differences appear. If you buy a new motor car, you can forget about the old one – you have completely replaced it. There is nothing about the older car that you need to carry across to the newer car. On the other hand, if you replace an information system, you *cannot* forget about the one you have replaced. An information system contains data that belongs to the company and this will have to be transferred across to the new information system. Also the information system will contain links to other information systems, maybe to a website. It is not as easy as replacing a motor car. In addition, development of new information systems has an incredibly bad track record. A system that is delivered on time and within budget is the exception rather than the rule. If new systems were as reliable as new motor cars, then there would not be a problem. However, history has made computer and business professionals extremely wary about new computer systems. As a result, you will often find that business-critical systems, for example billing systems, have not really changed much over the years because they work and 'if it ain't broke don't fix it'.

16.3 Which approach to use?

16.3.1 New and evolving

Information systems is a subject that is still quite new and evolving all the time. What is becoming apparent is that the subject is crossing disciplines – that is, sociology, psychology, ergonomics and computer science are all playing their part. Also, the subject is 'accumulating', for want of a better word. When a new approach appears on the scene, the temptation is to abandon the previous approach. What actually happens is that pieces of the old approach fuse into the new approach and an amalgamation eventually results.

To demonstrate this, let us consider the two main approaches covered by this book – object-oriented and structured – and one that we introduced in Chapter 1 and returned to briefly in Chapter 13 – that is, soft systems.

16.3.2 Object-orientation and persistent data

Object-oriented analysis and design is really derived from object-oriented programming languages, modern examples of which are C++ and JAVA. In order to write software in these languages, an analysis and design method is needed to describe systems that could easily be implemented using these languages. Languages such as these are often used in systems that control electronic or electro-mechanical machinery and increasingly nowadays, they are used in web-based systems. So, if you look at textbooks on object-oriented methods, many of the examples and case studies used are to do with systems that control lifts or entry to car parks using electronic swipe cards and that sort of thing. These systems do not tend to store a lot of data and so are very different from traditional information systems such as the student assessment system described in this book. Examples of web-based systems are also frequent. An example would be a system for selling goods over the Internet. Systems such as this *will* have a requirement to store large amounts of data – such as stock lists, and customer and order information.

It is this latter requirement for access to 'persistent data' that is still causing problems with object-oriented systems. Persistent data is data that exists before the system runs and still exists when it has finished. It is held in the files or databases that are part and parcel of all information systems. Languages such as JAVA and C++ do not really handle files – they are not file-handling languages such as COBOL or many of the traditional data processing languages. There are such things as object-oriented databases, but these tend to be good for handling multimedia such as graphics, sound and video files. What tends to happen is that files are often stored as non-object-oriented structures such as relational databases. Companies have a large investment in relational database technology and it is mature, sophisticated and successful. As a result you often find web-based systems that are written in JAVA but which access a relational database (such as Microsoft Access) through some sort of interface. In such cases, it is necessary to re-design a class diagram into an entity model using techniques like normalisation, the structured analysis technique that we covered in Chapter 8. This is an example of the compromises that are made between different approaches.

However, object-oriented analysis leads very naturally to object-oriented design and thence to implementation in an object-oriented programming language. In fact object-oriented analysis techniques are virtually the same as object-oriented design techniques; the boundary is unclear, if it exists at all.

16.3.3 Structured analysis . . . and design

The progression from structured analysis to structured design is not so automatic. In SSADM there are design techniques which take the products of structured analysis and convert them into structured program designs based on Jackson-like notation. However, these program designs are now regarded as very old-fashioned and more suited to implementation in languages such as COBOL. The design approach adopted by a development team depends very much on the implementation environment and so systems development departments tend to develop their own design methods or use the ones recommended by the vendors of their implementation environment.

16.3.4 Structured and object-oriented analysis

However, whatever the problems with structured design, it is our view that structured analysis is very, very powerful – more so than object-oriented analysis. Object-oriented analysis tends to look at the new computerised system. On the other hand, structured methods, like the ones described in the first part of this book, do spend a lot of time looking at the existing system. The object-oriented idea of self-contained objects with their own data and own responsibilities fits beautifully into a computer system. These objects communicate by sending messages to other objects telling them to do something which is their responsibility. But this idea does not fit naturally into an existing non-computerised system. One can relatively easily imagine a Customer object, for example, being responsible for sending and receiving orders, but it is much more difficult to imagine an Order object being responsible for adding lines to itself and cancelling itself. That is because an order is an inanimate object (excuse the pun) and is not a person who can do things in the real world. In an object-oriented computer system on the other hand, a Customer and an Order are equivalent as far as the system is concerned and they can do things. It is almost as though inanimate objects are anthropomorphised (we have been longing to use this word – it evidently means 'made human'!) in an object-oriented system.

In the structured approach it is *people* who do the processes. This is shown in the data flow diagram as a responsibility in the process box. As it is people who run the system and who are consulted in the analysis phase, it is a more natural analysis approach. So, it is a customer who cancels the order, not an order being told by a customer to cancel itself. This approach has added advantages as it allows a much broader view to be adopted than the object-oriented approach. It allows for the system to be manipulated and changed to make the processes more efficient. This comes through particularly strongly in the chapters on PISO.

16.3.5 Soft Systems

If we step back even further in the development process, we come to Soft Systems. We explained this approach briefly in Chapter 1 – and saw a use for it within certain types of PISO project, in Chapter 13. It is useful for dealing with complex, organisational and people-centred systems where problems exist but it is difficult to get agreement as to what these problems are. It does not attempt to design a system but does go some way towards identifying systems which will be needed to solve some of the problems which it unearths. Now, Soft Systems is being used as a front-end to structured approaches such as SSADM. It is used as a sort of feasibility study or business activity modelling phase.

The question can therefore be put. If Soft Systems can be used as a precursor to structured analysis, can structured analysis be used as a precursor to object-oriented design? Is it possible to change the products of structured analysis into products that are suitable for object-oriented design? Our bet is that there will be a few PhD theses that will attempt to do this!

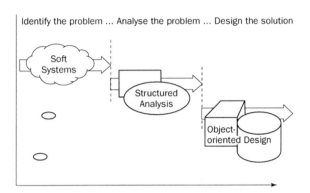

Figure 16.1   An all-encompassing approach to systems development?

16.4 A final finally

We would like to leave you with one of our favourite sayings by H.L. Mencken: 'To every complex question there is a simple answer – and it's always wrong'. This could not apply more to the questions raised in information systems.

A useful exercise

Reflect on the methods you have used in the development of your scenario and write a one-page critique outlining the advantages and disadvantages of each approach.

Further reading

N. Jayaratna, *Understanding and Evaluating Methodologies: NIMSAD a Systemic Framework*, McGraw-Hill, 1994.

Web addresses worth a visit

www.cee.hw.ac.uk/~lachlan/ism.html
www.bcs.org.uk/siggroup/sg27.htm
www.iap.org.uk

Bibliography

Avison, D. and Fitzgerald, G., *Information Systems Development,* 2nd edition, McGraw-Hill, Maidenhead, 1995.

Bennett, S., McRobb, S. and Farmer, R., *Object-oriented Systems Analysis and Design Using UML,* McGraw-Hill, 1999.

Bentley, C., *Practical PRINCE2,* Stationery Office Books, 1998.

Berztiss, A., *Software Methods for Business Re-engineering,* Springer-Verlag, New York, 1996.

Britton, C. and Doake, J., *Object-oriented Systems Development – a Gentle Introduction,* McGraw-Hill, Maidenhead, 2000.

Britton, C. and Doake, J., *Software Systems Development – a Gentle Introduction,* Alfred Waller, 1996.

Buzan, A., *The Mind Map Book,* Plume Books, 1996.

Checkland, P. and Scholes, P., *Soft Systems Methodology in Action,* Wiley, Chichester, 1999.

Checkland, P. and Scholes, P., *Systems Thinking, Systems Practice,* Wiley, Chichester, 1999.

Coad, J. and Yourdon, E., *Object-Oriented Design,* Yourdon Press; Prentice Hall, Englewood Cliffs, NJ, 1991.

Cutts, G., *Structured Systems Analysis and Design Methodology,* Blackwell, Oxford, 1991.

Date, C.J., *An Introduction to Database Systems,* 7th edition, Addison-Wesley, Reading, MA, 1999.

Deeks, D., *The Information Systems Group Project* (Teaching Pack), Business Education Publishers, Sunderland, 1999.

De Marco, T., *Structured Analysis and Systems Specification,* Prentice Hall International, Englewood Cliffs, NJ, 1980.

Dennis, A. and Haley, B., *Systems Analysis and Design in Action,* Wiley, Chichester, 2000.

Goodland, M. and Slater, C., *SSADM Version 4: A Practical Approach,* McGraw-Hill, London, 1995.

Howe, D., *Data Analysis for Database Design,* 3rd edition, Butterworth-Heinemann, 2001.

Jayaratna, N., *Understanding and Evaluating Methodologies: NIMSAD a Systemic Framework,* McGraw-Hill, 1994.

Maciaszek, L., *Requirements Analysis and Systems Design,* Addison-Wesley, Harlow, 2001.

Parkinson, J., *Making CASE Work,* NCC Blackwell, Oxford, 1991.

Peppard, J. and Rowland, P., *The Essence of Business Process Re-engineering,* Prentice Hall, Hemel Hempstead, 1995.

Plotkin, H., *Building a Winning Team*, Griffin Publishing, 1997.

Posner, K. and Applegarth, M., *The Project Management Pocketbook*, Management Pocketbooks, 1998.

Rumbaugh, J., Blaha, M., Premerlani, W., Eddy, F. and Lorensen, W., *Object-Oriented Modeling and Design*, Prentice Hall International, Englewood Cliffs, NJ, 1991.

Rumbaugh, J., Jacobson, I. and Booch, G., *The Unified Modeling Language Reference Manual*, Addison-Wesley, 1999.

Skidmore, S., *Introducing Systems Analysis*, Palgrave, 1997.

Tudor, J. and Tudor, I.J., *Systems Analysis and Design*, Palgrave, 1997.

Warner, T., *Communication Skills for Information Systems*, Pitman, London, 1996.

Williams, K., *Study Skills*, Palgrave, 1989.

Index